C-4734

CAREER EXAMINATION SERIES

THIS IS YOUR **PASSBOOK®** FOR ...

PARK POLICE OFFICER TRAINEE

NATIONAL LEARNING CORPORATION®
passbooks.com

EAST NORTHPORT PUBLIC LIBRARY
EAST NORTHPORT, NEW YORK

COPYRIGHT NOTICE

This book is SOLELY intended for, is sold ONLY to, and its use is RESTRICTED to individual, bona fide applicants or candidates who qualify by virtue of having seriously filed applications for appropriate license, certificate, professional and/or promotional advancement, higher school matriculation, scholarship, or other legitimate requirements of educational and/or governmental authorities.

This book is NOT intended for use, class instruction, tutoring, training, duplication, copying, reprinting, excerption, or adaptation, etc., by:

1) Other publishers
2) Proprietors and/or Instructors of «Coaching» and/or Preparatory Courses
3) Personnel and/or Training Divisions of commercial, industrial, and governmental organizations
4) Schools, colleges, or universities and/or their departments and staffs, including teachers and other personnel
5) Testing Agencies or Bureaus
6) Study groups which seek by the purchase of a single volume to copy and/or duplicate and/or adapt this material for use by the group as a whole without having purchased individual volumes for each of the members of the group
7) Et al.

Such persons would be in violation of appropriate Federal and State statutes.

PROVISION OF LICENSING AGREEMENTS. — Recognized educational, commercial, industrial, and governmental institutions and organizations, and others legitimately engaged in educational pursuits, including training, testing, and measurement activities, may address request for a licensing agreement to the copyright owners, who will determine whether, and under what conditions, including fees and charges, the materials in this book may be used them. In other words, a licensing facility exists for the legitimate use of the material in this book on other than an individual basis. However, it is asseverated and affirmed here that the material in this book CANNOT be used without the receipt of the express permission of such a licensing agreement from the Publishers. Inquiries re licensing should be addressed to the company, attention rights and permissions department.

All rights reserved, including the right of reproduction in whole or in part, in any form or by any means, electronic or mechanical, including photocopying, recording, or by any information storage and retrieval system, without permission in writing from the Publisher.

Copyright © 2020 by

NLC®

National Learning Corporation

212 Michael Drive, Syosset, NY 11791
(516) 921-8888 • www.passbooks.com
E-mail: info@passbooks.com

PUBLISHED IN THE UNITED STATES OF AMERICA

PASSBOOK® SERIES

THE *PASSBOOK® SERIES* has been created to prepare applicants and candidates for the ultimate academic battlefield – the examination room.

At some time in our lives, each and every one of us may be required to take an examination – for validation, matriculation, admission, qualification, registration, certification, or licensure.

Based on the assumption that every applicant or candidate has met the basic formal educational standards, has taken the required number of courses, and read the necessary texts, the *PASSBOOK® SERIES* furnishes the one special preparation which may assure passing with confidence, instead of failing with insecurity. Examination questions – together with answers – are furnished as the basic vehicle for study so that the mysteries of the examination and its compounding difficulties may be eliminated or diminished by a sure method.

This book is meant to help you pass your examination provided that you qualify and are serious in your objective.

The entire field is reviewed through the huge store of content information which is succinctly presented through a provocative and challenging approach – the question-and-answer method.

A climate of success is established by furnishing the correct answers at the end of each test.

You soon learn to recognize types of questions, forms of questions, and patterns of questioning. You may even begin to anticipate expected outcomes.

You perceive that many questions are repeated or adapted so that you can gain acute insights, which may enable you to score many sure points.

You learn how to confront new questions, or types of questions, and to attack them confidently and work out the correct answers.

You note objectives and emphases, and recognize pitfalls and dangers, so that you may make positive educational adjustments.

Moreover, you are kept fully informed in relation to new concepts, methods, practices, and directions in the field.

You discover that you arre actually taking the examination all the time: you are preparing for the examination by "taking" an examination, not by reading extraneous and/or supererogatory textbooks.

In short, this PASSBOOK®, used directedly, should be an important factor in helping you to pass your test.

PARK POLICE OFFICER TRAINEE

DUTIES:
As a Park Police Officer Trainee you will serve as a police officer. Your authority will extend throughout the state, although your prima responsibility will be to enforce laws and to provide information, assistance, and protection to visitors to State parks and historic sites. You will be responsible for the enforcement of all federal and state laws including, but not limited to, the penal, parks and recreation, vehicle and traffic, and environmental conservation laws. Your responsibilities might include assignment on foot, horseback, bicycle, all-terrain vehicle, boat, personal watercraft, snowmobile, or other patrol. You might also be assigned to patrol duty or other police responsibilities.

SUBJECT OF EXAMINATION:
The written test is designed to test for knowledge, skills, and/or abilities in such areas as:
1. **Applying written information (rules, regulations, policies, procedures, directives, etc.) in police situations** - These questions test for the ability to apply written rules in given situations similar to those typically experienced by police officers.
2. **Memory for facts and information** - These questions test for the ability to remember facts and information presented in written form.
3. **Reading, understanding and interpreting written information** - These questions test for the ability to read, understand, and interpret the kinds of written information that police officers are required to read during their formal training period and on the job.
4. **Preparing written material in a police setting** - These questions test for the ability to prepare the types of reports that police officers write. You will be presented with a page of notes followed by several questions. Each question will consist of four restatements of the information given in the notes. From each set of four, you must choose the version that presents the information most clearly and accurately.

HOW TO TAKE A TEST

I. YOU MUST PASS AN EXAMINATION

A. *WHAT EVERY CANDIDATE SHOULD KNOW*

Examination applicants often ask us for help in preparing for the written test. What can I study in advance? What kinds of questions will be asked? How will the test be given? How will the papers be graded?

As an applicant for a civil service examination, you may be wondering about some of these things. Our purpose here is to suggest effective methods of advance study and to describe civil service examinations.

Your chances for success on this examination can be increased if you know how to prepare. Those "pre-examination jitters" can be reduced if you know what to expect. You can even experience an adventure in good citizenship if you know why civil service exams are given.

B. *WHY ARE CIVIL SERVICE EXAMINATIONS GIVEN?*

Civil service examinations are important to you in two ways. As a citizen, you want public jobs filled by employees who know how to do their work. As a job seeker, you want a fair chance to compete for that job on an equal footing with other candidates. The best-known means of accomplishing this two-fold goal is the competitive examination.

Exams are widely publicized throughout the nation. They may be administered for jobs in federal, state, city, municipal, town or village governments or agencies.

Any citizen may apply, with some limitations, such as the age or residence of applicants. Your experience and education may be reviewed to see whether you meet the requirements for the particular examination. When these requirements exist, they are reasonable and applied consistently to all applicants. Thus, a competitive examination may cause you some uneasiness now, but it is your privilege and safeguard.

C. *HOW ARE CIVIL SERVICE EXAMS DEVELOPED?*

Examinations are carefully written by trained technicians who are specialists in the field known as "psychological measurement," in consultation with recognized authorities in the field of work that the test will cover. These experts recommend the subject matter areas or skills to be tested; only those knowledges or skills important to your success on the job are included. The most reliable books and source materials available are used as references. Together, the experts and technicians judge the difficulty level of the questions.

Test technicians know how to phrase questions so that the problem is clearly stated. Their ethics do not permit "trick" or "catch" questions. Questions may have been tried out on sample groups, or subjected to statistical analysis, to determine their usefulness.

Written tests are often used in combination with performance tests, ratings of training and experience, and oral interviews. All of these measures combine to form the best-known means of finding the right person for the right job.

II. HOW TO PASS THE WRITTEN TEST

A. NATURE OF THE EXAMINATION

To prepare intelligently for civil service examinations, you should know how they differ from school examinations you have taken. In school you were assigned certain definite pages to read or subjects to cover. The examination questions were quite detailed and usually emphasized memory. Civil service exams, on the other hand, try to discover your present ability to perform the duties of a position, plus your potentiality to learn these duties. In other words, a civil service exam attempts to predict how successful you will be. Questions cover such a broad area that they cannot be as minute and detailed as school exam questions.

In the public service similar kinds of work, or positions, are grouped together in one "class." This process is known as *position-classification*. All the positions in a class are paid according to the salary range for that class. One class title covers all of these positions, and they are all tested by the same examination.

B. FOUR BASIC STEPS

1) Study the announcement

How, then, can you know what subjects to study? Our best answer is: "Learn as much as possible about the class of positions for which you've applied." The exam will test the knowledge, skills and abilities needed to do the work.

Your most valuable source of information about the position you want is the official exam announcement. This announcement lists the training and experience qualifications. Check these standards and apply only if you come reasonably close to meeting them.

The brief description of the position in the examination announcement offers some clues to the subjects which will be tested. Think about the job itself. Review the duties in your mind. Can you perform them, or are there some in which you are rusty? Fill in the blank spots in your preparation.

Many jurisdictions preview the written test in the exam announcement by including a section called "Knowledge and Abilities Required," "Scope of the Examination," or some similar heading. Here you will find out specifically what fields will be tested.

2) Review your own background

Once you learn in general what the position is all about, and what you need to know to do the work, ask yourself which subjects you already know fairly well and which need improvement. You may wonder whether to concentrate on improving your strong areas or on building some background in your fields of weakness. When the announcement has specified "some knowledge" or "considerable knowledge," or has used adjectives like "beginning principles of..." or "advanced ... methods," you can get a clue as to the number and difficulty of questions to be asked in any given field. More questions, and hence broader coverage, would be included for those subjects which are more important in the work. Now weigh your strengths and weaknesses against the job requirements and prepare accordingly.

3) Determine the level of the position

Another way to tell how intensively you should prepare is to understand the level of the job for which you are applying. Is it the entering level? In other words, is this the position in which beginners in a field of work are hired? Or is it an intermediate or advanced level? Sometimes this is indicated by such words as "Junior" or "Senior" in the class title. Other jurisdictions use Roman numerals to designate the level – Clerk I, Clerk II, for example. The word "Supervisor" sometimes appears in the title. If the level is not indicated by the title, check the description of duties. Will you be working under very close supervision, or will you have responsibility for independent decisions in this work?

4) Choose appropriate study materials

Now that you know the subjects to be examined and the relative amount of each subject to be covered, you can choose suitable study materials. For beginning level jobs, or even advanced ones, if you have a pronounced weakness in some aspect of your training, read a modern, standard textbook in that field. Be sure it is up to date and has general coverage. Such books are normally available at your library, and the librarian will be glad to help you locate one. For entry-level positions, questions of appropriate difficulty are chosen – neither highly advanced questions, nor those too simple. Such questions require careful thought but not advanced training.

If the position for which you are applying is technical or advanced, you will read more advanced, specialized material. If you are already familiar with the basic principles of your field, elementary textbooks would waste your time. Concentrate on advanced textbooks and technical periodicals. Think through the concepts and review difficult problems in your field.

These are all general sources. You can get more ideas on your own initiative, following these leads. For example, training manuals and publications of the government agency which employs workers in your field can be useful, particularly for technical and professional positions. A letter or visit to the government department involved may result in more specific study suggestions, and certainly will provide you with a more definite idea of the exact nature of the position you are seeking.

III. KINDS OF TESTS

Tests are used for purposes other than measuring knowledge and ability to perform specified duties. For some positions, it is equally important to test ability to make adjustments to new situations or to profit from training. In others, basic mental abilities not dependent on information are essential. Questions which test these things may not appear as pertinent to the duties of the position as those which test for knowledge and information. Yet they are often highly important parts of a fair examination. For very general questions, it is almost impossible to help you direct your study efforts. What we can do is to point out some of the more common of these general abilities needed in public service positions and describe some typical questions.

1) General information

Broad, general information has been found useful for predicting job success in some kinds of work. This is tested in a variety of ways, from vocabulary lists to questions about current events. Basic background in some field of work, such as sociology or economics, may be sampled in a group of questions. Often these are principles which have become familiar to most persons through exposure rather than through formal training. It is difficult to advise you how to study for these questions; being alert to the world around you is our best suggestion.

2) Verbal ability

An example of an ability needed in many positions is verbal or language ability. Verbal ability is, in brief, the ability to use and understand words. Vocabulary and grammar tests are typical measures of this ability. Reading comprehension or paragraph interpretation questions are common in many kinds of civil service tests. You are given a paragraph of written material and asked to find its central meaning.

3) Numerical ability

Number skills can be tested by the familiar arithmetic problem, by checking paired lists of numbers to see which are alike and which are different, or by interpreting charts and graphs. In the latter test, a graph may be printed in the test booklet which you are asked to use as the basis for answering questions.

4) Observation

A popular test for law-enforcement positions is the observation test. A picture is shown to you for several minutes, then taken away. Questions about the picture test your ability to observe both details and larger elements.

5) Following directions

In many positions in the public service, the employee must be able to carry out written instructions dependably and accurately. You may be given a chart with several columns, each column listing a variety of information. The questions require you to carry out directions involving the information given in the chart.

6) Skills and aptitudes

Performance tests effectively measure some manual skills and aptitudes. When the skill is one in which you are trained, such as typing or shorthand, you can practice. These tests are often very much like those given in business school or high school courses. For many of the other skills and aptitudes, however, no short-time preparation can be made. Skills and abilities natural to you or that you have developed throughout your lifetime are being tested.

Many of the general questions just described provide all the data needed to answer the questions and ask you to use your reasoning ability to find the answers. Your best preparation for these tests, as well as for tests of facts and ideas, is to be at your physical and mental best. You, no doubt, have your own methods of getting into an exam-taking mood and keeping "in shape." The next section lists some ideas on this subject.

IV. KINDS OF QUESTIONS

Only rarely is the "essay" question, which you answer in narrative form, used in civil service tests. Civil service tests are usually of the short-answer type. Full instructions for answering these questions will be given to you at the examination. But in case this is your first experience with short-answer questions and separate answer sheets, here is what you need to know:

1) **Multiple-choice Questions**

Most popular of the short-answer questions is the "multiple choice" or "best answer" question. It can be used, for example, to test for factual knowledge, ability to solve problems or judgment in meeting situations found at work.

A multiple-choice question is normally one of three types—
- It can begin with an incomplete statement followed by several possible endings. You are to find the one ending which *best* completes the statement, although some of the others may not be entirely wrong.
- It can also be a complete statement in the form of a question which is answered by choosing one of the statements listed.
- It can be in the form of a problem – again you select the best answer.

Here is an example of a multiple-choice question with a discussion which should give you some clues as to the method for choosing the right answer:

When an employee has a complaint about his assignment, the action which will *best* help him overcome his difficulty is to
  A. discuss his difficulty with his coworkers
  B. take the problem to the head of the organization
  C. take the problem to the person who gave him the assignment
  D. say nothing to anyone about his complaint

In answering this question, you should study each of the choices to find which is best. Consider choice "A" – Certainly an employee may discuss his complaint with fellow employees, but no change or improvement can result, and the complaint remains unresolved. Choice "B" is a poor choice since the head of the organization probably does not know what assignment you have been given, and taking your problem to him is known as "going over the head" of the supervisor. The supervisor, or person who made the assignment, is the person who can clarify it or correct any injustice. Choice "C" is, therefore, correct. To say nothing, as in choice "D," is unwise. Supervisors have and interest in knowing the problems employees are facing, and the employee is seeking a solution to his problem.

2) **True/False Questions**

The "true/false" or "right/wrong" form of question is sometimes used. Here a complete statement is given. Your job is to decide whether the statement is right or wrong.

SAMPLE: A roaming cell-phone call to a nearby city costs less than a non-roaming call to a distant city.

This statement is wrong, or false, since roaming calls are more expensive.
This is not a complete list of all possible question forms, although most of the others are variations of these common types. You will always get complete directions for

answering questions. Be sure you understand *how* to mark your answers – ask questions until you do.

V. RECORDING YOUR ANSWERS

Computer terminals are used more and more today for many different kinds of exams.

For an examination with very few applicants, you may be told to record your answers in the test booklet itself. Separate answer sheets are much more common. If this separate answer sheet is to be scored by machine – and this is often the case – it is highly important that you mark your answers correctly in order to get credit.

An electronic scoring machine is often used in civil service offices because of the speed with which papers can be scored. Machine-scored answer sheets must be marked with a pencil, which will be given to you. This pencil has a high graphite content which responds to the electronic scoring machine. As a matter of fact, stray dots may register as answers, so do not let your pencil rest on the answer sheet while you are pondering the correct answer. Also, if your pencil lead breaks or is otherwise defective, ask for another.

Since the answer sheet will be dropped in a slot in the scoring machine, be careful not to bend the corners or get the paper crumpled.

The answer sheet normally has five vertical columns of numbers, with 30 numbers to a column. These numbers correspond to the question numbers in your test booklet. After each number, going across the page are four or five pairs of dotted lines. These short dotted lines have small letters or numbers above them. The first two pairs may also have a "T" or "F" above the letters. This indicates that the first two pairs only are to be used if the questions are of the true-false type. If the questions are multiple choice, disregard the "T" and "F" and pay attention only to the small letters or numbers.

Answer your questions in the manner of the sample that follows:

32. The largest city in the United States is
 A. Washington, D.C.
 B. New York City
 C. Chicago
 D. Detroit
 E. San Francisco

1) Choose the answer you think is best. (New York City is the largest, so "B" is correct.)
2) Find the row of dotted lines numbered the same as the question you are answering. (Find row number 32)
3) Find the pair of dotted lines corresponding to the answer. (Find the pair of lines under the mark "B.")
4) Make a solid black mark between the dotted lines.

VI. BEFORE THE TEST

Common sense will help you find procedures to follow to get ready for an examination. Too many of us, however, overlook these sensible measures. Indeed, nervousness and fatigue have been found to be the most serious reasons why applicants fail to do their best on civil service tests. Here is a list of reminders:

- Begin your preparation early – Don't wait until the last minute to go scurrying around for books and materials or to find out what the position is all about.
- Prepare continuously – An hour a night for a week is better than an all-night cram session. This has been definitely established. What is more, a night a week for a month will return better dividends than crowding your study into a shorter period of time.
- Locate the place of the exam – You have been sent a notice telling you when and where to report for the examination. If the location is in a different town or otherwise unfamiliar to you, it would be well to inquire the best route and learn something about the building.
- Relax the night before the test – Allow your mind to rest. Do not study at all that night. Plan some mild recreation or diversion; then go to bed early and get a good night's sleep.
- Get up early enough to make a leisurely trip to the place for the test – This way unforeseen events, traffic snarls, unfamiliar buildings, etc. will not upset you.
- Dress comfortably – A written test is not a fashion show. You will be known by number and not by name, so wear something comfortable.
- Leave excess paraphernalia at home – Shopping bags and odd bundles will get in your way. You need bring only the items mentioned in the official notice you received; usually everything you need is provided. Do not bring reference books to the exam. They will only confuse those last minutes and be taken away from you when in the test room.
- Arrive somewhat ahead of time – If because of transportation schedules you must get there very early, bring a newspaper or magazine to take your mind off yourself while waiting.
- Locate the examination room – When you have found the proper room, you will be directed to the seat or part of the room where you will sit. Sometimes you are given a sheet of instructions to read while you are waiting. Do not fill out any forms until you are told to do so; just read them and be prepared.
- Relax and prepare to listen to the instructions
- If you have any physical problem that may keep you from doing your best, be sure to tell the test administrator. If you are sick or in poor health, you really cannot do your best on the exam. You can come back and take the test some other time.

VII. AT THE TEST

The day of the test is here and you have the test booklet in your hand. The temptation to get going is very strong. Caution! There is more to success than knowing the right answers. You must know how to identify your papers and understand variations in the type of short-answer question used in this particular examination. Follow these suggestions for maximum results from your efforts:

1) Cooperate with the monitor

The test administrator has a duty to create a situation in which you can be as much at ease as possible. He will give instructions, tell you when to begin, check to see that you are marking your answer sheet correctly, and so on. He is not there to guard you, although he will see that your competitors do not take unfair advantage. He wants to help you do your best.

2) Listen to all instructions

Don't jump the gun! Wait until you understand all directions. In most civil service tests you get more time than you need to answer the questions. So don't be in a hurry. Read each word of instructions until you clearly understand the meaning. Study the examples, listen to all announcements and follow directions. Ask questions if you do not understand what to do.

3) Identify your papers

Civil service exams are usually identified by number only. You will be assigned a number; you must not put your name on your test papers. Be sure to copy your number correctly. Since more than one exam may be given, copy your exact examination title.

4) Plan your time

Unless you are told that a test is a "speed" or "rate of work" test, speed itself is usually not important. Time enough to answer all the questions will be provided, but this does not mean that you have all day. An overall time limit has been set. Divide the total time (in minutes) by the number of questions to determine the approximate time you have for each question.

5) Do not linger over difficult questions

If you come across a difficult question, mark it with a paper clip (useful to have along) and come back to it when you have been through the booklet. One caution if you do this – be sure to skip a number on your answer sheet as well. Check often to be sure that you have not lost your place and that you are marking in the row numbered the same as the question you are answering.

6) Read the questions

Be sure you know what the question asks! Many capable people are unsuccessful because they failed to *read* the questions correctly.

7) Answer all questions

Unless you have been instructed that a penalty will be deducted for incorrect answers, it is better to guess than to omit a question.

8) Speed tests

It is often better NOT to guess on speed tests. It has been found that on timed tests people are tempted to spend the last few seconds before time is called in marking answers at random – without even reading them – in the hope of picking up a few extra points. To discourage this practice, the instructions may warn you that your score will be "corrected" for guessing. That is, a penalty will be applied. The incorrect answers will be deducted from the correct ones, or some other penalty formula will be used.

9) Review your answers

If you finish before time is called, go back to the questions you guessed or omitted to give them further thought. Review other answers if you have time.

10) Return your test materials

If you are ready to leave before others have finished or time is called, take ALL your materials to the monitor and leave quietly. Never take any test material with you. The monitor can discover whose papers are not complete, and taking a test booklet may be grounds for disqualification.

VIII. EXAMINATION TECHNIQUES

1) Read the general instructions carefully. These are usually printed on the first page of the exam booklet. As a rule, these instructions refer to the timing of the examination; the fact that you should not start work until the signal and must stop work at a signal, etc. If there are any *special* instructions, such as a choice of questions to be answered, make sure that you note this instruction carefully.

2) When you are ready to start work on the examination, that is as soon as the signal has been given, read the instructions to each question booklet, underline any key words or phrases, such as *least, best, outline, describe* and the like. In this way you will tend to answer as requested rather than discover on reviewing your paper that you *listed without describing*, that you selected the *worst* choice rather than the *best* choice, etc.

3) If the examination is of the objective or multiple-choice type – that is, each question will also give a series of possible answers: A, B, C or D, and you are called upon to select the best answer and write the letter next to that answer on your answer paper – it is advisable to start answering each question in turn. There may be anywhere from 50 to 100 such questions in the three or four hours allotted and you can see how much time would be taken if you read through all the questions before beginning to answer any. Furthermore, if you come across a question or group of questions which you know would be difficult to answer, it would undoubtedly affect your handling of all the other questions.

4) If the examination is of the essay type and contains but a few questions, it is a moot point as to whether you should read all the questions before starting to answer any one. Of course, if you are given a choice – say five out of seven and the like – then it is essential to read all the questions so you can eliminate the two that are most difficult. If, however, you are asked to answer all the questions, there may be danger in trying to answer the easiest one first because you may find that you will spend too much time on it. The best technique is to answer the first question, then proceed to the second, etc.

5) Time your answers. Before the exam begins, write down the time it started, then add the time allowed for the examination and write down the time it must be completed, then divide the time available somewhat as follows:

- If 3-1/2 hours are allowed, that would be 210 minutes. If you have 80 objective-type questions, that would be an average of 2-1/2 minutes per question. Allow yourself no more than 2 minutes per question, or a total of 160 minutes, which will permit about 50 minutes to review.
- If for the time allotment of 210 minutes there are 7 essay questions to answer, that would average about 30 minutes a question. Give yourself only 25 minutes per question so that you have about 35 minutes to review.

6) The most important instruction is to *read each question* and make sure you know what is wanted. The second most important instruction is to *time yourself properly* so that you answer every question. The third most important instruction is to *answer every question.* Guess if you have to but include something for each question. Remember that you will receive no credit for a blank and will probably receive some credit if you write something in answer to an essay question. If you guess a letter – say "B" for a multiple-choice question – you may have guessed right. If you leave a blank as an answer to a multiple-choice question, the examiners may respect your feelings but it will not add a point to your score. Some exams may penalize you for wrong answers, so in such cases *only*, you may not want to guess unless you have some basis for your answer.

7) Suggestions
   a. Objective-type questions
      1. Examine the question booklet for proper sequence of pages and questions
      2. Read all instructions carefully
      3. Skip any question which seems too difficult; return to it after all other questions have been answered
      4. Apportion your time properly; do not spend too much time on any single question or group of questions
      5. Note and underline key words – *all, most, fewest, least, best, worst, same, opposite,* etc.
      6. Pay particular attention to negatives
      7. Note unusual option, e.g., unduly long, short, complex, different or similar in content to the body of the question
      8. Observe the use of "hedging" words – *probably, may, most likely,* etc.
      9. Make sure that your answer is put next to the same number as the question
      10. Do not second-guess unless you have good reason to believe the second answer is definitely more correct
      11. Cross out original answer if you decide another answer is more accurate; do not erase until you are ready to hand your paper in
      12. Answer all questions; guess unless instructed otherwise
      13. Leave time for review

   b. Essay questions
      1. Read each question carefully
      2. Determine exactly what is wanted. Underline key words or phrases.
      3. Decide on outline or paragraph answer

4. Include many different points and elements unless asked to develop any one or two points or elements
5. Show impartiality by giving pros and cons unless directed to select one side only
6. Make and write down any assumptions you find necessary to answer the questions
7. Watch your English, grammar, punctuation and choice of words
8. Time your answers; don't crowd material

8) Answering the essay question

Most essay questions can be answered by framing the specific response around several key words or ideas. Here are a few such key words or ideas:

M's: manpower, materials, methods, money, management
P's: purpose, program, policy, plan, procedure, practice, problems, pitfalls, personnel, public relations
 a. Six basic steps in handling problems:
  1. Preliminary plan and background development
  2. Collect information, data and facts
  3. Analyze and interpret information, data and facts
  4. Analyze and develop solutions as well as make recommendations
  5. Prepare report and sell recommendations
  6. Install recommendations and follow up effectiveness

 b. Pitfalls to avoid
  1. *Taking things for granted* – A statement of the situation does not necessarily imply that each of the elements is necessarily true; for example, a complaint may be invalid and biased so that all that can be taken for granted is that a complaint has been registered
  2. *Considering only one side of a situation* – Wherever possible, indicate several alternatives and then point out the reasons you selected the best one
  3. *Failing to indicate follow up* – Whenever your answer indicates action on your part, make certain that you will take proper follow-up action to see how successful your recommendations, procedures or actions turn out to be
  4. *Taking too long in answering any single question* – Remember to time your answers properly

IX. AFTER THE TEST

Scoring procedures differ in detail among civil service jurisdictions although the general principles are the same. Whether the papers are hand-scored or graded by machine we have described, they are nearly always graded by number. That is, the person who marks the paper knows only the number – never the name – of the applicant. Not until all the papers have been graded will they be matched with names. If other tests, such as training and experience or oral interview ratings have been given, scores will be combined. Different parts of the examination usually have different weights. For example, the written test might count 60 percent of the final grade, and a rating of training and experience 40 percent. In many jurisdictions, veterans will have a certain number of points added to their grades.

After the final grade has been determined, the names are placed in grade order and an eligible list is established. There are various methods for resolving ties between those who get the same final grade – probably the most common is to place first the name of the person whose application was received first. Job offers are made from the eligible list in the order the names appear on it. You will be notified of your grade and your rank as soon as all these computations have been made. This will be done as rapidly as possible.

People who are found to meet the requirements in the announcement are called "eligibles." Their names are put on a list of eligible candidates. An eligible's chances of getting a job depend on how high he stands on this list and how fast agencies are filling jobs from the list.

When a job is to be filled from a list of eligibles, the agency asks for the names of people on the list of eligibles for that job. When the civil service commission receives this request, it sends to the agency the names of the three people highest on this list. Or, if the job to be filled has specialized requirements, the office sends the agency the names of the top three persons who meet these requirements from the general list.

The appointing officer makes a choice from among the three people whose names were sent to him. If the selected person accepts the appointment, the names of the others are put back on the list to be considered for future openings.

That is the rule in hiring from all kinds of eligible lists, whether they are for typist, carpenter, chemist, or something else. For every vacancy, the appointing officer has his choice of any one of the top three eligibles on the list. This explains why the person whose name is on top of the list sometimes does not get an appointment when some of the persons lower on the list do. If the appointing officer chooses the second or third eligible, the No. 1 eligible does not get a job at once, but stays on the list until he is appointed or the list is terminated.

X. HOW TO PASS THE INTERVIEW TEST

The examination for which you applied requires an oral interview test. You have already taken the written test and you are now being called for the interview test – the final part of the formal examination.

You may think that it is not possible to prepare for an interview test and that there are no procedures to follow during an interview. Our purpose is to point out some things you can do in advance that will help you and some good rules to follow and pitfalls to avoid while you are being interviewed.

What is an interview supposed to test?

The written examination is designed to test the technical knowledge and competence of the candidate; the oral is designed to evaluate intangible qualities, not readily measured otherwise, and to establish a list showing the relative fitness of each candidate – as measured against his competitors – for the position sought. Scoring is not on the basis of "right" and "wrong," but on a sliding scale of values ranging from "not passable" to "outstanding." As a matter of fact, it is possible to achieve a relatively low score without a single "incorrect" answer because of evident weakness in the qualities being measured.

Occasionally, an examination may consist entirely of an oral test – either an individual or a group oral. In such cases, information is sought concerning the technical knowledges and abilities of the candidate, since there has been no written examination for this purpose. More commonly, however, an oral test is used to supplement a written examination.

Who conducts interviews?

The composition of oral boards varies among different jurisdictions. In nearly all, a representative of the personnel department serves as chairman. One of the members of the board may be a representative of the department in which the candidate would work. In some cases, "outside experts" are used, and, frequently, a businessman or some other representative of the general public is asked to serve. Labor and management or other special groups may be represented. The aim is to secure the services of experts in the appropriate field.

However the board is composed, it is a good idea (and not at all improper or unethical) to ascertain in advance of the interview who the members are and what groups they represent. When you are introduced to them, you will have some idea of their backgrounds and interests, and at least you will not stutter and stammer over their names.

What should be done before the interview?

While knowledge about the board members is useful and takes some of the surprise element out of the interview, there is other preparation which is more substantive. It *is* possible to prepare for an oral interview – in several ways:

1) Keep a copy of your application and review it carefully before the interview

This may be the only document before the oral board, and the starting point of the interview. Know what education and experience you have listed there, and the sequence and dates of all of it. Sometimes the board will ask you to review the highlights of your experience for them; you should not have to hem and haw doing it.

2) Study the class specification and the examination announcement

Usually, the oral board has one or both of these to guide them. The qualities, characteristics or knowledges required by the position sought are stated in these documents. They offer valuable clues as to the nature of the oral interview. For example, if the job involves supervisory responsibilities, the announcement will usually indicate that knowledge of modern supervisory methods and the qualifications of the candidate as a supervisor will be tested. If so, you can expect such questions, frequently in the form of a hypothetical situation which you are expected to solve. NEVER go into an oral without knowledge of the duties and responsibilities of the job you seek.

3) Think through each qualification required

Try to visualize the kind of questions you would ask if you were a board member. How well could you answer them? Try especially to appraise your own knowledge and background in each area, *measured against the job sought*, and identify any areas in which you are weak. Be critical and realistic – do not flatter yourself.

4) Do some general reading in areas in which you feel you may be weak

For example, if the job involves supervision and your past experience has NOT, some general reading in supervisory methods and practices, particularly in the field of human relations, might be useful. Do NOT study agency procedures or detailed manuals. The oral board will be testing your understanding and capacity, not your memory.

5) Get a good night's sleep and watch your general health and mental attitude

You will want a clear head at the interview. Take care of a cold or any other minor ailment, and of course, no hangovers.

What should be done on the day of the interview?

Now comes the day of the interview itself. Give yourself plenty of time to get there. Plan to arrive somewhat ahead of the scheduled time, particularly if your appointment is in the fore part of the day. If a previous candidate fails to appear, the board might be ready for you a bit early. By early afternoon an oral board is almost invariably behind schedule if there are many candidates, and you may have to wait. Take along a book or magazine to read, or your application to review, but leave any extraneous material in the waiting room when you go in for your interview. In any event, relax and compose yourself.

The matter of dress is important. The board is forming impressions about you – from your experience, your manners, your attitude, and your appearance. Give your personal appearance careful attention. Dress your best, but not your flashiest. Choose conservative, appropriate clothing, and be sure it is immaculate. This is a business interview, and your appearance should indicate that you regard it as such. Besides, being well groomed and properly dressed will help boost your confidence.

Sooner or later, someone will call your name and escort you into the interview room. *This is it.* From here on you are on your own. It is too late for any more preparation. But remember, you asked for this opportunity to prove your fitness, and you are here because your request was granted.

What happens when you go in?

The usual sequence of events will be as follows: The clerk (who is often the board stenographer) will introduce you to the chairman of the oral board, who will introduce you to the other members of the board. Acknowledge the introductions before you sit down. Do not be surprised if you find a microphone facing you or a stenotypist sitting by. Oral interviews are usually recorded in the event of an appeal or other review.

Usually the chairman of the board will open the interview by reviewing the highlights of your education and work experience from your application – primarily for the benefit of the other members of the board, as well as to get the material into the record. Do not interrupt or comment unless there is an error or significant misinterpretation; if that is the case, do not hesitate. But do not quibble about insignificant matters. Also, he will usually ask you some question about your education, experience or your present job – partly to get you to start talking and to establish the interviewing "rapport." He may start the actual questioning, or turn it over to one of the other members. Frequently, each member undertakes the questioning on a particular area, one in which he is perhaps most competent, so you can expect each member to participate in the examination. Because time is limited, you may also expect some rather abrupt switches in the direction the questioning takes, so do not be upset by it. Normally, a board member will not pursue a single line of questioning unless he discovers a particular strength or weakness.

After each member has participated, the chairman will usually ask whether any member has any further questions, then will ask you if you have anything you wish to add. Unless you are expecting this question, it may floor you. Worse, it may start you off on an extended, extemporaneous speech. The board is not usually seeking more information. The question is principally to offer you a last opportunity to present further qualifications or to indicate that you have nothing to add. So, if you feel that a significant qualification or characteristic has been overlooked, it is proper to point it out in a sentence or so. Do not compliment the board on the thoroughness of their examination – they have been sketchy, and you know it. If you wish, merely say, "No thank you, I have nothing further to add." This is a point where you can "talk yourself out" of a good impression or fail to present an important bit of information. Remember, *you close the interview yourself.*

The chairman will then say, "That is all, Mr. _____, thank you." Do not be startled; the interview is over, and quicker than you think. Thank him, gather your belongings and take your leave. Save your sigh of relief for the other side of the door.

How to put your best foot forward

Throughout this entire process, you may feel that the board individually and collectively is trying to pierce your defenses, seek out your hidden weaknesses and embarrass and confuse you. Actually, this is not true. They are obliged to make an appraisal of your qualifications for the job you are seeking, and they want to see you in your best light. Remember, they must interview all candidates and a non-cooperative candidate may become a failure in spite of their best efforts to bring out his qualifications. Here are 15 suggestions that will help you:

1) Be natural – Keep your attitude confident, not cocky

If you are not confident that you can do the job, do not expect the board to be. Do not apologize for your weaknesses, try to bring out your strong points. The board is interested in a positive, not negative, presentation. Cockiness will antagonize any board member and make him wonder if you are covering up a weakness by a false show of strength.

2) Get comfortable, but don't lounge or sprawl

Sit erectly but not stiffly. A careless posture may lead the board to conclude that you are careless in other things, or at least that you are not impressed by the importance of the occasion. Either conclusion is natural, even if incorrect. Do not fuss with your clothing, a pencil or an ashtray. Your hands may occasionally be useful to emphasize a point; do not let them become a point of distraction.

3) Do not wisecrack or make small talk

This is a serious situation, and your attitude should show that you consider it as such. Further, the time of the board is limited – they do not want to waste it, and neither should you.

4) Do not exaggerate your experience or abilities

In the first place, from information in the application or other interviews and sources, the board may know more about you than you think. Secondly, you probably will not get away with it. An experienced board is rather adept at spotting such a situation, so do not take the chance.

5) If you know a board member, do not make a point of it, yet do not hide it

Certainly you are not fooling him, and probably not the other members of the board. Do not try to take advantage of your acquaintanceship – it will probably do you little good.

6) Do not dominate the interview

Let the board do that. They will give you the clues – do not assume that you have to do all the talking. Realize that the board has a number of questions to ask you, and do not try to take up all the interview time by showing off your extensive knowledge of the answer to the first one.

7) Be attentive

You only have 20 minutes or so, and you should keep your attention at its sharpest throughout. When a member is addressing a problem or question to you, give him your undivided attention. Address your reply principally to him, but do not exclude the other board members.

8) Do not interrupt

A board member may be stating a problem for you to analyze. He will ask you a question when the time comes. Let him state the problem, and wait for the question.

9) Make sure you understand the question

Do not try to answer until you are sure what the question is. If it is not clear, restate it in your own words or ask the board member to clarify it for you. However, do not haggle about minor elements.

10) Reply promptly but not hastily

A common entry on oral board rating sheets is "candidate responded readily," or "candidate hesitated in replies." Respond as promptly and quickly as you can, but do not jump to a hasty, ill-considered answer.

11) Do not be peremptory in your answers

A brief answer is proper – but do not fire your answer back. That is a losing game from your point of view. The board member can probably ask questions much faster than you can answer them.

12) Do not try to create the answer you think the board member wants

He is interested in what kind of mind you have and how it works – not in playing games. Furthermore, he can usually spot this practice and will actually grade you down on it.

13) Do not switch sides in your reply merely to agree with a board member

Frequently, a member will take a contrary position merely to draw you out and to see if you are willing and able to defend your point of view. Do not start a debate, yet do not surrender a good position. If a position is worth taking, it is worth defending.

14) Do not be afraid to admit an error in judgment if you are shown to be wrong

The board knows that you are forced to reply without any opportunity for careful consideration. Your answer may be demonstrably wrong. If so, admit it and get on with the interview.

15) Do not dwell at length on your present job

The opening question may relate to your present assignment. Answer the question but do not go into an extended discussion. You are being examined for a *new* job, not your present one. As a matter of fact, try to phrase ALL your answers in terms of the job for which you are being examined.

Basis of Rating

Probably you will forget most of these "do's" and "don'ts" when you walk into the oral interview room. Even remembering them all will not ensure you a passing grade. Perhaps you did not have the qualifications in the first place. But remembering them will help you to put your best foot forward, without treading on the toes of the board members.

Rumor and popular opinion to the contrary notwithstanding, an oral board wants you to make the best appearance possible. They know you are under pressure – but they also want to see how you respond to it as a guide to what your reaction would be under the pressures of the job you seek. They will be influenced by the degree of poise you display, the personal traits you show and the manner in which you respond.

ABOUT THIS BOOK

This book contains tests divided into Examination Sections. Go through each test, answering every question in the margin. At the end of each test look at the answer key and check your answers. On the ones you got wrong, look at the right answer choice and learn. Do not fill in the answers first. Do not memorize the questions and answers, but understand the answer and principles involved. On your test, the questions will likely be different from the samples. Questions are changed and new ones added. If you understand these past questions you should have success with any changes that arise. Tests may consist of several types of questions. We have additional books on each subject should more study be advisable or necessary for you. Finally, the more you study, the better prepared you will be. This book is intended to be the last thing you study before you walk into the examination room. Prior study of relevant texts is also recommended. NLC publishes some of these in our Fundamental Series. Knowledge and good sense are important factors in passing your exam. Good luck also helps. So now study this Passbook, absorb the material contained within and take that knowledge into the examination. Then do your best to pass that exam.

EXAMINATION SECTION

MEMORY FOR FACTS AND INFORMATION

These questions test for the ability to remember facts and information presented in written form after you have been given a period to read and study the information.

TEST TASK: You will be given a Memory Booklet containing a story. The story will be considerably longer than the one presented here. You will have 5 minutes to read and study the information in the Memory Booklet. You will NOT be allowed to take notes. At the end of the study period, the monitor will collect the Memory Booklets containing the story and then will hand out the test booklets containing the test questions. The first group of questions in this test booklet will ask you to recall the facts and information presented in the Memory Booklet.

SAMPLE MEMORY STORY: Officer Gary Hanson of the Burke Police Department was questioning Mathew Meyers, the owner of Meyers Sporting Goods located at 321 Payne Avenue, about a burglary that occurred the previous evening. Meyers said that when he arrived at the store at 8:50 A.M., he noticed that the rear door had been broken into. Meyers said that, after he had checked his inventory, he was missing 20 rifles, 16 pellet guns, 12 shotguns, and 8 pistols.

SAMPLE QUESTION: How many shotguns did Meyers tell the Officer were missing from his store?

A. 8
B. 12
C. 16
D. 20

The answer is B.

SOLUTION: This question asks how many <u>shotguns</u> did Meyers tell the Officer were missing from his store. The last sentence in the Memory Story states, "...Meyers said that ... he was missing 20 rifles, 16 pellet guns, 12 shotguns, and 8 pistols."

Choice A: This is the number of missing <u>pistols</u>. Choice A is incorrect.

Choice B: This is the number of missing <u>shotguns</u>. Choice B is correct.

Choice C: This is the number of missing <u>pellet guns</u>. Choice C is incorrect.

Choice D: This is the number of <u>missing rifles</u>. Choice D is incorrect.

MEMORY FOR FACTS AND INFORMATION

EXAMINATION SECTION
TEST 1

DIRECTIONS: Questions 1 through 15 test your ability to remember key facts and details. You are given a rather long reading passage, which you will have approximately ten minutes to read. The reading selection should then be turned over. Then immediately answer the fifteen questions that refer to this passage. Please do NOT refer back to the reading passage at any time while you are answering the questions. Select the letter that represents the BEST of the four possible choices.

<u>THE CASE OF THE MISSING OVERTIME WAGES</u>

Melba Tolliber is a new Labor Standards Investigator assigned to investigate a complaint of nonpayment of some overtime wages. The complaint came in the form of a telephone call from Albert Brater, employed by the Whizzer Audio and Video Store in Dorchester. Whizzer Audio and Video, Inc. is a fast-growing and very successful chain in the Northeast. Their headquarters is in Dorchester.

Melba Tolliber drives the eight miles to Dorchester on a breezy Monday morning. She meets with Albert Brater, the employee who called. He is employed in the warehouse unit.

Hello, Mr. Brater, my name is Melba Tolliber, and I'm here to investigate whether you've been paid the proper amount of overtime wages.

Nice to meet you, Ms. Tolliber. I'm not the only one with this problem. Two salesclerks in the Dorchester store, Mary and Martin, have also gotten less for overtime than they should have.

Can I talk with them, too? Melba asks.

Well, the problem is, we're worried about getting into a lot of trouble with, the company. We were hoping you could talk just to me. I'm a little worried about talking with you myself.

This is a confidential interview; don't worry. It would be very helpful, however, if I could at least get copies of their pay stubs.

Albert hesitates and then says, *Gee, I hope I can find my last paystub. Anyway, we've been working forty-six hours a week the last four weeks, but only getting paid our usual rate of $5.25 an hour.*

Melba says, *But that's below the minimum wage.*

Maybe it's $5.35; I get confused; I'll have to check. I think it's $5.35. Yeah, I'm pretty sure it's $5.35. But you know what else? I was promised a raise of $.50 per hour after eight months of working here, and that's up next week. We'll see if I get it or not.

Have the other employees here gotten the raises they were promised?

Yeah, I think they have. But I know of at least one person, a truckdriver, who hasn't gotten his raise yet.

Do you know his name?

Just his first name. But the next time I see him, I'll ask him if he's gotten the raise yet. I'll let you know if he hasn't.

What day would be good for you to drop off the paystubs and have a second interview?

Well, you have to give me some time to get them from Mary and Martin, too. How about this Thursday afternoon at one?

Fine, heres my card. I'll see you this Thursday at one.

At the beginning of their next meeting, Albert gives Melba the paystubs for the last month's work for all three employees.

Let's do you first, Albert. What have your hours been each week for the last four weeks?

I've worked the same schedule for the past month, my usual forty hours - 8 to 5 with an hour for lunch, which I don't like, on Mondays, Tuesdays, and Thursdays. Wednesdays and Fridays I've worked from 8 A.M. to 9 P.M. because those are the days we do our most shipping. They give us from 5 to 6 P.M. as a dinner break on those days.

So that adds up to forty-six hours. Give me a few minutes to go over these figures with my calculator.

That's a great calculator; it's so small. Looks like a credit card.

Thanks, but I have to be careful how I hit the numbers; there's not much room.... Well, according to my calculations, you're owed $48.15 in overtime pay for the last four weeks. But there's something else wrong, too. It looks like they've been taking out a little too much money for Social Security. Let me recheck this.

1. In the passage, Melba Tolliber visited 1.____

    A. Midwood B. Dorchester
    C. Midale D. Midville

2. In the passage, Melba talked with 2.____

    A. Albert who works in the warehouse unit
    B. Albert who works in the warehouse unit and in the store
    C. Robert who works in the warehouse
    D. Robert, Martin, and Mary who work in the warehouse and the store

3. The organization whose payment of overtime wages is in question 3.____

    A. is struggling to succeed
    B. is the most successful of the new audio-visual store chains in the Northeast
    C. has its headquarters in the town that Melba travels to
    D. has successfully switched from selling just records to selling records, tapes, and video equipment

4. During their initial discussion, how sure of his rate of pay was the employee to whom Melba spoke? 4.____

    A. Not sure at all   B. Very sure
    C. Pretty sure   D. Totally unsure

5. What day of the week did Melba conduct the initial interview? 5.____

    A. Monday   B. Wednesday
    C. Tuesday   D. Thursday

6. When did Melba conduct the second interview? 6.____

    A. Monday at 1 P.M.   B. Thursday at 1 P.M.
    C. Wednesday at 1 P.M.   D. Friday at 1 P.M.

7. In order to calculate how much money the employee should have received, Melba used a 7.____

    A. credit card
    B. calculator
    C. credit card/calculator/watch combination
    D. desk top personal computer

8. According to the passage, what did Melba do to try to make the employee feel more at ease? 8.____
She

    A. gave him time to collect his thoughts
    B. assured him that she believed what he said
    C. assured him that the interview was confidential
    D. asked if she could speak with the other two employees affected

9. The initial complaint from the employee 9.____

    A. resulted in his receiving back pay
    B. came in the form of a phone call
    C. was anonymous
    D. resulted in a large-scale investigation

10. The name of the establishment the employee works for is the 10.____

    A. Whizzer
    B. Genuine Article
    C. Electronic Era
    D. Gizmos etcetera

4 (#1)

11. The other two employees who have questions about their overtime pay 11._____

   A. are truckdrivers
   B. work in the warehouse
   C. are salesclerks
   D. work in maintenance

12. The organization told the employee he would receive a 12._____

   A. $.60 per hour raise after eight months
   B. $.60 per hour raise after five months
   C. $.50 per hour raise after six months
   D. $.50 per hour raise after eight months

13. How many hours a week have the employees who are questioning their pay been working for the last month? 13._____

   A. Forty-four
   B. Forty-five
   C. Forty-six
   D. Forty-eight

14. In the last month, what hours did the employee Melba interviewed work on Wednesdays? 14._____

   A. 8 A.M. to 5 P.M.
   B. 9 A.M. to 10 P.M.
   C. 9 A.M. to 5 P.M.
   D. 8 A.M. to 9 P.M.

15. At the start of the second interview, 15._____

   A. the employee gives Melba the paystubs for the last month for all three workers involved
   B. the employee gives Melba the paystubs for the last month for all three workers involved, with the exception of his last paystub
   C. the employee gives Melba only his paystubs from the last month
   D. it cannot be determined if the employee gives Melba any paystubs

KEY (CORRECT ANSWERS)

1. B	6. B
2. A	7. B
3. C	8. C
4. C	9. B
5. A	10. A

11. C
12. D
13. C
14. D
15. A

TEST 2

DIRECTIONS: Questions 1 through 15 test your ability to remember key facts and details. You are given a rather long reading passage, which you will have approximately ten minutes to read. The reading selection should then be turned over. Then immediately answer the fifteen questions that refer to this passage. Please do NOT refer back to the reading passage at any time while you are answering these questions. Select the letter that represents the BEST of the four possible choices.

THE CASE OF THE DELINQUENT TAXPAYER

David Owens has been a Tax Investigator for five years. His unit has received another anonymous tip about possible sales tax abuse, and David's supervisor, William, has assigned David to conduct the investigation. The organization in question is Bob's News, a 24-hour newsstand and variety store. The store is located in Hillsdell, five miles away. The anonymous caller did not provide details, but stated that she was an employee, and that there was widespread abuse in the collection and reporting of sales tax by the store. The agency has had a series of crank calls regarding sales tax abuse in Hillsdell.

For this investigation, David has been instructed not to work undercover, but to go in, identify himself, and discuss the situation with the owner and some employees without divulging the reason for the visit. On Wednesday, David drives to the store in a government car, a 2004 Plymouth.

David arrives at the store and buys a magazine for which he is properly not charged sales tax. He speaks to the employee whose name tag says Susan.

Hello, Susan, my name is David Owens, and I'm from the State Tax Department. Here's my identification. We're doing a routine check-up to see if things are in order with regard to sales tax collection and reporting. Is the owner around?

No, Bob is out of town today. He'll be back tomorrow. You seem surprised that his name is Bob. Some people think he must not exist, sort of like a Betty Crocker or something. Can I help you with anything? I'm the Assistant Manager.

Well, it would be helpful if you could answer a few questions for me.

As long as it doesn't get me in trouble with my boss, I'd be glad to, Susan replied.

Don't worry, I won't ask you anything that could, get you in trouble.

OK, then.

Did someone tell employees how to go about collecting sales tax on items?

Bob has a list of items we're not allowed to collect tax on. It's right next to the cash register. Would you like to see it?

If you don't mind. Thanks. It says here not to collect tax on magazines, but there's no mention of newspapers.

I guess that's because he probably assumes we know better than that. I'll ask him to add it to the list.

This is a pretty good list, but what's this written on the bottom here about toilet paper? That's a taxable item.

Oh, I know. Henry who works nights put that in as a joke because he says toilet paper is a necessity, not a luxury, and shouldn't be taxed. I agree. So does Bob. But don't worry, we collect sales tax on it. Nine percent, right?

No, the rate is eight percent.

Just kidding, David. We know that. I guess I shouldn't joke about something like that; I don't want to end up in jail. What else do you need to know?

Who keeps the records and submits the sales tax money to Metro City every quarter?

Bob does that himself, but I'd rather you come back tomorrow to talk with him about that end of it....I think that would be best. I don't know much about it, except that he yells if I don't have everything - the records and stuff - ready for him when he wants it.

What time do you think Bob will be in tomorrow?

I think the morning would be best, you'll be sure to catch him then.

OK, I'll drop by tomorrow around nine. See you then. Thanks again.

The next day, David drives back to the store to meet with Bob at the time stated earlier. When he arrives, Susan immediately introduces him to Bob.

It's nice to meet you, Bob. Nice store you have here. How long have you been in business?

We've been open for five years. Time really flies, doesn't it?

It sure does. As Susan probably mentioned, I'm here on a routine type check-up about sales tax collection.

Sure thing.

Well, I just noticed you're not displaying the Sales Tax Certificate of Authority, that you need to show in order to collect sales tax.

That's strange; it was there yesterday. Here it is. It fell under the counter. We're off to a great start. Let me tape this thing back up.

How many employees work here. Bob?

We have six full-time and three part-time employees, plus myself. I understand you'd like to see our books. Come on in to my office. Stay in here as long as you need. I've got it all laid out for you.

Thanks.

Several hours later, David finishes looking through the books.

Well, Bob, things look in order. The only question I have is why your receipts for 2004 were so much lower than in other years?

A chain store moved in about eight blocks away, and we initially lost a lot of business. But eventually our customers started coming back. We do the little things - save them the Boston papers, things like that. The chain moved downtown in early 2005.

Well, listen, thanks very much for all of your time. I really appreciate it.

No problem. Anytime. Well, I wouldn't go that far, but it's been nice meeting you.

1. What was the name of the Tax Investigator in the above passage?

    A. David Allen
    B. Bob Williams
    C. Derwin Williams
    D. David Owens

2. What was the name of the city the investigator visited?

    A. Hillsville
    B. Hillsdale
    C. Hicksville
    D. Hillsdell

3. The store under investigation is a

    A. department store
    B. 24-hour massage parlor
    C. newsstand and variety store
    D. sporting goods store

4. The phone call received by the agency was

    A. placed by an anonymous employee of the store being accused of sales tax fraud
    B. received by the investigator handling the case
    C. placed by an anonymous caller
    D. received by the investigator's supervisor

5. The investigator on this case

    A. did not work undercover
    B. was instructed to work undercover, but refused because of the nature of the case
    C. worked undercover
    D. pretended to his supervisor that he worked undercover

6. According to the above passage, it is

    A. not correct to charge sales tax for a magazine
    B. correct to charge sales tax for pet food

C. correct to charge sales tax for a newspaper
D. correct to charge sales tax for a magazine

7. The Assistant Manager of the store is

   A. Susan
   B. David
   C. Bob
   D. Betty Crocker

   7.____

8. What day was the initial investigation conducted?

   A. Monday
   B. Wednesday
   C. Tuesday
   D. Thursday

   8.____

9. The list the investigator was shown contained

   A. a list of sales taxable items
   B. a list of non-taxable items
   C. a list of products on which sales tax was mistakenly charged
   D. the Certificate of Authority

   9.____

10. According to the above passage, sales tax was to be charged on

    A. pet food
    B. cigarettes
    C. gasoline
    D. toilet paper

    10.____

11. According to the above passage, the sales tax was ____%.

    A. seven   B. nine   C. eight   D. ten

    11.____

12. According to the passage, how often was the sales tax submitted?

    A. Every month
    B. Quarterly
    C. Twice a year
    D. Once every six months

    12.____

13. According to the passage, where are the sales tax monies sent?

    A. River City
    B. Metro City
    C. Metropolis
    D. Hillswood

    13.____

14. According to the passage, which of the following is TRUE? Bob's business, called Bob's

    A. News and Variety, has been open for five years
    B. Department Store, has been open for six years
    C. Variety, has been open for six years
    D. News, has been open for five years

    14.____

15. The only question the investigator had about Bob's books was why receipts for _____ than in other years.

    A. 2005 were so much lower
    B. 2004 were so much lower
    C. 2005 were so much higher
    D. 2004 were so much higher

    15.____

KEY (CORRECT ANSWERS)

1. D
2. D
3. C
4. C
5. A

6. A
7. A
8. B
9. B
10. D

11. C
12. B
13. B
14. D
15. B

———

EXAMINATION SECTION
TEST 1

DIRECTIONS: Each question or incomplete statement is followed by several suggested answers or completions. Select the one that BEST answers the question or completes the statement. *PRINT THE LETTER OF THE CORRECT ANSWER IN THE SPACE AT THE RIGHT.*

Questions 1-10.   MEMORY

DIRECTIONS: Questions 1 through 10 are to be answered SOLELY on the basis of the following passage, which contains a story about an incident involving police officers. You will have ten minutes to read and study the story. You may not write or make any notes while studying it. After ten minutes, close the memory booklet and do not look at it again. Then, answer the questions that follow.

You are one of a number of police officers who have been assigned to help control a demonstration inside Baldwin Square, a major square in the city. The demonstration is to protest the U.S. involvement in Iraq. As was expected, the demonstration has become nasty. You and nine other officers have been assigned to keep the demonstrators from going up Bell Street which enters the Square from the northwest. During the time you have been assigned to Bell Street, you have observed a number of things.

Before the demonstration began, three vans and a wagon entered the Square from the North on Howard Avenue. The first van was a 1989 blue Ford, plate number 897-JLK. The second van was a 1995 red Ford, plate number 899-LKK. The third van was a 1997 green Dodge step-van, plate number 997-KJL. The wagon was a blue 1998 Volvo with a luggage rack on the roof, plate number 989-LKK. The Dodge had a large dent in the left-hand rear door and was missing its radiator grill. The Ford that was painted red had markings under the paint which made you believe that it had once been a telephone company truck. Equipment for the speakers' platform was unloaded from the van, along with a number of demonstration signs. As soon as the vans and wagon were unloaded, a number of demonstrators picked up the signs and started marching around the square. A sign reading *U.S. Out Now* was carried by a woman wearing red jeans, a black tee shirt, and blue sneakers. A man with a beard, a blue shirt, and Army pants began carrying a poster reading *To Hell With Davis*. A tall, Black male and a Hispanic male had been carrying a large sign with *This Is How Vietnam Started* in big black letters with red dripping off the bottom of each letter.

A number of the demonstrators are wearing black armbands and green tee shirts with the peace symbol on the front. A woman with very short hair who was dressed in green and yellow fatigues is carrying a triangular-shaped blue sign with white letters. The sign says *Out Of Iraq*.

A group of 12 demonstrators have been carrying six fake coffins back and forth across the Square between Apple Street on the West and Webb Street on the East. They are shouting *Death to Hollis and his Henchmen*. Over where Victor Avenue enters the Square from the South, a small group of demonstrators (two men and three women) just started painting slogans on the walls surrounding the construction of the First National Union Bank and Trust.

1. Which street is on the opposite side of the Square from Victor Avenue?
   A. Bell B. Howard C. Apple D. Webb

2. How many officers are assigned with you?
   A. 8 B. 6 C. 9 D. 5

3. Howard Avenue enters the Square from which direction?
   A. Northwest B. North C. East D. Southwest

4. The van that had PROBABLY been a telephone truck had plate number
   A. 899-LKK B. 989-LKK C. 897-JKL D. 997-KJL

5. What is the color of the sign carried by the woman with very short hair?
   A. Blue B. White C. Black D. Red

6. The man wearing the army pants has a(n)
   A. Afro
   B. beard
   C. triangular-shaped sign
   D. black armband

7. Which vehicle had plate number 989-LKK? The
   A. red Ford B. blue Ford C. Volvo D. Dodge

8. The bank under construction is located _____ of the Square.
   A. north B. south C. east D. west

9. How many people are painting slogans on the walls surrounding the construction site?
   A. 4 B. 5 C. 6 D. 7

10. What is the name of the bank under construction?
    A. National Union Bank and Trust
    B. First National Bank and Trust
    C. First Union National Bank and Trust
    D. First National Union Bank and Trust

KEY (CORRECT ANSWERS)

1. B
2. C
3. B
4. A
5. A
6. B
7. C
8. B
9. B
10. D

TEST 2

DIRECTIONS: Each question or incomplete statement is followed by several suggested answers or completions. Select the one that BEST answers the question or completes the statement. *PRINT THE LETTER OF THE CORRECT ANSWER IN THE SPACE AT THE RIGHT.*

Questions 1-15.

DIRECTIONS: Questions 1 through 15 are to be answered SOLELY on the basis of the Memory Booklet given below.

MEMORY BOOKLET

The following passage contains a story about an incident involving police officers. You will have ten minutes to read and study the story. You may not write or make any notes while studying it. The first questions in the examination will be based on the passage. After ten minutes, close the memory booklet, and do not look at it again. Then, answer the questions that follow.

Police Officers Boggs and Thomas are patrolling in a radio squad car on a late Saturday afternoon in the spring. They are told by radio that a burglary is taking place on the top floor of a six-story building on the corner of 5th Street and Essex and that they should deal with the incident.

The police officers know the location and know that the Gold Jewelry Company occupies the entire sixth floor. They also know that, over the weekends, the owner has gold bricks in his office safe worth $500,000.

When the officers arrive at the location, they lock their radio car. They then find the superintendent of the building who opens the front door for them. He indicates he has neither seen nor heard anything suspicious in the building. However, he had just returned from a long lunch hour. The officers take the elevator to the sixth floor. As the door of the elevator with the officers opens on the sixth floor, the officers hear the door of the freight elevator in the rear of the building closing and the freight elevator beginning to move. They leave the elevator and proceed quickly through the open door of the office of the Gold Jewelry Company. They see that the office safe is open and empty. The officers quickly proceed to the rear staircase. They run down six flights of stairs, and they see four suspects leaving through the rear entrance of the building.

They run through the rear door and out of the building after the suspects. The four suspects are running quickly through the parking lot at the back of the building. The suspects then make a right-hand turn onto 5th Street and are clearly seen by the officers. The officers see one white male, one Hispanic male, one Black male, and one white female.

15

The white male has a beard and sunglasses. He is wearing blue jeans, a dark red and blue jacket, and white jogging shoes. He is carrying a large green duffel bag over his shoulder.

The Hispanic male limps slightly and has a dark moustache. He is wearing dark brown slacks, a dark green sweat shirt, and brown shoes. He is carrying a large blue duffel bag.

The Black male is clean-shaven, wearing black corduroy pants, a multi-colored shirt, a green beret, and black boots. He is carrying a tool box.

The white female has long dark hair and is wear-ing light-colored blue jeans, a white blouse, sneakers, and a red kerchief around her neck. She is carrying a shotgun.

The officers chase the suspects for three long blocks without getting any closer to them. At the intersection of 5th Street and Pennsylvania Avenue, the suspects separate. The white male and the Black male rapidly get into a 1992 brown Ford stationwagon. The stationwagon has a roof rack on top and a Connecticut license plate with the letters *JEAN* on it. The stationwagon departs even before the occupants close the door completely.

The Hispanic male and the white female get into an old blue Dodge van. The van has a CB antenna on top, a picture of a cougar on the back doors, a dented right rear fender, and a New Jersey license plate. The officers are not able to read the plate numbers on the van.

The officers then observe the stationwagon turn left and enter an expressway going to Connecticut. The van turns right onto Illinois Avenue and proceeds toward the tunnel to New Jersey.

The officers immediately run back to their radio car to radio in what happened.

1. Which one of the following suspects had sunglasses on?

    A. White male   B. Hispanic male
    C. Black male   D. White female

2. Which one of the following suspects was carrying a shotgun?

    A. White male   B. Hispanic male
    C. Black male   D. White female

3. Which one of the following suspects was wearing a green beret?

    A. White male   B. Hispanic male
    C. Black male   D. White femal

4. Which one of the following suspects limped slightly?

    A. White male   B. Hispanic male
    C. Black male   D. White female

5. Which one of the following BEST describes the stationwagon used?
   A

    A. 1992 brown Ford   B. 1992 blue Dodge
    C. 1979 brown Ford   D. 1979 blue Dodge

6. Which one of the following BEST describes the suspect or suspects who used the sta-   6.____
   tionwagon?
   A

   A. Black male and a Hispanic male
   B. white male and a Hispanic male
   C. Black male and a white male
   D. Black male and a white female

7. The van had a license plate from which of the following states?   7.____

   A. Connecticut   B. New Jersey
   C. New York   D. Pennsylvania

8. The license plate on the stationwagon read as follows: 8.____

   A. JANE   B. JOAN   C. JEAN   D. JUNE

9. The van used had a dented _____ fender.   9.____

   A. left rear   B. right rear
   C. right front   D. left front

10. When last seen by the officers, the van was headed toward   10.____

    A. Connecticut   B. New Jersey
    C. Pennsylvania   D. Long Island

11. The female suspect's hair can BEST be described as   11.____

    A. long and dark-colored   B. short and dark-colored
    C. long and light-colored   D. short and light-colored

12. Which one of the following suspects was wearing a multicolored shirt?   12.____

    A. White male   B. Hispanic male
    C. Black male   D. White female

13. Blue jeans were worn by the _____ male suspect and the suspect.   13.____

    A. Hispanic; white female   B. Black; Hispanic male
    C. white; white female   D. Black; white male

14. The color of the duffel bag carried by the Hispanic male suspect was   14.____

    A. blue   B. green   C. brown   D. red

15. The Hispanic male suspect was wearing   15.____

    A. brown shoes   B. black shoes
    C. black boots   D. jogging shoes

KEY (CORRECT ANSWERS)

1. A
2. D
3. C
4. B
5. A

6. C
7. B
8. C
9. B
10. B

11. A
12. C
13. C
14. A
15. A

EXAMINATION SECTION
TEST 1

DIRECTIONS: Each question or incomplete statement is followed by several suggested answers or completions. Select the one that BEST answers the question or completes the statement. *PRINT THE LETTER OF THE CORRECT ANSWER IN THE SPACE AT THE RIGHT.*

Questions 1-3.

DIRECTIONS: Questions 1 to 3 measure your ability to fill out forms correctly and to remember information and ideas. Below and on the following two pages are directions for completing two kinds of forms, a correctly completed sample of each form, and a section from a procedures manual. You should memorize the sets of directions and the section from the procedures manual.

In the test, you will be (1) asked questions about the information and ideas in the manual and (2) presented with completed forms and asked to identify entries that are INCORRECT (contain wrong information, incomplete information, information in wrong order, etc.).

DIRECTIONS FOR COMPLETING CASE REPORT FORM

A case report form (see completed sample) is to be filled out by each officer at the time of the preliminary investigation. The entry for each numbered box is as follows:

Box 1 - The time the assignment was received.

Box 2 - The day, date, and time of the occurrence, in that order. Names of months and days may be abbreviated.

Box 3 - The manner in which the report was received. Use P = person, TOC = Through Official Channels (911 or other emergency numbers), M = mail, or T = telephone.

Box 4 - Name of the person notifying the department.

Box 5 - The address of the occurrence. include number, street, and village, and name of establishment, if appropriate. Do NOT abbreviate the name of a street, village, or establishment. If no street address is available, supply directions.

Box 6 - Victim's name, last name first.

Box 7 - Victim's birthdate - month, day, and year. Use the style shown in the completed sample.

Box 8 - Victim's sex and race: F = female, M = male, B = black, W = white, Y = yellow, O = other.

Box 9 - Relationship of victim to the offender (be as specific as possible):
HU = husband, WI = wife, MO = mother, FA = father,

SO = son, DA = daughter, BR = brother, SI = sister,
AQ = acquaintance, ST = stranger, UN = unknown.

SAMPLE OF COMPLETED CASE REPORT FORM

1. Time Received 5:57 PM	2. Date and Time of Occurrence Wed., Oct. 17, 2017, 1:00 PM	
3. Original Complaint Received TOC	4. Reported by Jeffrey Greene	
5. Place of Occurrence Sam's Stationery Shop, 130 Main St., Brooketown		
6. Victim's Name Silver, Sam	7. Date of Birth 3/17/72	8. Sex and Race M - W
7. Relationship to the Offender ST		

DIRECTIONS FOR COMPLETING
AUTOMOBILE FIELD INTERVIEW FORM

An automobile field interview form (see completed sample on the following page) is to be filled out when a car is stopped under suspicious circumstances, but no arrests are made. The entry for each numbered box is as follows:

Box 1 - Driver's name, last name first.

Box 2 - Village of residence, if within the county

Box 3 - Type of vehicle: S = sedan, C = convertible, SW = station wagon, V = van, T = truck.

Box 4 - Vehicle registration number.

Box 5 - Time and place of interview: location (street address only), time (per 24-hour clock), date, in that order.

Box 6 - Type of area: C = commercial, H = highway, R = residential, I = industrial, S = school

Box 7 - Patrol post number: precinct number is first digit; sector number is last two digits.

Box 8 - Officer's name and shield number, in that order.

SAMPLE OF COMPLETED AUTOMOBILE FIELD INTERVIEW FORM

1. Operator Robbins, Susan		2. Village Shady Brook	
3. Type of Vehicle C		4. Registration C 7237	
5. Time and Place of Interview Merry Road at Elm Street, 1428, 2/7/17			
6. Type of Area R	7. Post No. 221	8. Officer Sally Dodd, 2212	

CASE REPORT MANUAL
Section 1 - Solvability Factors

A solvability factor can be defined as any information about a crime that can provide a means to determine who committed it. In other words, a solvability factor is a useful clue to the identity of the perpetrator.

Based on national-level research, the following twelve universal factors have been identified:

1. Existence of witnesses to the crime
2. Knowledge of a perpetrator's name
3. Knowledge of a perpetrator's whereabouts
4. Description of a perpetrator
5. Identification of a perpetrator
6. Property that has traceable characteristics such as a registration number
7. Existence of a distinctive MO
8. Presence of significant physical evidence such as a set of burglar's tools
9. Description of a perpetrator's automobile
10. Positive results from a crime scene evidence search, such as fingerprints or footprints
11. Belief that a crime may be solved with publicity and/or reasonable investigative effort
12. Opportunity for only one person to have committed the crime

The presence of at least one of these solvability factors is necessary for there to be a reasonable chance for a solution to the crime. When there is no solvability factor, the chance of crime solution is limited. Therefore, the police officer who arrives at the scene of a crime first must make the greatest possible effort to identify solvability factors. This effort should include identification of witnesses and a thorough search of the crime scene.

DIRECTIONS: After you have memorized the directions and manual section, try to answer the following questions without referring to the study materials.

1. Which of the following crimes is *most likely* to have a solvability factor?

    A. A pickpocket takes several wallets on a crowded bus.
    B. Two muggers take money from a blind man in an alley.
    C. A hospital drug cabinet is broken into during a major emergency.
    D. A kidnapper escapes in a van decorated with pink, yellow, and avocado-green paint.

2. At 7:30 AM on Wednesday, February 6, 2017, Patrol Officer Alex White was assigned to investigate a suspected child-beating. The boy had been brought to the hospital, and Dr. Paul Cohen called the local station house at 7:20 AM. David Pepson, a White boy born on June 27, 2015, was brought from his home by his mother, who claims that her husband had punished David an hour earlier for making loud noises. David resides with his parents at 86 Whitewood Lane in Middletown.

4 (#1)

CASE REPORT FORM			
1. Time Received 7:30 AM		2. Date and Time of Occurrence Wed., February 6, 2017, 5:00 AM	
3. Original Complaint Received T		4. Reported by Dr. Paul Cohen	
5. Place of Occurrence 86 Whitewood Lane, Middletown			
6. Victim's Name David Pepson	7. Date of Birth 6/27/15		8. Sex and Race M - W
9. Relationship to the Offender FA			

Of the following, the box in the form above which is filled out INCORRECTLY is Box
   A. 3   B. 4   C. 8   D. 9

3. Officer Steven Brown, 7234, stopped a station wagon in the business section of Westville. He talked to the driver, John Caseman, on Rocky Road near South Bend and the western boundary of section 16 of precinct 2 at 8:20 PM on 3/8/17. The vehicle, registration number 2729H belongs to Mr. Caseman, who resides in Silverton.

3.____

AUTOMOBILE FIELD INTERVIEW FORM

1. Operator Caseman, John		2. Village Westville	
3. Type of Vehicle V		4. Registration 2729H	
5. Time and Place of Interview Rocky Road near South Bend, 2020, 3/8/17			
6. Type of Area C	7. Post No. 216		8. Officer Steven Brown, 7234

Of the following, the box in the form above which is filled out INCORRECTLY is Box
   A. 1   B. 3   C. 5   D. 7

Questions 4-6.

DIRECTIONS: Questions 4 to 6 measure your ability to recall information in a set of bulletins. To do well in the test, you must memorize both the pictorial and the written portions of each of the following eight bulletins.

Date of Issuance 5/13/17

INFORMATION WANTED

by

Police Department. County of Allamin
Hooblertown, Indiana 43102

The Allamin County Police Department homicide squad requests all auto repair shops, dealers and General Motors parts dealers in the precinct be contacted and questioned relative to the below described vehicle which is wanted for a felony - leaving the scene of a fatality. If vehicle is located, contact the homicide squad, (731) 624-1372. Refer to Homicide Case 130.

Place of Occurrence:	Midway State Road, South Strata, Indiana
Time of Occurrence:	0240 hours on March 3, 2017
Vehicle Wanted:	1980 Oldsmobile Cutlass Supreme, color green
Damage:	The Vehicle will have damage to the plastic grill located in the vicinity of the right front headlights. The chrome strip which is affixed to the center of the hood was recovered at the scene.
Parts:	The following parts will be needed to repair the vehicle: 1. Hood - GM Part No. 557547 or 557557 2. Plastic Grill - GM Part No. 22503156

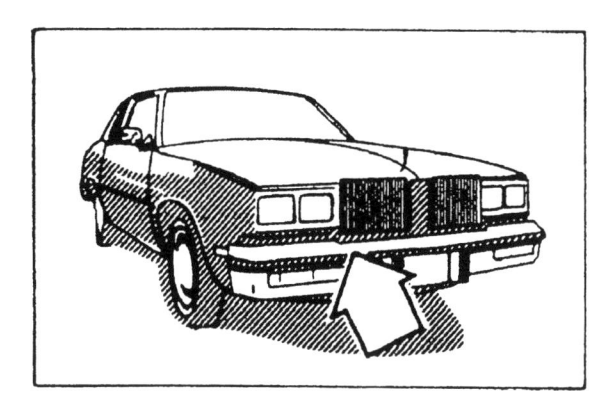

6 (#1)

WANTED
by

Police Department. County of Paradise
Cobbs Cove, Louisiana 41723
for
MURDER

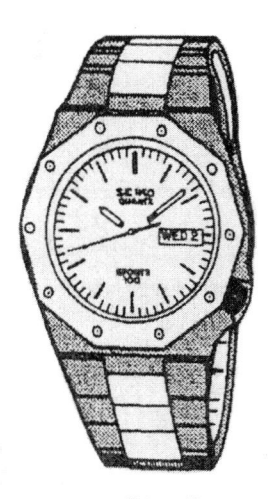

BULLETIN NO.
9-17

No. FJ110M

Note
Seiko watch with Gold Face and three section band is not a standard import into this area.

Occurrence:	Blue Jay Way and Nickel Drive, Yellowbird, 0530 hours on April 12, 2017.
Modus Operandi:	The deceased returned to his home at 2 Blue Jay Way, Yellowbird, at about 0530 hours, April 12, 2017. Four male whites were waiting in the vicinity of his garage and robbed him of U.S. currency and the above watch. They ran to the intersection of Blue Jay Way and Nickel Drive and got into a late model, shiny dark color, four door sedan with large tail-lights. The deceased chased them to the corner. One shot was fired causing his death.
Subjects:	Four Male Whites, dark hair.
Property:	One Seiko Quartz - Sports 100 - wrist watch, yellow metal face and crystal retainer. The band is an expandable three-section, white, yellow, white metal.
Note:	Anyone with information is requested to contact the Paradise County Homicide Squad.

7 (#1)

<u>W A N T E D</u>
<u>by</u>
<u>Police Department. County of Whitewall</u>
<u>Short Hills, Kentucky 27135</u>

for
MURDER

BULLETIN NO.
15-17

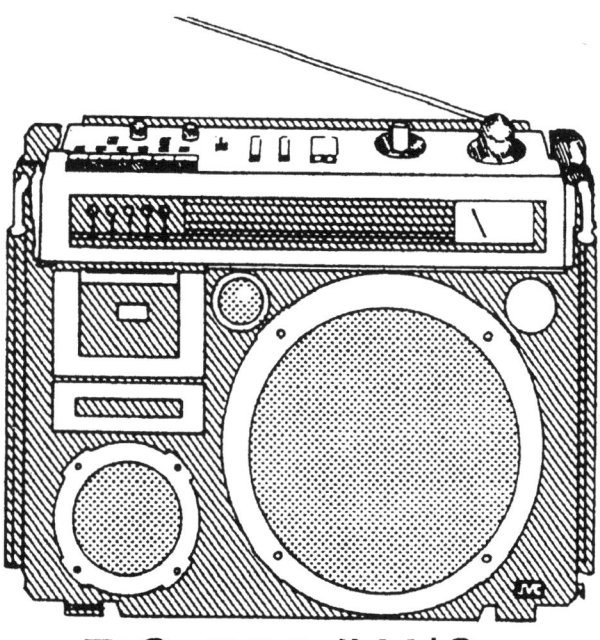

RC-550JW/C

Occurrence:	Public street, Brown Avenue, 60 ft. north of Camino Street, South Hill, KY, at 2340 hours, 6/25/17.
Modus Operandi:	The victim of the murder was walking south on Brown Avenue when he was accosted by the suspect and shot in the head by the suspect.
Subject:	Male, Black, 25-28 years, 5'9"-6' tall, thin build, short dark hair, medium dark skin, wearing a dark waist-length jacket, sneakers - armed with a gun.
Property:	The above property, a JVC AM-FM cassette radio, Model RC 550JW/C made of black plastic with chrome trim was stolen during the commission of a murder on Brown Avenue in South Hill. The battery compartment door is missing from the radio.
Note:	Anyone with information concerning the murder or the radio is asked to call the Whitewall Homicide Squad.

8 (#1)

W A N T E D
by
Police Department, County of Larinda
Blue Ridge. CA 97235

BULLETIN NO.
6-17

for
BURGLARY

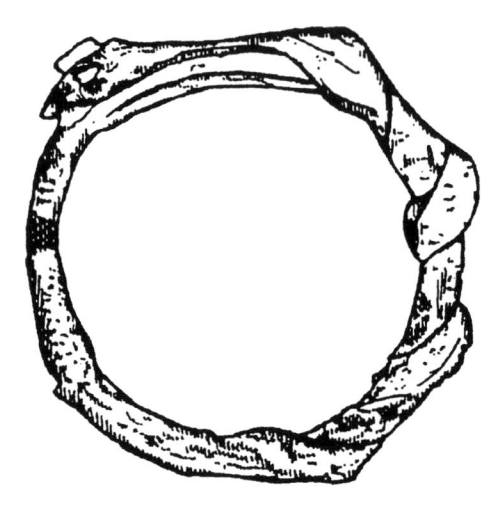

#1   #2

Date of Occurrence:	August 17, 2017 - 1930 to 2230 hours.
Place of Occurrence:	Private home, 37 Cliffmount Dr., Palasino, CA
Property:	Two distinctive, original designer rings taken.

    1. Ladies, yellow gold, 18K ring, size 8, an alligator with green emerald eye.
    2. Mans, yellow gold ring, a snake with 1/4 carat white diamond head and white diamond chips for eyes.

Value:	1. $5,000 2. $7,500
Note:	Any information - contact Burglary Squad, Refer to DD 4-25.

9 (#1)

WANTED
by

BULLETIN NO.
12-17

Police Department, County of Canton
Midship. Texas 84290

for
BURGLARY

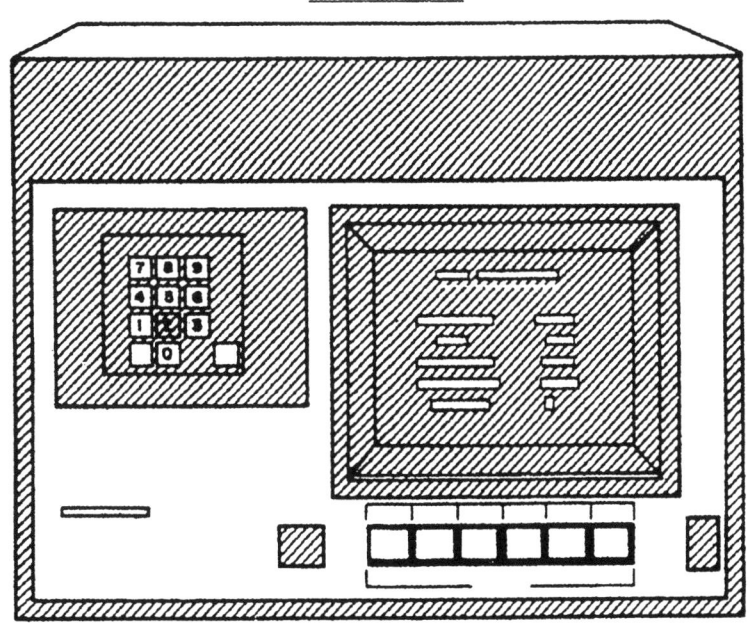

Date of Occurrence:	July 31, 2017 - 1640 hours to August 1 - 0720 hours.
Place of Occurrence:	606 Hillmont Drive, Alston, TX Freemont Testing Systems
Property:	Three engine analysers, color red, measuring 14" x 20" x 19"
Serial Numbers:	1. AN-0059 2. BP-0079 3. CR-0099
Value:	$6,666.00 each.
Note:	Request officers on patrol check service stations on post for the above items. Any information contact Detective Bryant, Third Squad, and refer to DD 3-52.

10 (#1)

<u>W A N T E D</u>
<u>by</u>

BULLETIN NO.
5-17

<u>Police Department, County of Marina</u>
<u>Waterford, CT 03612</u>

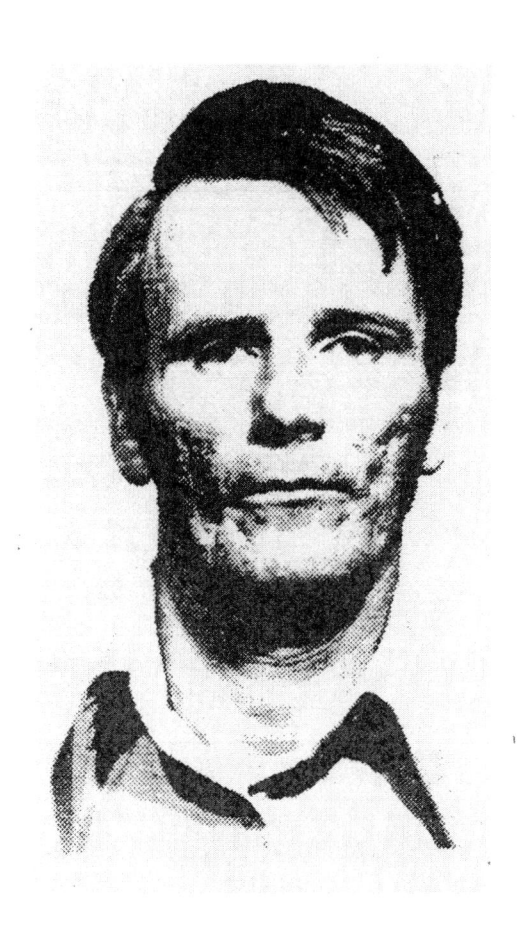

<u>for</u>
<u>ROBBERY</u>

2014 PHOTO

Occurrences:	Robberies of gas stations and boutiques in North End precincts of Marina County.
Modus Operandi:	Subject enters store and uses telephone or shops. He then produces sawed-off shotgun or revolver from under his coat and announces robbery.
Subject:	Harry Hamilton, Male, White, DOB 6/22/73, 5'10", 180 lbs., medium complexion, severely pockmarked face.
Further Details:	Contact Robbery Squad at (203) 832-7663. Refer to Robbery Case 782. Robbery Squad has warrant for subject. IF THIS PERSON ENTERS YOUR STORE <u>DIAL 911</u> OR THE ABOVE NUMBER

11 (#1)

WANTED
by

BULLETIN NO. 30-17

Police Department, County of Panfield
Lanser, South Carolina 30012

for
ROBBERY

2014 PHOTO
#1   #2

Occurrence:	3 North Avenue, Anita, South Carolina, on 11/26/17 at 2310 hours.
Modus Operandi:	The above subjects forced their way into the private residence of a rug dealer, accosted the dealer, his wife, and brother, demanding jewelry, currency, escaped on foot after binding victims.
Subjects:	No. 1 - Male, White, 40-45 years, 200 lbs., heavy build, bald shaved head, fair complexion, mustache, goatee, large hooked nose, black leather jacket, armed with a knife. No. 2 - Male, White, 6'1" tall, medium build, brown hair, subject identified as Mark Nine, DOB 4/16/78, last known address 1275 East 61st Street, Brooklyn, NY in 2011, hard drug user, armed with a hand gun, subject has been indicted for residence robbery. See Wanted Bulletin 21-12.
Possible 3rd Suspect:	Male, Hispanic, 30-35 years, 5'6", thin build, collar-length black wavy hair, eyes close together, with a large Doberman. Subject observed in the area before robbery talking to bald, stocky male. Also seen entering a vehicle containing 3 or 4 males after the robbery.
Loss:	U.S. currency and jewelry valued at $3,000 to $4,000.

Further Details: Contact Robbery Squad.

12 (#1)

WANTED	BULLETIN NO.
by	1-17
Police Department, County of Fantail	
Sweet Waters, Vermont 04610	

for
HI-JACKING

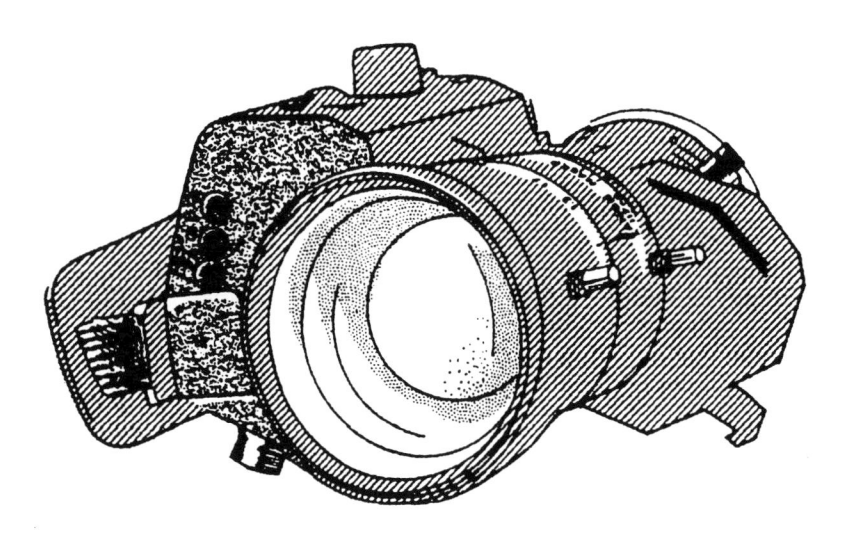

Occurrence: Vicinity of Nikon Plaza, off Jewel Avenue & Brook Bubble Road, Sweet Waters, VT at 1820 hours, 2/6/17.

Modus Operandi: Subjects accosted the driver of a United Parcel tractor/trailer, forcing him into a pale yellow van-type vehicle, make and year unknown. Vehicle contained a black and yellow leopard rug. Driver released after two (2) hours, in the vicinity of West Lake, VT. Tractor/ trailer recovered in White River, New Hampshire.

Subjects: Four (4) male Whites, one possibly named Joe, armed with hand guns. No further description.

Loss: Photo of above item: one (1) of four (4) broadcasting TV zoom lenses made by Nikon, valued at $7,000. Also included in the Nikon loss were current models of cameras, lenses, calculators, valued at $196,000. Medical supplies, mfg. by True Tell Inc., value $49,000. High quality medical examination scopes, industrial fiberscopes, cassette recorders and cameras, all mgf. by Canon Inc. valued at over $250,000. Sweaters, young mens, vee-neck design, mfg. Milford, Inc., labeled Dimension, Robt. Klein, J.C. Penney. Valued at over $20,450. Above items bearing serial numbers have been entered in NCIC.

Further Details: Contact Robbery Squad.

DIRECTIONS: After you have memorized both the pictorial and written portions of the bulletins, try to answer the following questions WITHOUT referring to the study materials.

4. Which of the following statements about the contents of the *Information Wanted* bulletin is or are true?
   I. The subject vehicle is involved in a felony.
   II. The subject vehicle is green-colored.
The CORRECT answer is:

   A. I *only*
   B. II *only*
   C. Both I and II
   D. Neither I nor II

4._____

5.

5._____

Which of the following statements about the object above is or are true?
   I. It was taken in the robbery of a residence.
   II. Its value is between $1,000 and $2,000.
The CORRECT answer is:

   A. I *only*
   B. II *only*
   C. Both I and II
   D. Neither I nor II

6. Which of the following, if any, fits the description of the individual who is wanted for the robbery of several gas stations?

6._____

   A.

   B.

C.   D. None of these

Questions 7-10.

DIRECTIONS: Questions 7 to 10 measure your ability to memorize and recall addresses, identification numbers and codes, and similar data.
In the test, you will be asked questions about the following body of information. You will NOT have the information in front of you when you take the test.

RADIO SIGNALS
01 - Back in Service
02 - Acknowledgement(OK)
06 - On Coffee
08 - Off Meal, Coffee, Personal
27 - Valid License
33 - Clear Channel (Any Emergency Request)
41 - One-Car Assistance Request
63 - Responding to Command
78 - Police Officer in Danger
99 - Possible Emergency Situation, Respond Quietly

TRUCK-TRACTOR IDENTIFICATION NUMBERS
VIN* Plate

Make	Location
Autocar	8
Brockway	2
Diamond Reo	9
Ford	10
GMC	4
Kenworth	1
Peterbuilt	7
White	5

*Vehicle Identification Number

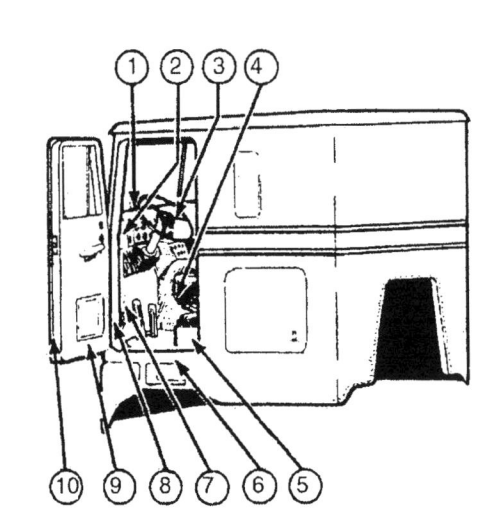

Location of County Precinct Houses

First -   In H,* on S side of Merrick Rd., just E of Grand Avenue.
Second - In OB,* 1/8 mi. E of Seaford-Oyster Bay Expressway, 1/8 mi.S. of Jericho Trnpk.
Third -   In NH,* 1/8 mi. N of Hillside Ave., 1/8 mi. W of Willis Avenue
Fourth - In H, on E side of Broadway, just N of Rockaway Avenue
Fifth -   In H, on S side of Dutch Broadway, 1/4 mi. N of Exit 14 of Southern State Parkway
Six -   In NH, just E of Community Drive, and just S of Whitney Pond Park. Seventh - In H,
          on side of Merrick Rd., just W of Seaford-Oyster Bay Expressway
Eighth - In H, on E side of Wantagh Ave., just N of Hempstead Farmingdale Trnpk.

Location of Universities, Colleges, and Institutes

Adelphi U. -   In H,* 1/4 mi. E of Nassau Blvd., 1/4 mi. S of Stewart Ave.
Hofstra U. -   In H, at Oak and Fulton Streets.
Molloy College -   In H, on Hempstead Ave., just S of Southern State Pkway., and midway
                          between Exits 19 and 20.
C. W. Post College -   In OB,* on Northern Blvd., 1 1/2 mi. W of Massapequa-Glen Cove Rd.
Nassau Community College - In H, on Stewart Ave., 1/2 mi. E of Clinton Rd.
Long Island Agri. & Tech. Institute - In OB, 1/2 mi. E of Round Swamp Rd., between Bethpage
       State Park and Old Bethpage Village Restoration.
N.Y. Inst. of Technology - In OB, on Northern Blvd., just E of line dividing OB and NH.
U.S. Merchant Marine Acad. - In NH,* at NW end of Elm Point Rd.

*H - Town of Hempstead; NH - Town of North Hempstead; OB - Town of Oyster Bay.

DIRECTIONS: After you have memorized the listed data, try to answer the following questions
              WITHOUT referring to the list.

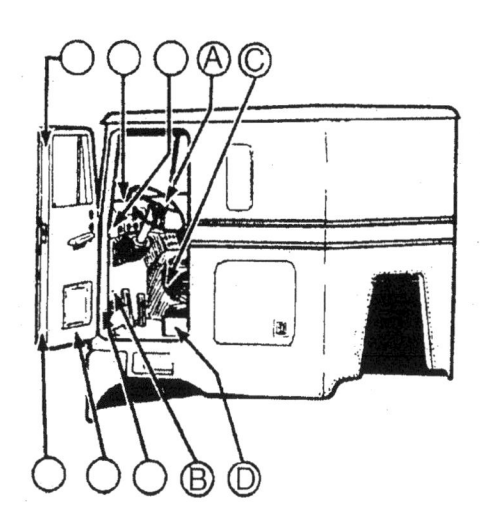

7. On a GMC truck-tractor, above, the VIN is located at

   A. A   B. B   C. C   D. D

8. The radio signal for *back in service* is

   A. 01   B. 04   C. 08   D. none of these

9. The Third Precinct House is located in   9.____
    A. NH, 1/8 mi. N of Hillside Ave., 1/8 mi. W of Willis Ave.
    B. NH, 1/4 mi. S of I.U. Willets Rd., 1/4 mi. E of Herricks Rd.
    C. Williston Park, on Willis Ave., 1/4 mi. S of Northern State Parkway
    D. Mineola, on Mineola Blvd., 1/2 mi. N of Jericho Trnpk.

10. The U.S. Merchant Marine Academy is at the NW end of _____ Rd.   10.____
    A. Sands Point   B. Mill Neck
    C. Kings Point   D. Elm Point

KEY (CORRECT ANSWERS)

1. D
2. D
3. B
4. C
5. A

6. D
7. C
8. A
9. A
10. D

VISUAL RECALL

EXAMINATION SECTION
TEST 1

DIRECTIONS: Each question or incomplete statement is followed by several suggested answers or completions. Select the one that BEST answers the question or completes the statement. *PRINT THE LETTER OF THE CORRECT ANSWER IN THE SPACE AT THE RIGHT.* This test consists of four(4) pictures with questions following each picture. Study each picture for three (3) minutes. Then answer the questions based upon what you remember without looking back at the pictures.

Questions 1-5

DIRECTIONS: Questions 1 through 5 are based on the drawing below showing a view of a waiting area in a public building.

1. A desk is shown in the drawing. Which of the following is on the desk? A(n)

   A. plant
   B. telephone
   C. in-out file
   D. *Information* sign

2. On which floor is the waiting area?

   A. Basement
   B. Main floor
   C. Second floor
   D. Third floor

3. The door <u>immediately to the right</u> of the desk is a(n)

   A. door to the Personnel Office
   B. elevator door
   C. door to another corridor
   D. door to the stairs

4. Among the magazines on the tables in the waiting area are

   A. TIME and NEWSWEEK
   B. READER'S DIGEST and T.V. GUIDE
   C. NEW YORK and READER'S DIGEST
   D. TIME and T.V. GUIDE

5. One door is partly open.
   This is the door to

   A. the Director's office
   B. the Personnel Manager's office
   C. the stairs
   D. an unmarked office

Questions 6-9.

DIRECTIONS: Questions 6 through 9 are based on the drawing below showing the contents of a male suspect's pockets.

6. The suspect had a slip in his pockets showing an appointment at an out-patient clinic on   6.____
   A. February 9, 2009   B. September 2, 2008
   C. February 19, 2008   D. September 12, 2009

7. The transistor radio that was found on the suspect was made by   7.____
   A. RCA   B. GE   C. Sony   D. Zenith

8. The coins found in the suspect's pockets have a TOTAL value of   8.____
   A. 56¢   B. 77¢   C. $1.05   D. $1.26

9. All except one of the following were found in the suspect's pockets.   9.____
   Which was NOT found?
   A
   A. ticket stub   B. comb
   C. subway token   D. pen

Questions 10-13.

DIRECTIONS: Questions 10 through 13 are based on the picture showing the contents of a woman's handbag. Assume that all of the contents are shown in the picture.

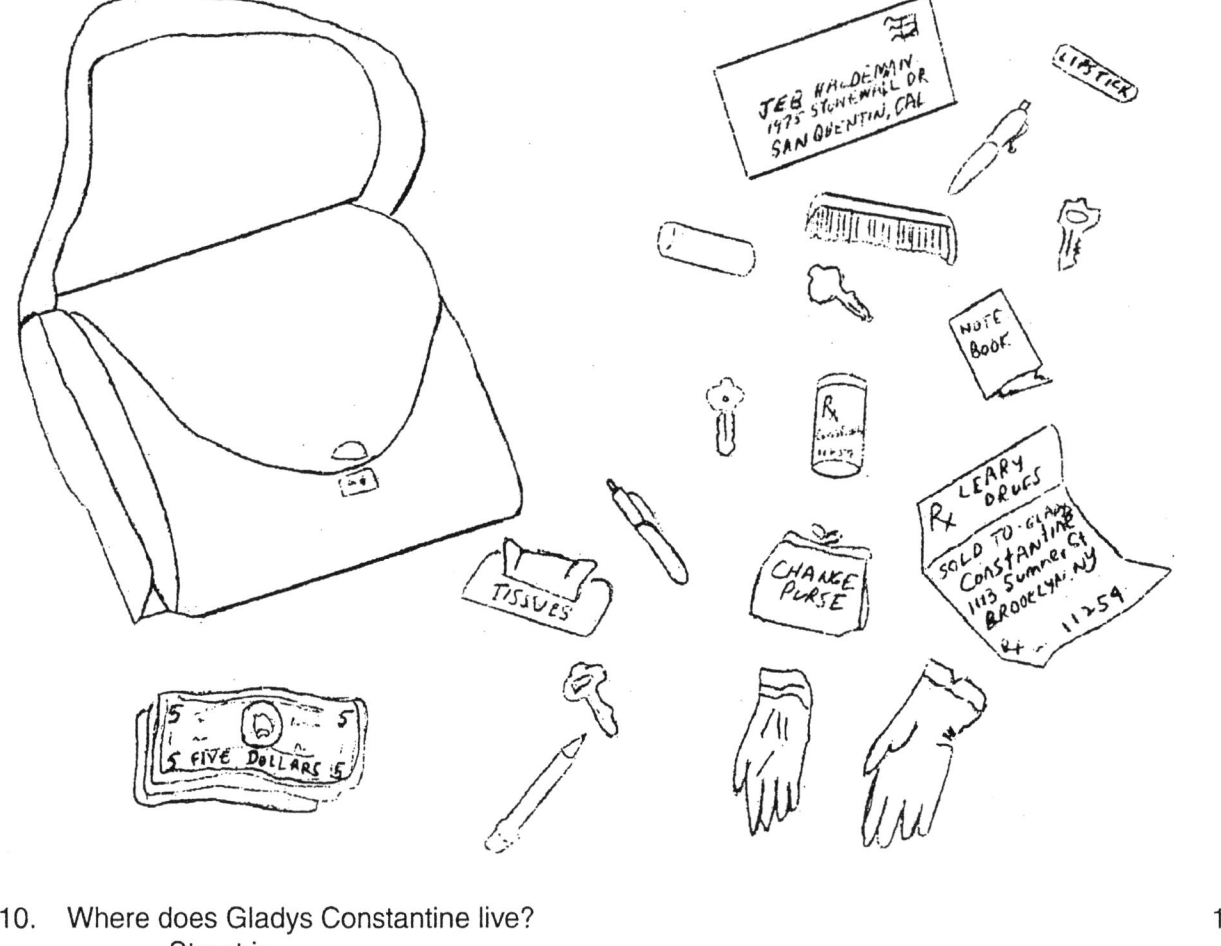

10. Where does Gladys Constantine live? _____ Street in _____.   10.____

    A. Chalmers; Manhattan   B. Summer; Manhattan
    C. Summer; Brooklyn   D. Chalmers; Brooklyn

11. How many keys were in the handbag?   11.____

    A. 2   B. 3   C. 4   D. 5

12. How much money was in the handbag? _____ dollar(s).   12.____

    A. Exactly five   B. More than five
    C. Exactly ten   D. Less than one

13. The sales slip found in the handbag shows the purchase of which of the following?   13.____

    A. The handbag   B. Lipstick
    C. Tissues   D. Prescription medicine

Questions 14-18.

DIRECTIONS: Questions 14 through 18 are based on the street scene on the following page. A robbery may be in progress down the block from where you are standing. Study and memorize the details before answering these questions.

40

14. The man carrying the two shopping bags is wearing 14._____

    A. khaki shorts and work boots
    B. a hat and black jacket
    C. a zip-up fleece and glasses
    D. a casual shirt and jeans

15. The building at the center of the photo is a(n) 15._____

    A. hotel   B. bank   C. restaurant   D. office building

16. The sidewalk is lined on the street side with 16._____

    A. parking meters   B. safety pillars
    C. street vendors   D. flower beds

17. Among the people standing in front of the center building is a 17._____

    A. man wearing khaki pants
    B. woman wearing knee-high boots
    C. young boy chasing another young boy
    D. man wearing a sports jersey

18. Reflections in the store windows indicate that 18._____

   A. there are food carts parked in the street
   B. a white truck is driving nearby
   C. it is a very sunny day
   D. a man is sitting on a curb nearby

KEY (CORRECT ANSWERS)

1.	D		11.	C
2.	C		12.	B
3.	B		13.	D
4.	D		14.	C
5.	B		15.	A
6.	A		16.	D
7.	C		17.	A
8.	D		18.	B
9.	D			
10.	C			

POLICE PROCEDURES & INFORMATION

Police Officers must be able to understand information and follow specified police procedures. One portion of the exam will test your ability to remember the information presented in this booklet. You are to assume that the police procedures presented here are the procedures that must be followed. The procedures and information to be memorized are:

> Hospital Cases
> Use of Police Radio
> Responsibilities of Police Officers at Crime Scenes
> Transporting Prisoners
> Reporting Vehicular Accidents
> Job Specification for Police Officer Trainee

Carefully learn these police procedures. If there are any words in these procedures you do not understand, look them up in a dictionary. You will NOT have these materials in front of you when you take the test. It is important to learn carefully this information or you will not be able to answer the questions on this section of the test.

Hospital Cases

Police personnel may be assigned to or encounter a hospital case. These cases will be considered emergencies unless a doctor or other medically trained person states otherwise. Hospital cases will be transported to the nearest hospital. In the case of a patient needing specialized care not available at the nearest hospital, a patrol supervisor will be contacted and will make the final decision.

Whenever possible, such as in cases where a stretcher is not needed, hospital cases will be transported by patrol car instead of by patrol wagon. In the case of life-threatening situations, the City Paramedic Unit will be notified immediately. The paramedics will assume the care and transportation of the patient. Police officers will direct traffic and assist paramedics as required.

Use of Police Radio

The purpose of police radio is to receive calls from the general public and dispatch unit, and to aid and inform police personnel in the field. Police dispatchers can give out assignments, relay information, and dispatch supervisors when requested or needed by field officers. Dispatchers cannot make command decisions but can relay the information to the proper command personnel. Police dispatchers also will broadcast information of general interest to police such as names of wanted and missing persons, and information on crimes. In addition, they will assign an identification number to each incident for which an officer is to file a report. This number will be recorded in the proper block on the Incident Report (82-7) and on all subsequent reports resulting from the original incident.

Dispatchers will make assignments by broadcasting the vehicle number, location of assignment and reason (e.g., "214, 2200 Connecticut Avenue, possible child abuse"). Each assignment will be repeated at least three times. If a unit is in-service and does not acknowledge an assignment, the dispatcher will record this and the officer will be required to submit a written memo stating the reason he/she did not respond. Disciplinary action may result.

Units will respond to dispatchers by stating their vehicle number and "Okay" if they can respond to the call. If not, they will state their vehicle number and the reason they are not available. Then the dispatcher may assign another officer. Patrol officers will notify police radio upon arrival at the scene by stating the vehicle number and "on scene." Officers will again notify police radio at the completion of the assignment by stating the vehicle number and "available."

All uniformed officers will remain in radio range at all times unless they are out-of-service or there is a shortage of hand-held units. Officers who will be out of radio range will report to the dispatcher their vehicle number, location, and reason for being out of range (e.g., "214, 2414 Down Drive, no portable unit") and will report back in as soon as they have radio access.

When an officer wishes to contact the dispatcher in a non-emergency situation, he/she will wait for a break in communications and state the vehicle number. The officer will wait for dispatcher acknowledgement (i.e., "214 go ahead") before proceeding. The officer will acknowledge information and assignments by stating vehicle number and "Okay."

In emergency situations, the officer will state his/her vehicle number and "emergency." These calls take precedence and all other transmissions will stop until the emergency call is ended. Emergency calls include: assist officer calls, reports of crimes-in-progress, car accidents involving serious injury, riotous situations, and life-endangering situations.

Responsibilities of Police Officers at Crime Scenes

The first officer on the scene is responsible for protecting the scene and telling the police dispatcher to send the necessary assistance. The officer also will take responsibility for the following:

1. Give first aid to the injured and make arrangements for transportation of the injured immediately. The officer should try to outline the position of the body before removal.

2. Question victim(s), if possible, to find out what happened. Notify police radio so information can be broadcast.

3. Detain all persons at the scene and try to prevent conversations among witnesses.

4. Do not let <u>anyone</u> touch or move anything at the scene or enter the crime scene except:

   A. Those transporting the injured.
   B. Personnel from the investigative unit and crime lab unit. I.D. <u>must</u> be displayed on outer garment.
   C. Police officers guarding the scene.
   D. An object such as a motor vehicle at the scene may be moved if it is a danger to public safety. Before moving it, outline its position and why and when moved. Give this information to the chief investigator on the scene.

5. Maintain a log of the names and badge numbers of all persons entering the scene and the reason for entering.

6. <u>No</u> other personnel, including supervisors not involved in the investigation, are allowed on the crime scene.

Transporting Prisoners

All persons will be searched by the arresting officer in accordance with procedures in section 11.07 of the Patrol Officer's Manual.

All prisoners will be taken to the district station by patrol wagon. If no wagons are available, prisoners will be transported in a patrol car after the officers receive permission from their sergeant. Two officers must be present in the car. The prisoner will sit in the rear seat behind the passenger side and the second officer will sit behind the driver.

All prisoners will be handcuffed behind their backs.

Prisoners should be kept in the rear seat of the patrol car while waiting for the wagon. Officers riding in the wagon will search the prisoner again in accordance with section 11.07 of the Patrol Officer's Manual.

After prisoners have been handed over to other authorities, officers will check their vehicles for contraband or weapons left behind or hidden by the prisoner. Officers should check behind and under seats. In patrol wagons, officers also should check the canvas stretchers and blankets if so equipped. Officers should exercise caution in case razor blades or other dangerous and exposed materials have been left behind.

Reporting Vehicular Accidents

The following procedures will be followed by police officers responding to or observing a vehicular accident:

1. Check to see if there are any injured people who require hospital treatment. If so, use police radio to request transportation.

2. Obtain operator's license(s), registration card(s), and insurance card(s) from the operator(s).

3. Fill out Incident Report for <u>all</u> accidents.

4. If the accident is reportable, also fill out a Police Accident Report. Reportable accidents are those in which any of the following occur:

    A. There is death or injury.
    B. Any vehicle is so damaged that it cannot be driven from the scene of the accident without further damage or danger, and towing is required.
    C. There is any damage to state or local government property or vehicles.
    D. The operator involved leaves the scene of the accident.
    E. It is believed that the operator involved is under the influence of drugs or alcohol.

5. Give operator(s) involved the report number of the completed Police Accident Form.

6. Give each operator an officer's business card containing the officer's rank, name, district of assignment, badge number, and district phone number.

7. Request police radio to send an officer from the Accident Investigation Unit in all cases where there has been fatal or potentially fatal injuries, or a local or state government vehicle is involved.

Note: The job specifications are not official with respect to the position for which you are applying. They are included to test your ability to read, understand, and recall information.

Job Specification for Police Officer Trainee

<u>Nature of Work:</u>

This work applies to entry and training level positions in law enforcement. The officer is trained in all aspects of law enforcement. Often, considerable public contact is involved, therefore, the officer is required to exercise the immediate practical judgment necessary to cope with unusual or emergency situations. The officer is expected to place emphasis on courteous explanation and personal persuasiveness in routinely seeking the compliance of others in obeying the laws. However, situations arise in which the officer must restrain and/or arrest persons threatening the security of the public.

Performance of the work is guided by written procedures. The officer receives close supervision from a higher level police officer. Officers in the trainee class normally do not hold supervisory positions.

Examples of Work:

    Patrols assigned areas.
    Searches for missing persons.
    Compiles data, keeps records, and prepares written reports on enforcement activities.
    Enforces federal, state, and local laws.
    Issues warnings or summonses and arrests those apprehended for violations.
    Investigates accidents and criminal acts.
    Presents evidence and gives testimony in court.
    Renders emergency first aid.
    Gives motorists directions and assistance.
    Attends formal training courses.

Required Knowledge and Abilities:

Introductory knowledge of criminal, civil, and traffic laws; and, knowledge of the care and use of firearms.

Ability to handle firearms safely, to comprehend oral and written instructions; to write narrative reports; to meet situations requiring tact, understanding, and good judgment; to detect situations imperiling security and safety; to remember names and faces; to learn.

Minimum Qualifications:

    Education: Graduation from high school or possession of a State high school equivalence certificate.

    License: A valid Motor Vehicle Operator license.

Conditions of Employment:

1. Candidates will be given a medical examination to determine physical ability to perform the job. This examination may include strength and agility tests. Good vision is required.

2. Due to provisions in the Retirement System Law, candidates aged 70 or over will not be appointed.

3. Duties necessitate being outdoors in all types of weather, standing and walking, or in assigned vehicles.

4. Due to the nature and condition of the work, a criminal conviction record may be a bar to employment. Candidates who have a conviction record will not be prevented from taking the test. If an investigation determines that a criminal conviction record is job-related, the candidate will not be selected and the Department of Personnel will authorize the passing over of such names on the eligible lists as provided by State law.

5. Persons appointed to the position of police officer may be required to be present for duty on Saturdays, Sundays, and holidays. Officers in this position may be assigned to any one of three shifts on a permanent or rotating basis and are required to report to work when called in during emergencies.

6. Demonstration of practical knowledge and proficiency in the safe use and care of firearms may be required of applicants prior to appointment or upon completion of the Police Training Commission course.

7. Prior to appointment being made permanent, a person appointed to a position of police officer trainee must have successfully completed, within the first year of employment, a training course approved by the Police Training Commission. Candidates must, therefore, be able to meet the minimum standards as determined by the Police Training Commission.

8. Candidates receiving a passing rating on all parts of the test will be interviewed before appointment. Also, candidates are subject to investigation by the State Police in order to establish eligibility to be commissioned to make arrests and to obtain a gun permit.

9. Persons appointed to this position may be required to have a telephone in their residence so that they may be contacted at any time.

Sample Questions

The following question is based on "Responsibilities of Police Officers at Crime Scenes."

1. You are the first officer on the scene. Your sergeant, who is not part of the investigation, wants to enter the crime scene. You should:

    A. let him enter.
    B. let him enter but caution him not to move or touch anything.
    C. let him enter and record his name and badge number in the log.
    D. not let him enter.

The following question is based on "Reporting Vehicular Accidents."

2. You arrive at the scene of an accident at the intersection of Apple Street and Orange Avenue. The owner of a badly damaged car tells you she saw a man in a van run into her parked car. You should:

   A. use police radio to broadcast the description of the van.
   B. fill out an Incident Report and a Police Accident Report.
   C. put a tag on the car with the name of the owner and the date of the accident.
   D. question witnesses to verify the car owner's account of the accident.

KEY (CORRECT ANSWERS)

1. D

2. B

EVALUATING INFORMATION AND EVIDENCE
EXAMINATION SECTION
TEST 1

DIRECTIONS: Each question or incomplete statement is followed by several suggested answers or completions. Select the one that BEST answers the question or completes the statement. *PRINT THE LETTER OF THE CORRECT ANSWER IN THE SPACE AT THE RIGHT.*

Questions 1-4.

DIRECTIONS: Questions 1 to 4 measure your ability (1) to determine whether statements from witnesses say essentially the same thing and (2) to determine the evidence needed to make it reasonably certain that a particular conclusion is true.

To do well in this part of the test, you do NOT have to have a working knowledge of police procedures and techniques or to have any more familiarity with crimes and criminal behavior than that acquired from reading newspapers, listening to radio, or watching TV. To do well in this part, you must read carefully and reason closely. Sloppy reading or sloppy reasoning will lead to a low score.

1. In which of the following do the two statements made say essentially the same thing in two different ways?
    I. All members of the pro-x group are free from persecution. No person that is persecuted is a member of the pro-x group.
    II. Some responsible employees of the police department are not supervisors. Some police department supervisors are not responsible employees.

    The CORRECT answer is:

    A. I *only*
    B. II *only*
    C. Both I and II
    D. Neither I nor II

2. In which of the following do the two statements made say essentially the same thing in two different ways?
    I. All Nassau County police officers weigh less than 225 pounds.
    II. No police officer weighs more than 225 pounds.
    No police officer is an alcoholic. No alcoholic is a police officer.

    The CORRECT answer is:

    A. I *only*
    B. II *only*
    C. Both I and II
    D. Neither I nor II

3. Summary of Evidence Collected to Date: All pimps in the precinct own pink-colored cars and carry knives.
   Prematurely Drawn Conclusion: Any person in the precinct who carries a knife is a pimp.
   Which one of the following additional pieces of evidence, if any, would make it *reasonably certain* that the conclusion drawn is TRUE?

   A. Each person who carries a knife owns a pink-colored car.
   B. All persons who own pink-colored cars pimp.

51

C. No one who carries a knife has a vocation other than pimping.
D. None of these

4. Summary of Evidence Collected to Date:
   1. Some of the robbery suspects have served time as convicted felons.
   2. Some of the robbery suspects are female.

   Prematurely Drawn Conclusion: Some of the female suspects have never served time as convicted felons.

   Which one of the following additional pieces of evidence, if any, would make it *reasonably certain* that the conclusion drawn is TRUE?

   A. The number of female suspects is the same as the number of robbery suspects who have served time as convicted felons.
   B. The number of female suspects is smaller than the number of convicted felons.
   C. The number of suspects that have served time is smaller than the number of suspects that have been convicted of a felony.
   D. None of these

Questions 5-8.

DIRECTIONS: Questions 5 to 8 measure your ability to orient yourself within a given section of a town, neighborhood, or particular area. Each of the questions describes a starting point and a destination. Assume that you are driving a patrol car in the area shown on the map accompanying the questions. Use the map as a basis for choosing the shortest way to get from one point to another without breaking the law.

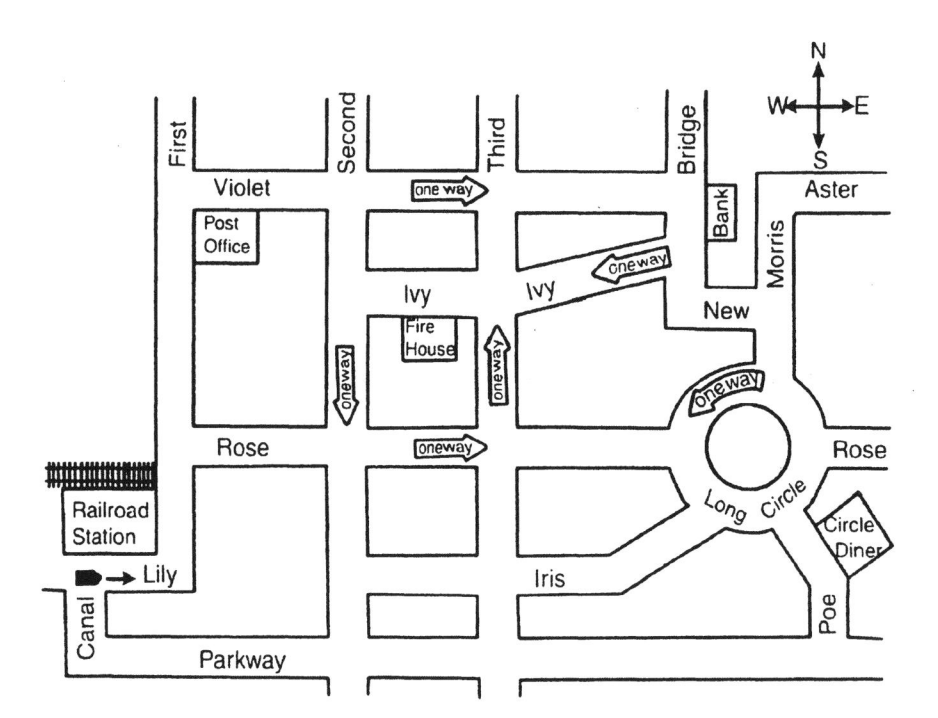

A street marked *one way* is one-way for the full length, even when there are breaks or jogs in the street. EXCEPTION: A street that does not have the same name over the full length.

5. A patrol car at the train station is sent to the bank to investigate a robbery. The SHORT-   5.____
   EST way to get there without breaking any traffic laws is to go

   A. east on Lily, north on First, east on Rose, north on Third, and east on Ivy to bank
   B. east on Lily, north on First, east on Violet, and south on Bridge to bank
   C. south on Canal, east on Parkway, north on Poe, around Long Circle to Morris, west on New, and north on Bridge to bank
   D. south on Canal, east on Parkway, north on Third, and east on Ivy to bank

6. At the bank, the patrol car receives a call to hurry to the post office. The SHORTEST way   6.____
   to get there without breaking any traffic laws is to go

   A. west on Ivy, south on Second, west on Rose, and north on First to post office
   B. west on Ivy, south on Second, west on Rose, and south on First to post office
   C. south on Bridge, east on New, south on Morris, around Long Circle, south on Poe, west on Parkway, north on Canal, east on Lily, and north on First to post office
   D. north on Bridge, west on Violet, and south on First to post office.

7. On leaving the post office, the police officers decide to go to the Circle Diner. The   7.____
   SHORTEST way to get there without breaking any traffic laws is to go

   A. south on First, left on Rose, right on Second, left on Parkway, and right on Poe to diner
   B. south on First, left on Rose, around Long Circle, and right on Poe to diner
   C. south on First, left on Rose, right on Second, right on Iris, around Long Circle, and left on Poe to diner
   D. west on Violet, right on Bridge, right on New, right on Morris, around Long Circle, and left on Poe to diner

8. During lunch break, a fire siren sounds and the police officers rush to their patrol car and   8.____
   head for the fire-house. The SHORTEST way to get there without breaking any traffic laws is to go

   A. north on Poe, around Long Circle, west on Iris, north on Third, and west on Ivy to firehouse
   B. north on Poe, around Long Circle, north on Morris, west on New, north on Bridge, and west on Ivy to firehouse
   C. north on Poe, around Long Circle, west on Rose, north on Third, and west on Ivy to firehouse
   D. south on Poe, west on Parkway, north on Third, and east on Ivy to firehouse

Questions 9-13.

DIRECTIONS: Questions 9 to 13 measure your ability to understand written descriptions of events. Each question presents you with a description of an accident, a crime, or an event and asks you which of four drawings BEST represent it.

In the drawings, the following symbols are used (these symbols and their meanings will be repeated in the test):

A moving vehicle is represented by this symbol: (front) ◁ (rear)

A parked vehicle is represented by this symbol: (front) ◀ (rear)

A pedestrian or a bicyclist is represented by this symbol: •

The path and direction of travel of a vehicle or pedestrian is indicated by a solid line: ⟶

EXCEPTION: The path and direction of travel of each vehicle or person directly involved in a collision from the point of impact is indicated by a dotted line: --→

9. A driver pulling out from between two parked cars on Magic is struck by a vehicle heading east which turns left onto Maple and flees.
Which of the following depicts the accident?

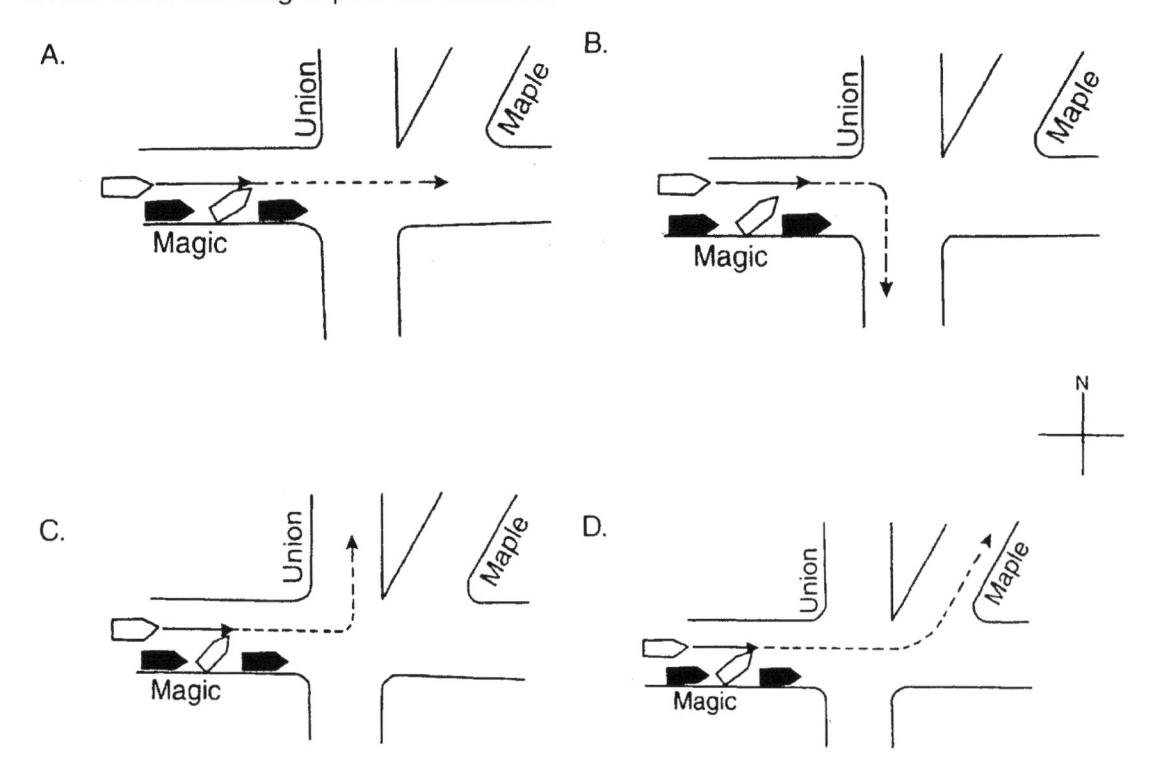

9.____

10. As Mr. Jones is driving south on Side. St., he falls asleep at the wheel. His car goes out of control and sideswipes an oncoming car, goes through an intersection, and hits a pedestrian on the southeast corner of Main Street.
Which of the following depicts the accident?

10.____

A. 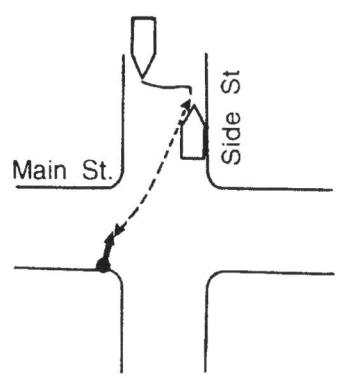
B. 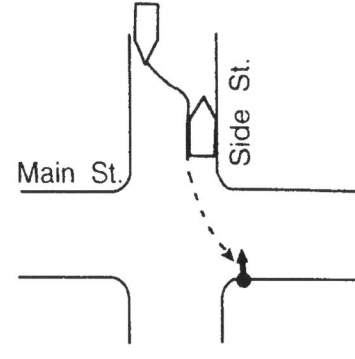
C. 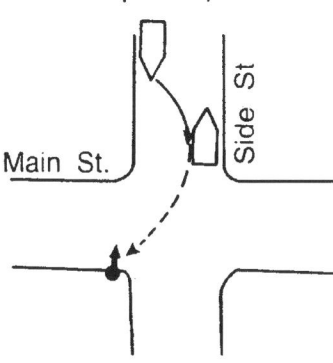
D.

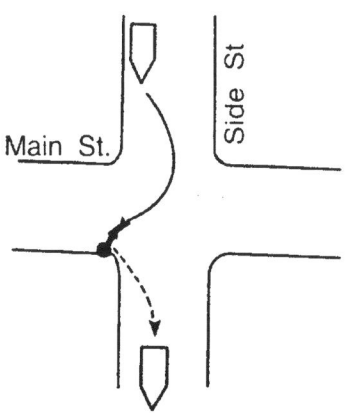

11. A car traveling south on Baltic skids through a red light at the intersection of Baltic and Atlantic, sideswipes a car stopped for a light in the northbound lane, skids 180 degrees, and stops on the west sidewalk of Baltic.
Which of the following depicts the accident?

11.____

A. 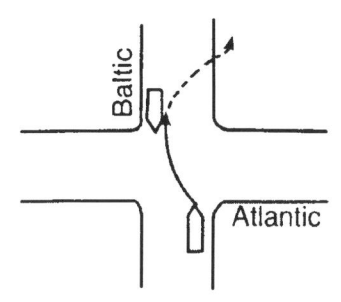
B. 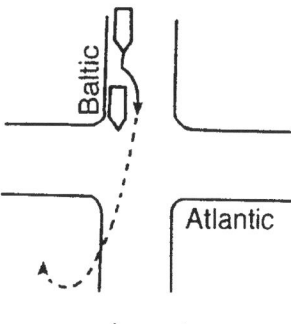
C. 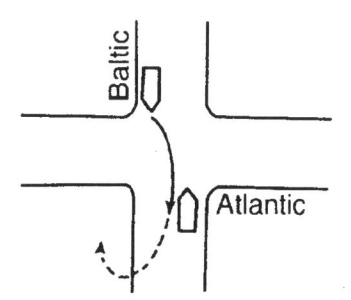
D.

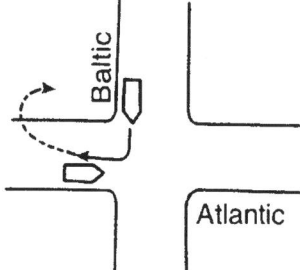

12. When found, the right front end of an automobile was smashed and bent around a post, and the hood was buckled.
Which of the following cars on a service lot is the car described?

A.

B.

C.

D.

12.____

13. An open floor safe with its door bent out of shape was found at the scene. It was empty. An electric drill and several envelopes and papers were found on the floor near the safe.
Which of the following shows the scene described?

A.

B.

C.

D.

13.____

Questions 14-16.

DIRECTIONS: In Questions 14 to 16, you are to pick the word or phrase CLOSEST in meaning to the word or phrase printed in capital letters.

14. HAZARDOUS 14.____
    A. uncertain   B. threatening   C. difficult   D. dangerous

15. NEGLIGENT 15.____
    A. careless   B. fearless   C. ruthless   D. useless

16. PROVOKE 16.____
    A. accuse   B. arouse   C. insist   D. suspend

Questions 17-20.

DIRECTIONS: Questions 17 to 20 measure your ability to do arithmetic related to police work. Each question presents a separate arithmetic problem to be solved.

17. To the nearest hour, how long can a specialized police vehicle with a 40-gallon fuel tank be on the road before heading for a service facility, assuming that the vehicle consumes 8 gallons per hour and must head for a service facility when there are only 8 gallons in the tank?

    A. 3   B. 4   C. 5   D. None of these

17.____

18. A man with a history of vagrancy was found dead under a bridge with the following U.S. currency in a band around his belly:

    7 $5 bills
    3 $10 bills
   11 $20 bills
    9 $50 bills
    4 $100 bills

What is the total amount of the money that was found in the band?

    A. $1,015   B. $1,135   C. $2,710   D. None of these

18.____

19. X is 110 dimes.
Y is 1,111 pennies.
Which of the following statements about the values of X and Y above is TRUE?

    A. X is greater than Y.
    B. Y is greater than X.
    C. X equals Y.
    D. The relationship of X to Y cannot be determined from the information given.

19.____

20. Which of the following individuals drinking hard liquor in a bar was 21 years old at the time of the incident?

    A. One born August 26, 1989 - Date of incident is March 17, 2010
    B. One born January 6, 1989 - Date of incident is New Year's Eve 2009
    C. One born 3/17/89 - Date of incident is 2/14/10
    D. None of these

20.____

KEY (CORRECT ANSWERS)

1.	A	11.	C
2.	B	12.	D
3.	C	13.	B
4.	D	14.	D
5.	B	15.	A
6.	C	16.	B
7.	B	17.	B
8.	B	18.	B
9.	D	19.	B
10.	B	20.	D

EVALUATING INFORMATION AND EVIDENCE
EXAMINATION SECTION
TEST 1

DIRECTIONS: Each question or incomplete statement is followed by several suggested answers or completions. Select the one that BEST answers the question or completes the statement. *PRINT THE LETTER OF THE CORRECT ANSWER IN THE SPACE AT THE RIGHT.*

Questions 1-9

Questions 1 through 9 measure your ability to (1) determine whether statements from witnesses say essentially the same thing and (2) determine the evidence needed to make it reasonably certain that a particular conclusion is true.

1. Which of the following pairs of statements say essentially the same thing in two different ways?

    I. The only time the machine's red light is on is when the door is locked. If the machine's door is locked, the red light is on.
    II. Some gray-jacketed cables are connected to the blower. If a cable is connected to the blower, it must be gray-jacketed.

    A. I only
    B. I and II
    C. II only
    D. Neither I nor II

1. _____

2. Which of the following pairs of statements say essentially the same thing in two different ways?

    I. If you live on Maple Street, your child is in the Valley District. If your child is in the Valley District, you must live on Maple Street.
    II. All the Smith children are brown-eyed.
    If a child is brown-eyed, it is not one of the Smith children.

    A. I only
    B. I and II
    C. II only
    D. Neither I nor II

2. _____

3. Which of the following pairs of statements say essentially the same thing in two different ways?

   I. If it's Monday, Mrs. James will be here.
   Mrs. James is here every Monday.
   II. Most people in the Drama Club do not have stage fright, but everyone in the Drama Club wants to be noticed.
   Some people in the Drama Club have stage fright and want to be noticed.

   A. I only
   B. I and II
   C. II only
   D. Neither I nor II

4. Which of the following pairs of statements say essentially the same thing in two different ways?

   I. If you are older than 65, you will get a senior's discount.
   Either you will get a senior's discount, or you are not older than 65.
   II. Every cadet in Officer Johnson's class has passed the firearms safety course.
   No cadet that has failed the firearms safety course is in Officer Johnson's class.

   A. I only
   B. I and II
   C. II only
   D. Neither I nor II

5. <u>Summary of Evidence Collected to Date:</u>

   Most people in the Greenlawn housing project do not have criminal records.

   <u>Prematurely Drawn Conclusion:</u> Some people in Greenlawn who have been crime victims have criminal records themselves.

   Which of the following pieces of evidence, if any, would make it *reasonably certain* that the conclusion drawn is true?

   A. Some of those who live in the Greenlawn project have been arrested or convicted of "victimless" crimes
   B. Most people in Greenlawn have been the victims of crime
   C. Everyone in Greenlawn has been the victim of crime
   D. None of these

6. Summary of Evidence Collected to Date:

    Every drug dealer in the Oak Lawn neighborhood wears blue and carries a Glock.

    Prematurely Drawn Conclusion: A person in the Oak Lawn neighborhood who carries a Glock is a drug dealer.

    Which of the following pieces of evidence, if any, would make it *reasonably certain* that the conclusion drawn is true?

    A. In the Oak Lawn neighborhood, only drug dealers wear blue
    B. Drug dealers in Oak Lawn only carry Glocks when they're dealing drugs
    C. In the Oak Lawn neighborhood, only drug dealers carry Glocks
    D. None of these

7. Summary of Evidence Collected to Date:

    I. Dr. Jones is older than Dr. Gupta.
    II. Dr. Gupta and Dr. Unruh were born on the same day.

    Prematurely Drawn Conclusion: Dr. Gupta does not work in the emergency room.

    Which of the following pieces of evidence, if any, would make it *reasonably certain* that the conclusion drawn is true?

    A. Dr. Jones is older than Dr. Unruh
    B. Dr. Jones works in the emergency room
    C. Every doctor in the emergency room is older then Dr. Unruh
    D. None of these

8. Summary of Evidence Collected to Date:

    I. On the street, a "dose" of a certain drug contains four "drams."
    II. A person can trade three "rolls" of a drug for a "plunk."

    Prematurely Drawn Conclusion: A plunk is the most valuable amount of the drug on the street.

    Which of the following pieces of evidence, if any, would make it *reasonably certain* that the conclusion drawn is true?

    A. A person can trade five doses for two rolls
    B. A dram contains two rolls
    C. A roll is larger than a dram
    D. None of these

9. Summary of Evidence Collected to Date:

   Sam is a good writer and editor.

   Prematurely Drawn Conclusion: Sam is qualified for the job.

   Which of the following pieces of evidence, if any, would make it *reasonably certain* that the conclusion drawn is true?

   A. The job calls for good writing and editing skills
   B. A person who is not a good editor could still apply for the job on the strength of his/her writing skills
   C. If Sam applies for the job, he must be both a good writer and editor
   D. None of these

5 (#1)

Questions 10-14

Questions 10 through 14 refer to Map #7 and measure your ability to orient yourself within a given section of town, neighborhood or particular area. Each of the questions describes a starting point and a destination. Assume that you are driving a car in the area shown on the map accompanying the questions. Use the map as a basis for the shortest way to get from one point to another without breaking the law.

On the map, a street marked by arrows, or by arrows and the words "One Way," indicates one-way travel, and should be assumed to be one-way for the entire length, even when there are breaks or jogs in the street. EXCEPTION: A street that does not have the same name over the full length.

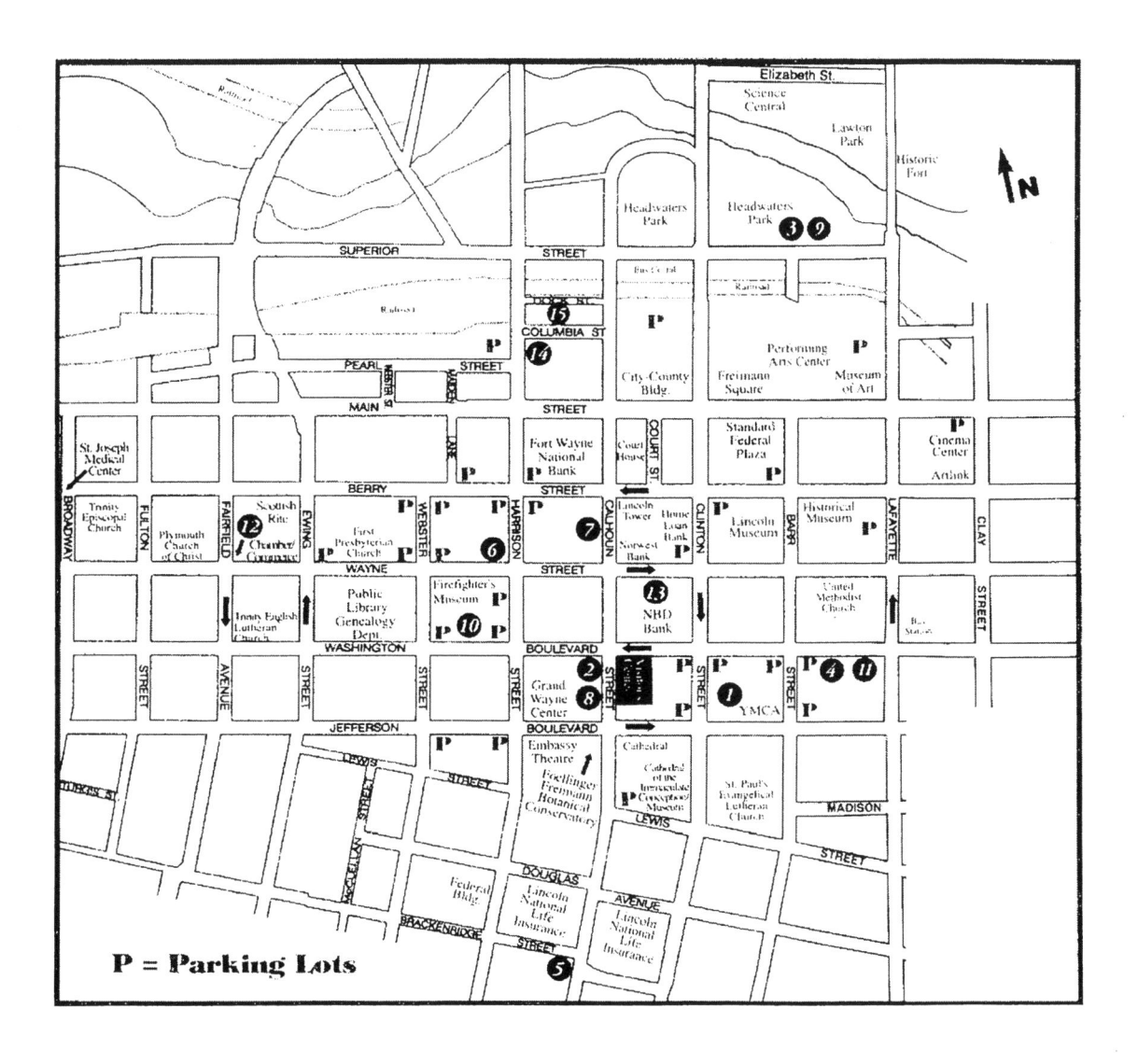

Map #7

10. The shortest legal way from Trinity Episcopal Church to Science Central is

    A. east on Berry, north on Clinton, east on Elizabeth
    B. east on Berry, north on Lafayette, west on Elizabeth
    C. north on Fulton, east on Main, north on Lafayette, west on Elizabeth
    D. north on Fulton, east on Main, north on Calhoun

10._____

11. The shortest legal way from the Grand Wayne Center to the Museum of Art is

    A. north on Harrison, east on Superior, south on Lafayette
    B. east on Washington Blvd., north on Lafayette
    C. east on Jefferson Blvd., north on Clinton, east on Main
    D. east on Jefferson Blvd., north on Lafayette

11._____

12. The shortest legal way from the Embassy Theatre to the City/County Building is

    A. west on Jefferson Blvd., north on Ewing, east on Main
    B. east on Jefferson Blvd., north on Lafayette, west on Main
    C. east on Jefferson Blvd., north on Clinton
    D. north on Harrison, east on Main

12._____

13. The shortest legal way from the YMCA to the Firefighter's Museum is

    A. west on Jefferson Blvd., north on Webster
    B. north on Barr, west on Washington Blvd., north on Webster
    C. north on Barr, west on Wayne
    D. north on Barr, west on Berry, south on Webster

13._____

14. The shortest legal way from the Historic Fort to Freimann Square is

    A. north on Lafayette, west on Elizabeth, south on Clinton
    B. north on Lafayette, west on Elizabeth, west/south on Calhoun, east on Main
    C. south on Lafayette, west on Main
    D. south on Lafayette, west on Superior, south on Clinton

14._____

7 (#1)

Questions 15-19

Questions 15 through 19 refer to Figure #7, on the following page, and measure your ability to understand written descriptions of events. Each question presents a description of an accident or event and asks you which of the five drawings in Figure #7 BEST represents it.

In the drawings, the following symbols are used:

    Moving vehicle: ⌂   Non-moving vehicle: ⬛

    Pedestrian or bicyclist: ●

The path and direction of travel of a vehicle or pedestrian is indicated by a solid line.

The path and direction of travel of each vehicle or pedestrian directly involved in a collision from the point of impact is indicated by a dotted line.

In the space at the right, print the letter of the drawing that best fits the descriptions written below:

15. A driver headed northeast on Cary strikes a car in the intersection and is diverted north, where he collides with the rear of a car that is traveling north on Park. The northbound car is knocked into the rear of another car that is traveling north ahead of it.

15._____

16. A driver headed northeast on Cary strikes a car in the intersection and is diverted north, where he collides head-on with a car stopped at a traffic light in the southbound lane on Park.

16._____

17. A driver headed northeast on Cary strikes a car in the intersection and is diverted east, where he collides head-on with a car stopped at a traffic light in the westbound lane on Roble.

17._____

18. A driver headed east on Roble collides with the left front of a car that is turning right from Knox onto Roble. The driver swerves right after the collision and collides head-on with another car headed north on Park.

18._____

19. A driver headed northeast on Cary strikes a car in the intersection and is diverted north, where he collides with the rear of a car parked in the northbound lane on Park.

19._____

FIGURE #7   8 (#1)

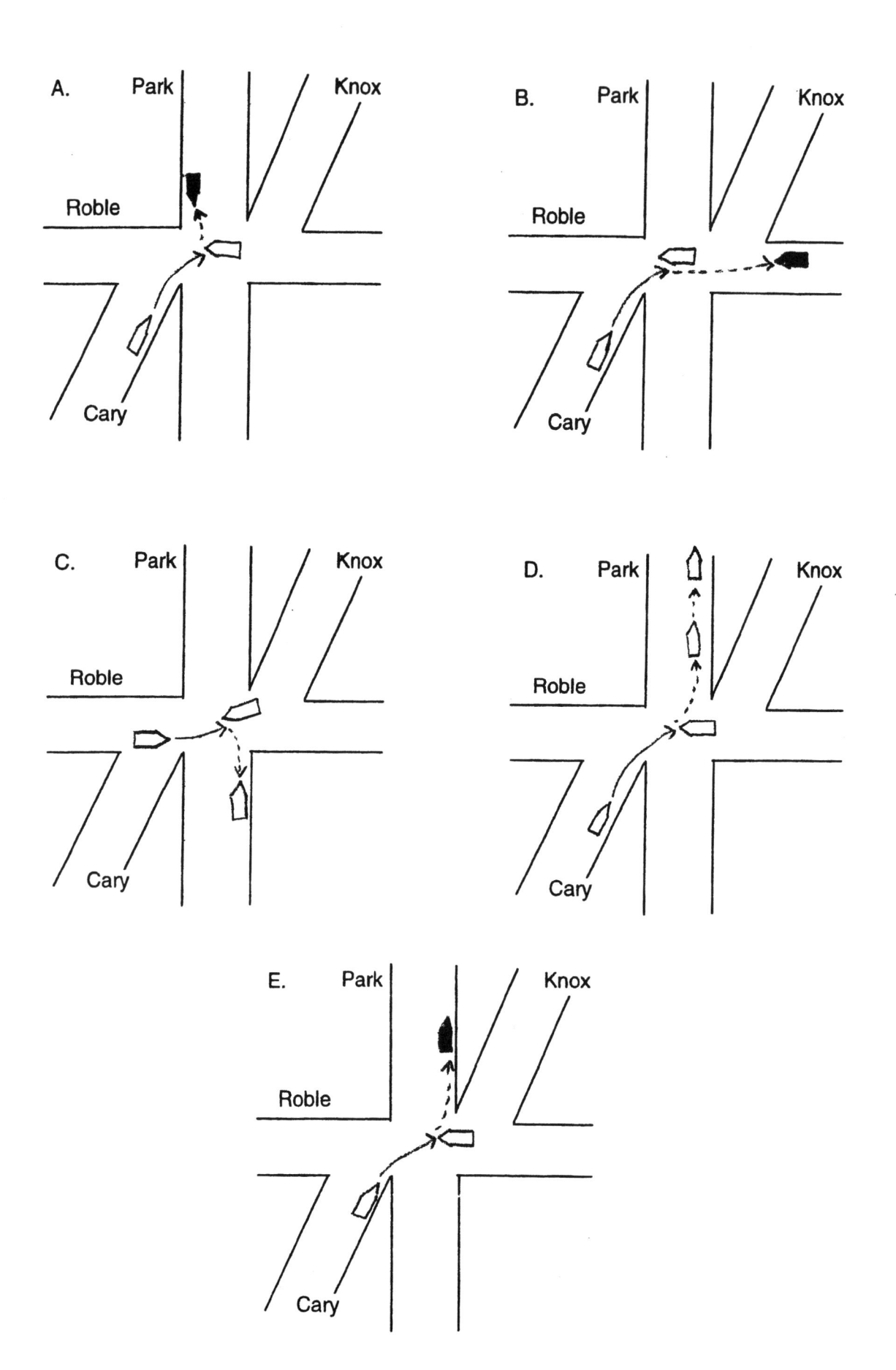

N ↑

A. Park / Knox / Roble / Cary

B. Park / Knox / Roble / Cary

C. Park / Knox / Roble / Cary

D. Park / Knox / Roble / Cary

E. Park / Knox / Roble / Cary

Questions 20-22

In questions 20 through 22, choose the word or phrase CLOSEST in meaning to the word or phrase printed in capital letters.

20. JURISDICTION
    A. authority
    B. decision
    C. judgment
    D. argument

21. PROXY
    A. neighbor
    B. agent
    C. enforcer
    D. impostor

22. LARCENY
    A. theft
    B. assault
    C. deceit
    D. gentleness

Questions 23-25

Questions 23 through 25 measure your ability to do fieldwork-related arithmetic. Each question presents a separate arithmetic problem for you to solve.

23. Mr. Long has 14 employees. He has four more male employees than female employees. How many female employees does he have?
    A. 4   B. 5   C. 9   D. 10

24. A box of latex gloves costs $18. A crate has 12 boxes, each of which contains 48 gloves. How much does a crate of latex gloves cost?
    A. $216   B. $328   C. $576   D. $864

25. In a single week, the Department of Parking collected 540 quarters, 623 dimes and 146 nickels from its parking meters. What was the total revenue collected from the meters during the week?
    A. $135.00   B. $154.00   C. $204.60   D. $270.30

KEY (CORRECT ANSWERS)

1. A	11. D	21. B
2. D	12. D	22. A
3. B	13. B	23. B
4. B	14. A	24. A
5. C	15. D	25. C
6. C	16. A	
7. C	17. B	
8. A	18. C	
9. A	19. E	
10. C	20. A	

SOLUTIONS (QUESTIONS 1 - 9)

P implies Q = original statement

Not Q implies not P = contrapositive of the original statement. A statement and its contrapositive are logically equivalent.

Q implies P = converse of the original statement.

Not P implies not 0 = inverse of the original statement. The converse and inverse of an original statement are logically equivalent.

P implies 0 = Not P or Q.

#1. The correct answer is **A**. For item I, the equivalent of the first statement would be "If the red light is on, the door is locked." This is the converse of the second statement, so it is not equivalent to the first statement. For item II, the first statement does not guarantee that all cables that are connected to the blower must be gray-jacketed. There may very well be other cables that are connected to the blower that are not gray-jacketed. Equally possible, some gray-jacketed cables are not necessarily connected to the blower.

#2. The correct answer is **D**. For item I, the second statement is the converse of the first statement, so it is not logically equivalent. For item II, the equivalent of the first statement is "If a child is not brown-eyed, then it is not one of the Smith children." Thus, statement II as it stands is not equivalent to statement I.

#3. The correct answer is **B**. For item I, Mrs. James is here every Monday, so we conclude that if it is Monday, she is here. (She may be here on other days as well.) For item II, we can conclude that there are some people in the Drama club who do have stage fright. Since everyone in the Drama Club wants to be noticed, this would include those who have stage fright.

#4. The correct answer is **B**. For item I, these two statements represent " **P** implies Q" and "Not P or Q," where P = Older than 65 and Q = Get a senior discount. These are equivalent statements. For item II, these statements are contrapositives of each other and so must be equivalent. (P = Cadet in Johnson's class and Q = Passes the safety course.)

#5. The correct answer is **C**. If everyone in the housing project has been a victim of crime and most of these people do not have a criminal record, we can conclude that some of them do have a criminal record. Thus, we have the situation that some of the people who live in this housing project are both a victim of crime as well as a perpetrator of crime.

#6. The correct answer is **C**. This choice can be written as "In this neighborhood, if a person carries a Glock, he is a drug dealer. This would lead directly to the drawn conclusion.

#7. The correct answer is **C**. We know that every doctor in the emergency room is older than Dr. Unruh; it is not possible for Dr. Gupta to be working in the emergency room since he is the same age as Dr. Unruh.

#8. The correct answer is **A**. From statement I, a dose is worth more than a dram. If 5 doses is equal to 2 rolls, than a roll is worth more than a dose. So of these three, a roll is worth the most.

Finally, statement II tells us that a plunk is worth more than a roll. This means that a plunk is worth the most among all four of these categories.

#9. The correct answer is **A**. Sam has the qualifications of being a good writer and editor, which is exactly what is needed for the job. Therefore, Sam is qualified for this job.

TEST 2

DIRECTIONS: Each question or incomplete statement is followed by several suggested answers or completions. Select the one that BEST answers the question or completes the statement. *PRINT THE LETTER OF THE CORRECT ANSWER IN THE SPACE AT THE RIGHT.*

Questions 1-9

Questions 1 through 9 measure your ability to (1) determine whether statements from witnesses say essentially the same thing and (2) determine the evidence needed to make it reasonably certain that a particular conclusion is true.

To do well on this part of the test, you do NOT have to have a working knowledge of police procedures and techniques. Nor do you have to have any more familiarity with criminals and criminal behavior than that acquired from reading newspapers, listening to radio or watching TV. To do well in this part, you must read and reason carefully.

1. Which of the following pairs of statements say essentially the same thing in two different ways?

    I. If the garbage is collected today, it is definitely Wednesday.
       The garbage is collected every Wednesday.
    II. Nobody has no answer to the question.
        Everybody has at least one answer to the question.

    A. I only
    B. I and II
    C. II only
    D. Neither I nor II

    1._____

2. Which of the following pairs of statements say essentially the same thing in two different ways?

    I. If it rains, the streets will be wet.
       If the streets are wet, it has rained.
    II. All of the Duluth Five are immune from prosecution.
        No member of the Duluth Five can be prosecuted.

    A. I only
    B. I and II
    C. II only
    D. Neither I nor II

    2._____

3. Which of the following pairs of statements say essentially the same thing in two different ways?

   I. Ms. Friar will accept her promotion if and only if she is offered a 10% raise.
   For Ms. Friar to accept her promotion, it is necessary that she be offered a 10% raise.
   II. If the hydraulic lines are flushed, it is definitely inspection day.
   The hydraulic lines are flushed only on inspection days.

   A. I only
   B. I and II
   C. II only
   D. Neither I nor II

4. Which of the following pairs of statements say essentially the same thing in two different ways?

   I. If you are tall you will get onto the basketball team.
   Unless you are tall you will not get onto the basketball team.
   II. That raven is black.
   If that bird is black, it's a raven.

   A. I only
   B. I and II
   C. II only
   D. Neither I nor II

5. <u>Summary of Evidence Collected to Date:</u>

   Every member of the Rotary Club is retired.

   <u>Prematurely Drawn Conclusion:</u> At least some people in the planning commission are retired.

   Which of the following pieces of evidence, if any, would make it *reasonably certain* that the conclusion drawn is true?

   A. Retirement is a condition for membership in the Rotary Club
   B. Every member of the planning commission has been in the Rotary Club at one time
   C. Every member of the Rotary Club is also on the planning commission
   D. None of these

6. Summary of Evidence Collected to Date:

   Some of the SWAT team snipers have poor aim.

   Prematurely Drawn Conclusion: The snipers on the SWAT team with the worst aim also have 20/20 vision.

   Which of the following pieces of evidence, if any, would make it *reasonably certain* that the conclusion drawn is true?

   A. Some of the SWAT team snipers have 20/20 vision
   B. Every sniper on the SWAT team has 20/20 vision
   C. Some snipers on the SWAT team wear corrective lenses
   D. None of these

7. Summary of Evidence Collected to Date:

   The only time Garson hears voices is on a day when he doesn't take his medication.

   Prematurely Drawn Conclusion: On Fridays, Garson never hears voices.

   Which of the following pieces of evidence, if any, would make it *reasonably certain* that the conclusion drawn is true?

   A. Garson is supposed to take his medication every day
   B. Garson usually undergoes shock therapy on Fridays
   C. Garson usually takes his medication and undergoes shock therapy on Fridays
   D. None of these

8. Summary of Evidence Collected to Date:

   Among the three maintenance workers—Frank, Lily and Jean—Frank is not the tallest.

   Prematurely Drawn Conclusion: Lily is the tallest.

   Which of the following pieces of evidence, if any, would make it *reasonably certain* that the conclusion drawn is true?

   A. Jean is not the tallest
   B. Frank is the shortest
   C. Jean is the shortest
   D. None of these

9. Summary of Evidence Collected to Date: 9._____

   Doctor Lyons went to the cafeteria for lunch today and did not eat dessert.

   Prematurely Drawn Conclusion: The cafeteria did not serve dessert.

   Which of the following pieces of evidence, if any, would make it *reasonably certain* that the conclusion drawn is true?

   A. Dr. Lyons never eats dessert
   B. When the cafeteria serves dessert, Dr. Lyons always eats it
   C. The cafeteria rarely serves dessert when Dr. Lyons eats there
   D. None of these

Questions 10-14

Questions 10 through 14 refer to Map #8 and measure your ability to orient yourself within a given section of town, neighborhood or particular area. Each of the questions describes a starting point and a destination. Assume that you are driving a car in the area shown on the map accompanying the questions. Use the map as a basis for the shortest way to get from one point to another without breaking the law.

On the map, a street marked by arrows, or by arrows and the words "One Way," indicates one-way travel, and should be assumed to be one-way for the entire length, even when there are breaks or jogs in the street. EXCEPTION: A street that does not have the same name over the full length.

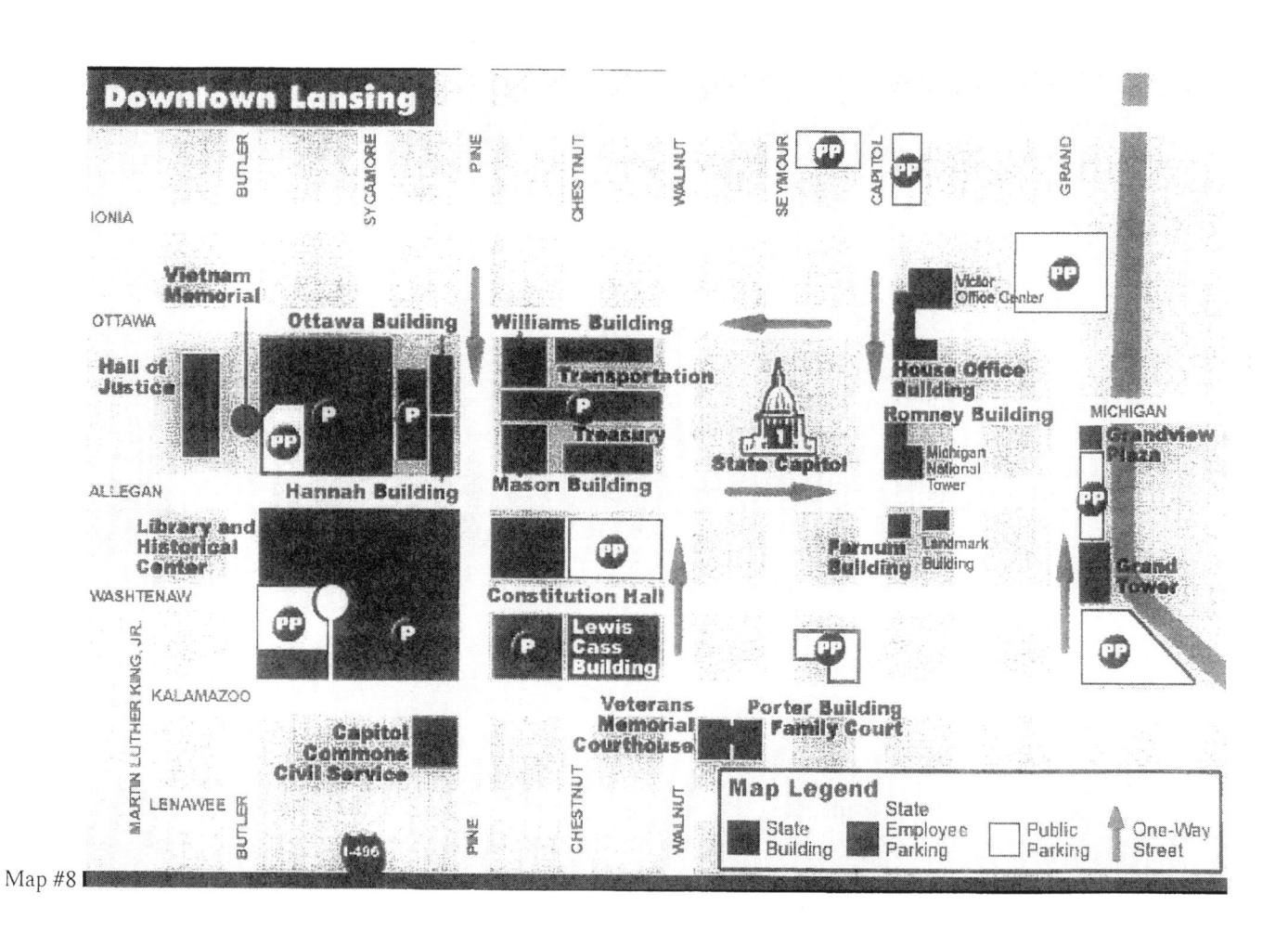

Map #8

10. The shortest legal way from the Library and Historical Center to Grandview Plaza is
    A. south on Butler, east on Kalamazoo, north on Grand
    B. east on Allegan, north on Grand
    C. north on Butler, east on Ionia, south on Grand
    D. north on Martin Luther King, Jr., east on Ottawa, south on Pine, east on Allegan, north on Grand

10._____

11. The shortest legal way from the Victor Office Center to the Mason Building is
    A. west on Ottawa, south on Pine
    B. south on Capitol, west on Allegan, north on Pine
    C. south on Capitol, west on Washtenaw, north on Walnut, west on Allegan
    D. west on Ottawa, north on Seymour, west on Ionia, south on Pine

11._____

12. The shortest legal way from the Treasury to the Hall of Justice is
    A. north on Walnut, west on Ottawa, south on Martin Luther King, Jr.
    B. west on Allegan
    C. east on Allegan, north on Grand, west on Ottawa, south on Martin Luther King, Jr.
    D. south on Walnut, west on Kalamazoo, north on Martin Luther King, Jr.

12._____

13. The shortest legal way from the Veterans Memorial Courthouse to the House Office Building is
    A. north on Walnut, east on Ottawa
    B. east on Kalamazoo, north on Capitol
    C. east on Kalamazoo, north on Grand, west on Ottawa
    D. north on Walnut, east on Allegan, north on Capitol

13._____

14. The shortest legal way from Grand Tower to Constitution Hall is
    A. west on Washtenaw
    B. north on Grand, west on Allegan, south on Pine
    C. north on Grand, west on Ottawa, south on Pine
    D. south on Grand, west on Kalamazoo, north on Pine

14._____

7 (#2)

Questions 15-19

Questions 15 through 19 refer to Figure #8, on the following page, and measure your ability to understand written descriptions of events. Each question presents a description of an accident or event and asks you which of the five drawings in Figure #8 BEST represents it.

In the drawings, the following symbols are used:

Moving vehicle: ⌂   Non-moving vehicle: ⬛

Pedestrian or bicyclist: ●

The path and direction of travel of a vehicle or pedestrian is indicated by a solid line.

The path and direction of travel of each vehicle or pedestrian directly involved in a collision from the point of impact is indicated by a dotted line.

In the space at the right, print the letter of the drawing that best fits the descriptions written below:

15. A driver headed west on Holly runs a red light and turns left. He sideswipes a car headed south in the intersection, and then flees south on Bay. The southbound car is diverted into the rear end of a car parked in the southbound lane on Bay.

15._____

16. A driver headed east on Holly runs a red light. Another driver headed south through the intersection slams on her brakes just in time to avoid a serious collision. The eastbound driver glances off the front of the southbound car and continues east, where he collides with a car parked in the eastbound lane on Holly.

16._____

17. A driver headed east on Holly runs a red light. She strikes the left front of a westbound car that is turning left from Holly onto Bay, and then veers left and strikes the rear end of a car parked in the northbound lane on Bay.

17._____

18. A driver headed north on Bay strikes the right front of a car heading south in the intersection of Bay and Holly. After the collision, the driver veers left and collides with the rear end of a car parked in the westbound lane of Holly. The southbound car veers left and collides with the rear end of a car in the eastbound lane on Holly.

18._____

19. A driver headed north on Bay strikes the left front of a car heading south in the intersection of Bay and Holly. After the collision, the driver continues north and collides with the rear end of a car parked in the northbound lane. The southbound car continues south and collides with the rear end of a car in the southbound lane.

19._____

FIGURE #8

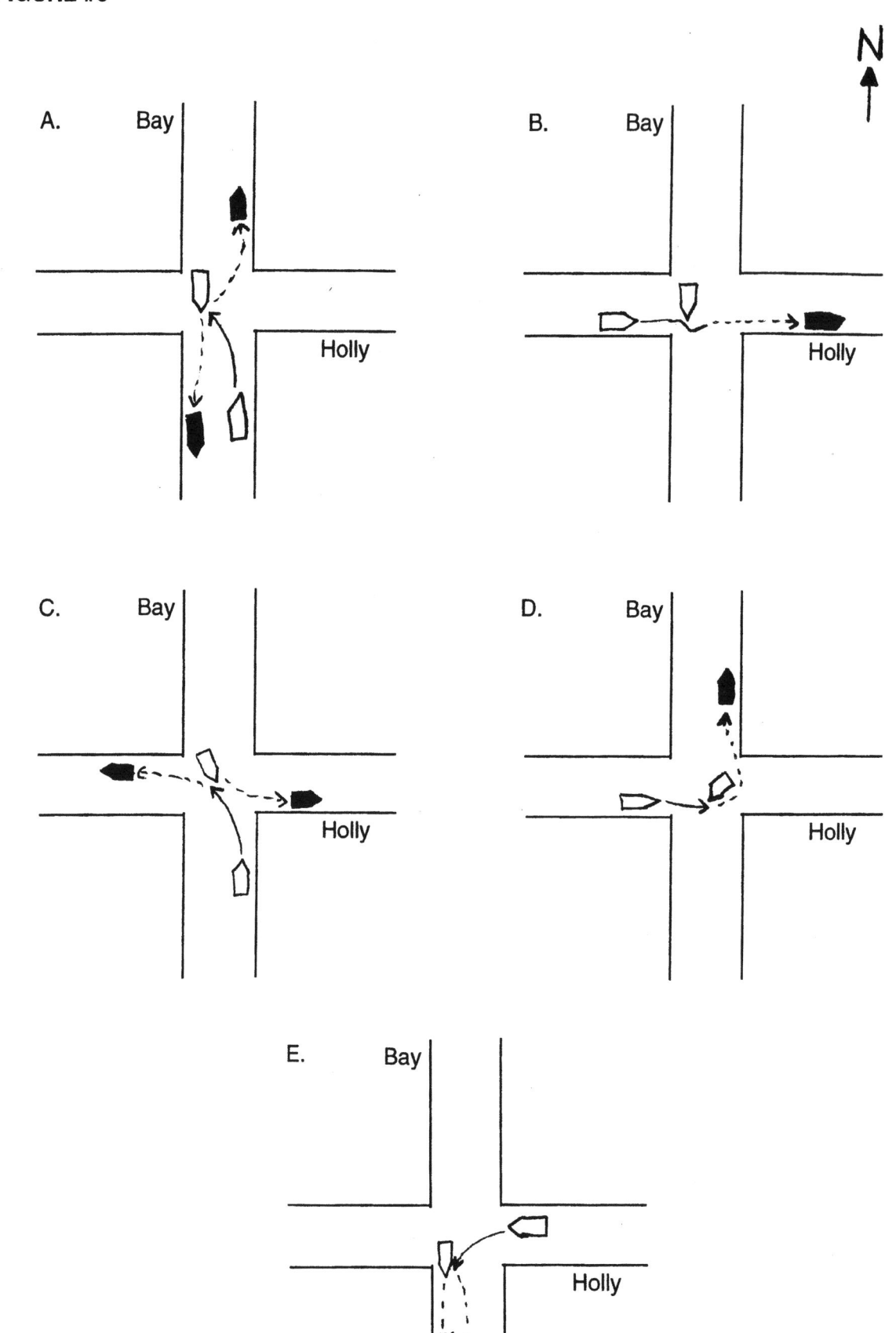

8 (#2)

Questions 20-22

In questions 20 through 22, choose the word or phrase CLOSEST in meaning to the word or phrase printed in capital letters.

20. LIABLE
    A. sensitive
    B. dishonest
    C. responsible
    D. valid

21. CLAIM
    A. debt
    B. period
    C. denial
    D. banishment

22. ADMISSIBLE
    A. false
    B. conclusive
    C. acceptable
    D. indisputable

Questions 23-25

Questions 23 through 25 measure your ability to do fieldwork-related arithmetic. Each question presents a separate arithmetic problem for you to solve.

23. Three departments divide an $800 payment. Department 1 takes $270, and Department 2 takes $150 more than Department 3. How much does Department 2 take?
    A. $150   B. $190   C. $340   D. $490

24. Detective Smalley cleared 100 murder cases in five years. Each year he cleared six more than he cleared in the previous year. How many cases did he clear during the first year?
    A. 6   B. 8   C. 12   D. 18

25. The purchasing agent bought three binders for $2 each, four reams of copier paper for $3 each and five packs of black pens for $7 each. How much did the agent spend?
    A. $12.00   B. $25.20   C. $53.00   D. $72.00

KEY (CORRECT ANSWERS)

1. B	11. A	21. A
2. C	12. A	22. C
3. B	13. C	23. C
4. D	14. A	24. B
5. C	15. E	25. C
6. B	16. B	
7. D	17. D	
8. A	18. C	
9. B	19. A	
10. B	20. C	

SOLUTIONS (QUESTIONS 1 - 9)

P implies Q = original statement

Not Q implies not P = contrapositive of the original statement. A statement and its contrapositive are logically equivalent.

Q implies P = converse of the original statement.

Not P implies not Q = inverse of the original statement. The converse and inverse of an original statement are logically equivalent.

P implies Q = Not P or Q.

#1. The correct answer is **B**. For item I, we can conclude that it is Wednesday if and only if the garbage is collected. For item II, the phrase "nobody has no" is equivalent to 'everybody has at least one."

#2. The correct answer is C. For item I, each statement is the converse of the other. Thus, they are not equivalent. For item II, each statement says that each member of the Duluth Five is immune from prosecution.

#3. The correct answer is **B**. For item I, accepting a promotion is a necessary and sufficient condition for receiving a 10% raise. For item II, we have the P implies Q condition, where P = hydraulic lines are flushed and Q = it is an inspection day.

#4. The correct answer is **D**. For item I, each statement is the converse of the other (so they not equivalent). For item II, the first statement simply states that a particular raven is black. The second statement says that all black birds are ravens. They are not equivalent.

#5. The correct answer is C. The two scenarios are (a) a Rotary Club member is a subset of the set of all retirees, which is a subset of all planning commission members or (b) a Rotary Club member is a subset of all planning commission members, which is a subset of all retirees. In either case, each member of the Rotary Club is also a member of the planning commission.

#6. The correct answer is **B**. We know that some SWAT sniper members have poor aim. If we also know that all snipers on the SWAT team also have 20/20 vision, then we conclude that any sniper (including those with the worst aim) must have 20/20 vision.

#7. The correct answer is **D**. The only way that Garson will not hear voices is if he takes his medication. The premature conclusion can only be correct if he takes his medication every Friday. None of choices A, **B**, or C mentions this specifically.

#8. The correct answer is **A**. If Frank is not the tallest and Jean is not the tallest, then the conclusion that Lily is the tallest is correct. This is a reasonable conclusion, unless all three are the same height (very unlikely).

#9. The correct answer is **B**. We are given that Dr. Lyons went to the cafeteria for lunch and that he did not have dessert. If Dr. Lyons always eats dessert when it is served in the cafeteria, we can conclude that the cafeteria did not serve dessert.

APPLYING WRITTEN INFORMATION
(RULES, REGULATIONS, POLICIES, PROCEDURES, DIRECTIVES, ETC.) IN POLICE SITUATIONS

These questions test for the ability to apply written rules to given situations similar to those typically experienced by police officers.

TEST TASK: You will be given a set of rules, regulations, or other written information to read. You will then be asked a question which requires you to apply the rule to a given situation.

SAMPLE QUESTION:

RULE: Patrol vehicles should be checked at the start of each shift. Do not assume that the vehicle is in satisfactory condition. Check all of the lighting equipment, all emergency equipment, siren, engine, oil, transmission fluid, battery, radiator and gasoline levels, tire pressure and condition (including spare), lug wrench, jack, windshield wipers and windshield washer fluid level. Check the body of the vehicle for damaged or missing parts and report any problems, damage, or discrepancies to your supervisor. At the end of your shift, leave the vehicle in optimum condition for emergency use by the next officer.

SITUATION: Officer Burton is about to begin her patrol shift when she discovers that her police vehicle has a large dent in the left rear bumper. She knows that the vehicle did not have this dent yesterday, when she last drove it.

QUESTION: According to the above Rule, Officer Burton should most properly

A. request that she be assigned a different vehicle
B. begin her shift and be alert to any operating problems
C. find out what other officers have used the vehicle since her last shift
D. inform her supervisor about the dented bumper

The answer is D.

SOLUTION: *The Situation states that Officer Burton has discovered a dent in the bumper of her patrol vehicle that did not exist when she last used it. The question asks what she should do about it. To answer the question, evaluate all of the choices.*

Choice A states that the officer should request a different vehicle. There is nothing in the rule that states that the officer should do this. Choice A is incorrect.

Choice B states that the officer should begin her shift and be alert to any operating problems. The rule states that the officer should report any problems with the vehicle to her supervisor. Choice B is incorrect.

Choice C states that the officer should find out what other officers have used the vehicle since her last shift. There is nothing in the rule that states that the officer should do this. Choice C is incorrect.

Choice D states that the officer should inform her supervisor about the damaged bumper. This conforms to the given rule that states that the officer should report any problems, damage, or discrepancies to her supervisor. Choice D is the correct answer.

POLICE SCIENCE

EXAMINATION SECTION
TEST 1

DIRECTIONS: Each question or incomplete statement is followed by several suggested answers or completions. Select the one that BEST answers the question or completes the statement. *PRINT THE LETTER OF THE CORRECT ANSWER IN THE SPACE AT THE RIGHT.*

1. As you are patrolling your post, you observe two men running toward a parked automobile in which a driver is seated. You question the three men and you note the license number. You *should*

    A. let them go if you see nothing suspicious
    B. warn them not to be caught loitering again
    C. arrest them because they have probably committed a crime
    D. take them back with you to the place from which the two men came

    1.____

2. While you are patrolling your post, you find a flashlight and a screwdriver lying near a closed bar and grill. You notice further some jimmy marks on the door.
You *should*

    A. continue patrolling your post after noting in your memorandum book what you have seen
    B. arrest any persons standing in the vicinity
    C. try to enter the bar and grill to investigate whether it has been robbed
    D. telephone the owner of the bar and grill and inform him of what you have seen outside the door

    2.____

3. While you are patrolling your post, you notice that a peddler is vending merchandise. As you approach, he gathers up his wares and begins to run.
You *should*

    A. shoot at him as he is a violator of the law
    B. blow your whistle to summon other patrolmen in order to apprehend him
    C. remain for some time at this place so as to be certain that he does not return
    D. pursue him and continue patrolling your post

    3.____

4. You have been assigned to a patrol post in a park during the winter months. You hear the cries of a boy who has fallen through the ice.
The FIRST thing you should do is to

    A. rush to the nearest call telephone and summon the Emergency Squad
    B. call upon passersby to summon additional patrolmen
    C. rush to the spot from which the cries came and try to save the boy
    D. rush to the spot from which the cries came and question the boy concerning his identity so that you can summon his parents

    4.____

5. You have been summoned about a robbery in a station. Three men are grappling with each other. Two of the men are plainclothesmen, but their identity is not known to you. The FIRST thing you should do is to

    A. advance with your nightstick and be ready to use it as soon as you know which one is the thief
    B. use karate to stop the fighting
    C. ask any bystanders to identify the thief before you use your gun
    D. shoot the one who is most likely to be the thief, letting yourself be guided by your own experience as to the thief's identity

6. Upon arriving at the scene of an accident in which a pedestrian was struck and killed by an automobile, a police officer's first action was to clear the scene of spectators. Of the following, the PRINCIPAL reason for this action is that

    A. important evidence may be inadvertently destroyed by the crowd
    B. this is a fundamental procedure in first aid work
    C. the operator of the vehicle may escape in the crowd
    D. witnesses will speak more freely if other persons are not present

7. In questioning witnesses a police officer is instructed to avoid leading questions or questions that will suggest the answer.
Accordingly, when questioning a witness about the appearance of a suspect, it would be BEST for him to ask:

    A. What kind of hat did he wear?
    B. Did he wear a felt hat?
    C. What did he wear?
    D. Didn't he wear a hat?

8. The only personal description the police have of a particular criminal was made several years ago.
Of the following, the item in the description that will be MOST useful in identifying him at the present time is the

    A. color of his eyes   B. color of his hair
    C. number of teeth   D. weight

9. Crime statistics indicate that property crimes such as larceny, burglary and robbery, are more numerous during winter months than in summer.
The one of the following explanations that MOST adequately accounts for this situation is that

    A. human needs, such as clothing, food, heat and shelter, are greater in summer
    B. criminal tendencies are aggravated by climatic changes generally
    C. there are more hours of darkness in winter and such crimes are usually committed under cover of darkness
    D. urban areas are more densely populated during winter months, affording greater opportunity for such crimes

10. When automobile tire tracks are to be used as evidence, a plaster cast is made of them. Before the cast is made, however, a photograph of the tracks is taken. Of the following, the MOST probable reason for taking a photograph is that

    A. photographs can be duplicated more easily than castings
    B. less skill is required for photographing than casting
    C. the tracks may be damaged in the casting process
    D. photographs are more easily transported than castings

    10.____

11. It is generally recommended that a patrolman, in lifting a revolver that is to be sent to the Police Laboratory for ballistics tests and fingerprint examination, do so by inserting a pencil through the trigger guard rather than into the barrel of the weapon. The reason for PREFERRING this procedure is that

    A. every precaution must be taken not to obliterate fingerprints on the weapon
    B. there is a danger of accidentally discharging the weapon by placing the pencil in the barrel
    C. the pencil may make scratches inside the barrel that will interfere with the ballistics tests
    D. a weapon can more easily be lifted by the trigger guard

    11.____

12. In addressing a class of recruits, a police captain remarked: "Carelessness and failure are twins."
    The one of the following that *most nearly* expresses his meaning is:

    A. Negligence seldom accompanies success
    B. Incomplete work is careless work
    C. Conscientious work is never attended by failure
    D. A conscientious person never makes mistakes

    12.____

13. In taking a statement from a person who has been shot by an assailant and is not expected to live, police are instructed to ask the person: "Do you believe you are about to die?"
    Of the following, the MOST probable reason for this question is

    A. the theory that a person about to die and meet his Maker will tell the truth
    B. to determine if the victim is conscious and capable of making a statement
    C. to put the victim mentally at ease and more willing to talk
    D. that the statement could not be used in court if his mind was distraught by the fear of impending death

    13.____

14. If, while you are on traffic duty at a busy intersection, a pedestrian asks you for directions to a particular place, the BEST course of conduct is to

    A. ignore the question and continue directing traffic
    B. tell the pedestrian to ask a patrolman on foot patrol
    C. answer the question in a brief, courteous manner
    D. leave your traffic post only long enough to give clear and adequate directions

    14.____

15. In lecturing on the law of arrest, an instructor remarked: "To go beyond is as bad as to fall short."
The one of the following which MOST nearly expresses his meaning is:

   A. Never undertake the impossible
   B. Extremes are not desirable
   C. Look before you leap
   D. Too much success is dangerous

16. Suppose you are a police officer assigned to a patrol precinct. While you are patrolling your post in the vicinity of a school, your attention is called to a man who is selling small packages to school children. You are told that this man distributes similar packages to these same children daily and that he is suspected of dealing in narcotics. Of the following, the BEST action for you to take is to

   A. pretend to be an addict and attempt to purchase narcotics from him
   B. observe the man's action yourself for several days in order to obtain grounds for arrest
   C. stop and question one or more of the children after they have transacted business with the man
   D. stop and question the man as he leaves the children

17. In the event of a poison gas attack, civil defense authorities advise civilians to

   A. open doors and windows and go to upper floors
   B. close doors and windows and go to upper floors
   C. open doors and windows and go to the basement
   D. close doors and windows and go to the basement

18. As an intelligent police officer, you should know that, of the following, the one which is LEAST likely to be followed by an increase in crime is

   A. war   B. depression
   C. poor housing   D. prosperity

19. As a police officer interested in the promotion of traffic safety, you should know that, according to recent statistics, the one group which has the *highest* number of deaths as a result of being struck in traffic is

   A. adults over 55 years of age
   B. adults between 36 and 55 years of age
   C. adults between 22 and 35 years old
   D. children up to 4 years old

20. As an intelligent police officer having a knowledge of the various types of crimes, you should know that, in recent years, the age group 16 through 25 showed the *greatest* number of arrests for

   A. grand larceny from highways and vehicles
   B. burglary
   C. rape
   D. homicide

21. As a well-informed police officer, you should know that the *greatest* number of arrests made and summonses served in recent years was for

   A. offenses against property rights
   B. general criminality
   C. bestial criminality
   D. offenses against public health, safety and policy

21.____

22. As a police officer interested in the reduction of unnecessary traffic accidents, you should know that two of the *chief* sources of such accidents to pedestrians in recent years were crossing a street

   A. against the light, and crossing past a parked car
   B. at a point other than the crossing, and crossing against the light
   C. at a point other than the crossing, and running off the sidewalk
   D. against the light, and failing to observe whether cars were making right or left turns

22.____

23. A "modus operandi" file will be MOST valuable to a new patrolman as a means of showing the

   A. methods used by criminals
   B. various bureaus and divisions of the Police Department
   C. number and nature of vehicular accidents
   D. forms used by the Police Department

23.____

24. A police officer is frequently advised to lie down before returning fire, if a person is shooting at him. This is PRIMARILY because

   A. a smaller target will thus be presented to the assailant
   B. he can return fire more quickly while in the prone position
   C. the assailant will think he has struck the police officer and cease firing
   D. it will indicate that the police officer is not the aggressor

24.____

25. In making arrests during a large riot, it is the practice of the police to take the ringleaders into custody as soon as possible. This is PRIMARILY because

   A. the police can obtain valuable information from them
   B. they deserve punishment more than the other rioters
   C. rioters need leadership and, without it, will disperse more quickly
   D. arrests of wrongdoers should always be in order of their importance

25.____

KEY (CORRECT ANSWERS)

1.	A	11.	C
2.	C	12.	A
3.	C	13.	A
4.	C	14.	C
5.	A	15.	B
6.	A	16.	C
7.	C	17.	B
8.	A	18.	D
9.	C	19.	A
10.	C	20.	B

21.	D
22.	B
23.	A
24.	A
25.	C

TEST 2

DIRECTIONS: Each question or incomplete statement is followed by several suggested answers or completions. Select the one that BEST answers the question or completes the statement. *PRINT THE LETTER OF THE CORRECT ANSWER IN THE SPACE AT THE RIGHT.*

1. Assume that you are a police officer. A woman has complained to you about a man's indecent exposure in front of a house. As you approach the house, the man begins to run. You *should*

    A. shoot to kill as the man may be a dangerous maniac
    B. fire a warning shot to try to halt the man
    C. summon other patrolmen in order to apprehend him
    D. question the woman regarding the man's identity

    1.____

2. You are patrolling a parkway in a radio car with another police officer. A maroon car coming from the opposite direction signals you to stop and the driver informs you that he was robbed by three men speeding ahead of him in a black sedan. Your radio car cannot cross the center abutment.
You *should*

    A. request the driver to make a report to the nearest precinct as your car cannot cross over to the other side
    B. make a U turn in your radio car and give chase on the wrong side of the parkway
    C. fire warning shots in the air to summon other patrolmen
    D. flash police headquarters over your radio system

    2.____

3. You are on patrol duty in a crowded part of the city. You hear the traffic patrolman fire four shots in the air and cry, "Get out of his way. He's got a gun." You see a man tearing along the street dodging traffic.
You *should*

    A. fire several shots in the air to alert other police officers
    B. give chase to the man and shoot, as it is possible that one of your shots may hit him
    C. wait for an opening in the crowds and then shoot at the man from one knee
    D. wade through the crowds and then shout at the man to stop

    3.____

4. Assume that you have been assigned to a traffic post at a busy intersection. A car bearing out-of-town license plates is about to turn into a one-way street going in the opposite direction. You blow your whistle and stop the car.
You *should then*

    A. hand out a summons to the driver in order to make an example of him, since out-of-town drivers notoriously disregard our traffic regulations
    B. pay no attention to him and let him continue in the proper direction
    C. ask him to pull over to the curb and advise him to drive to the nearest precinct to get a copy of the latest city traffic regulations
    D. call his attention to the fact that he was violating a traffic regulation and permit him to continue in the proper direction

    4.____

5. A storekeeper has complained to you that every day at noon several peddlers congregate outside his store in order to sell their merchandise. You *should*

    A. inform him that such complaints must be made directly to the Police Commissioner
    B. inform him that peddlers have a right to earn their living, too
    C. make it your business to patrol that part of your post around noon
    D. pay no attention to him as this storekeeper is probably a crank inasmuch as nobody else has complained

6. You notice that a man is limping hurriedly, leaving a trail of blood behind him. You question him, and his explanation is that he was hurt accidentally while he was watching a man clean a gun.
You *should*

    A. let him go as you have no proof that his story is not true
    B. have him sent to the nearest city hospital under police escort so that he may be questioned again after treatment
    C. ask him whether the man had a license for his gun
    D. ask him to lead you to the man who cleaned his gun so that you may question him further about the accident

7. There have been a series of burglaries in a certain residential area consisting of one-family houses. You have been assigned to select a house in this area in which detectives can wait secretly for the attempt to burglarize that house so that the burglars can be apprehended in the act.
Which of the following would be the *BEST* house to select for this purpose? The house

    A. that was recently burglarized and from which several thousand dollars worth of clothing and personal property were taken
    B. whose owner reports that several times the telephone has rung but the person making the call hung up as soon as the telephone was answered
    C. that is smaller and looks much less pretentious than other houses in the same area
    D. that is occupied by a widower who works long hours but who lives with an invalid mother requiring constant nursing service

8. The two detectives noticed the man climb a ladder to the roof of a loft building. The detectives followed the same route. They saw him break a skylight and lower himself into the building. Through the broken skylight, one of the detectives covered the man with his gun and told him to throw up his hands.
The action of the detectives in this situation was *faulty CHIEFLY* because

    A. one of the detectives should have remained on the ladder
    B. criminals should be caught red-handed
    C. the detectives should have made sure of the identity of the man before following him
    D. the possibility of another means of escape from the building should have been foreseen

9. Suppose that, while you are patrolling your post, a middle-aged woman informs you that three men are holding up a nearby express office. You rush immediately to the scene of the holdup. While you are still about 75 feet away, you see the three men, revolvers in their hands, emerge from the office and make for what is apparently their getaway car, which is pointed in the opposite direction. Of the following, your FIRST consideration in this situation should be to

   A. enter the express office in order to find out what the men have taken
   B. maneuver quickly so as to get the getaway car between you and the express office
   C. make a mental note of the descriptions of the escaping men for immediate alarm
   D. attempt to overtake the car in which the holdup men seek to escape.

10. Which of the following situations, if observed by you while on patrol, should you consider MOST suspicious and deserving of further investigation?

    A. A shabbily dressed youth is driving a new Cadillac
    B. An old Plymouth has been parked without lights outside an apartment house for several hours
    C. A light is on in the rear of a one-family, luxurious residence
    D. Two well-dressed men are standing at a bus stop at 2 A.M. and arguing heatedly

11. Suppose that, while on patrol late at night, you find a woman lying in the street, apparently the victim of a hit-and-run driver. She seems to be injured seriously but you wish to ask her one or two questions in order to help apprehend the hit-and-run car.
    Of the following, the BEST question to ask is:

    A. In what direction did the car go?
    B. What time did it happen?
    C. What kind of car was it?
    D. How many persons were in the car?

12. Assume that you are driving a police car, equipped with two-way radio, along an isolated section of a parkway at 3 A.M. You note that the headlights of a car are blinking rapidly. When you stop to investigate, the driver of the car informs you that he was just forced to the side of the road by two men in a green convertible, who robbed him of a large amount of cash and jewelry at the point of a gun and then sped away. Your FIRST consideration in this situation should be to

    A. drive rapidly along the parkway in the direction taken by the criminals in an effort to apprehend them before they escape
    B. question the driver carefully, looking for inconsistencies indicating that he made up the whole story
    C. obtain a complete listing and identification of all materials lost
    D. notify your superior to have the parkway exits watched for a car answering the description of the getaway car

13. Suppose that you have been assigned to check the story of a witness in a holdup case. The witness states that, while sitting at her window, she observed the suspect loitering outside a cigar store. As she watched, the suspect entered a nearby liquor store. He remained there only a minute or two. Then she saw him walk out rapidly, hurry to the corner and hail a cab. Assume that Figure 1 is a scale drawing of the scene. All four corners of the intersection are occupied by tall buildings. W indicates the window at which the witness sat, C indicates the cigar store and L indicates the liquor store. On the basis of this sketch, the BEST reason for doubting the truthfulness of the witness is that
    A. the window is far removed from the cigar store
    B. the cigar store and the window are not on the same street
    C. distances may be distorted by a high angle of observation
    D. the liquor store cannot be seen from the window

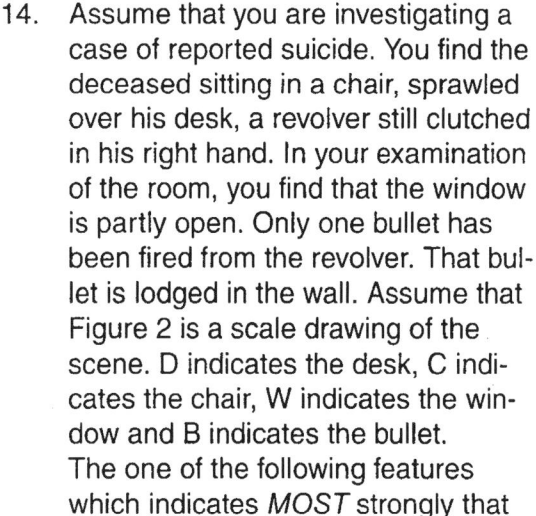

14. Assume that you are investigating a case of reported suicide. You find the deceased sitting in a chair, sprawled over his desk, a revolver still clutched in his right hand. In your examination of the room, you find that the window is partly open. Only one bullet has been fired from the revolver. That bullet is lodged in the wall. Assume that Figure 2 is a scale drawing of the scene. D indicates the desk, C indicates the chair, W indicates the window and B indicates the bullet. The one of the following features which indicates MOST strongly that the deceased did not commit suicide is the
    A. distance between the desk and the bullet hole
    B. relative position of the bullet hole and the chair
    C. fact that the window was partly open
    D. relative position of the desk and the window

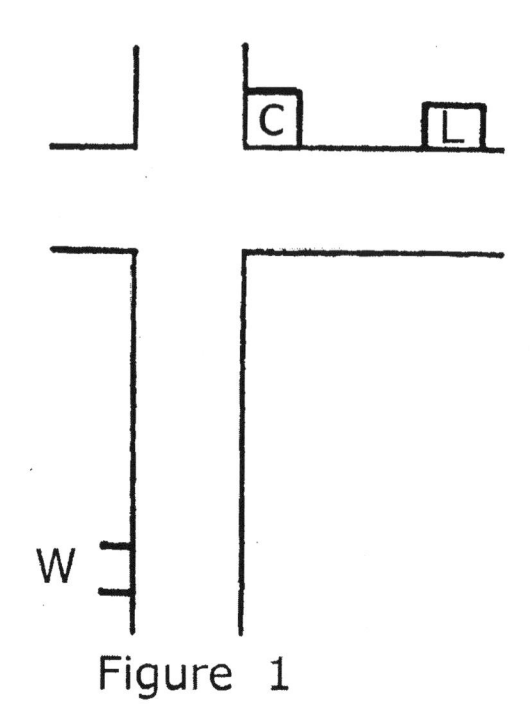

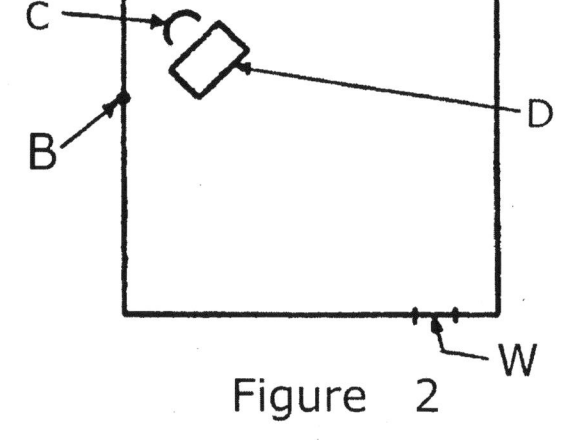

15. Driver 1 claimed that the collision occurred because, as he approached the intersection, Driver 2 started to make a left turn suddenly and at high speed, even though the light had been red against him for 15 or 20 seconds.
Suppose that you have been assigned to make a report on this accident. The position of the vehicles after the accident is indicated in Figure 3, the point in each case indicating the front of the vehicle. On the basis of this sketch, the *BEST* reason for concluding that Driver 1's statement is *false* is that Driver
    A. 2's car is beyond the center of the intersection
    B. 2's car is making the turn on the proper side of the road
    C. 1's car is beyond the sidewalk line
    D. 1's car is on the right hand side of the road

Figure 3

16. Suppose that you are a police officer investigating a complaint that a gunman is brandishing an automatic revolver in the back room of a bar and grill. Of the following, the *BEST* reason for you to exercise caution as you enter the back room is that

    A. there may be a second means of exit from the room
    B. the complaint may have been exaggerated
    C. an automatic revolver may easily become jammed
    D. the complaint mentioned only one gunman
    E. the gunman may open fire without warning

17. Suppose that you have arrested a man for attempting to break into a fur shop and that you are about to escort him to a nearby precinct station.
Of the following, the *FIRST important* precaution for you to take is to make certain that

    A. the man is carrying proper identification
    B. no furs are missing
    C. the man has a criminal record
    D. the man is unarmed
    E. the man's fingerprints have been carefully checked

18. While you are patrolling your post in a busy midtown area, you notice the gasoline tank of a bus burst into flame. The passengers see the fire and begin to leave the bus at once. The street is crowded with pedestrians.
Of the following, the *BEST* reason for you to clear the area of pedestrians immediately is to

    A. avoid panic among the bus passengers
    B. reduce the possibility of injuries due to an explosion
    C. prevent the fire from spreading
    D. leave room for the bus driver to maneuver the bus
    E. avoid possible fatalities due to carbon monoxide fumes

6 (#2)

19. Detectives had been following the two men for some time. At 8:10 P.M., Sunday, the suspects entered a four-story apartment house. They went to the roof of the building, walked across to an adjoining warehouse, and went down the fire escape to the second floor, where they forced a warehouse window. Meanwhile, although the temperature was below freezing, other detectives waited in the street below. Under the circumstances described above, for several detectives to wait in the street was *wise CHIEFLY* because it was

   A. possible that the suspects lived in the apartment building
   B. unlikely that the suspects would again venture out into the street
   C. desirable to block all possible avenues of escape by the suspects
   D. obvious that the warehouse windows were unlocked
   E. necessary to know the exact location of the suspects every minute of the time

19._____

20. Jones was found lying in the kitchen of his bungalow, two feet from the window. A bullet had passed through hsi heart and was found lodged in the wall. Death must have been instantaneous. There was a bullet hole in the lower part of the glass of the kitchen window. All doors and windows were closed and locked from within. No weapon was found in the bungalow.
Of the following, the *MOST* valid conclusion on the basis of the above facts is that

   A. Jones was killed by a friend who escaped through the window
   B. the murderer must have had an accomplice
   C. the window was closed and locked after the murder had been committed
   D. Jones probably committed suicide
   E. Jones was shot by a person standing outside the kitchen window

20._____

21. Looking through the window of a jewelry store, a police officer sees a man take a watch from the counter and drop it into his pocket while the jeweler is busy talking to someone else. The man looks around the store and then walks out.
The officer should

   A. *follow* the man to see what he does with the watch as thieves of this type usually work in pairs
   B. *ignore* the incident; if the man were performing an illegal act, the jeweler would have called for help
   C. *arrest* the man, take him to the station house, and then return to obtain the jeweler's statement
   D. *ignore* the incident; if the man were a thief, the jeweler would not have left the watches unattended
   E. *stop* the man and bring him back into the shop so that both he and the jeweler can be questioned

21._____

22. It is quite possible to set up a general procedure which will result in the rehabilitation of all juvenile delinquents.
This statment is, *in general,*

   A. *correct;* the major causes of all juvenile delinquency are improper home life and a general lack of morals; cure these and there will be no problem of juvenile delinquency
   B. *not correct;* juvenile delinquency results from the generally lower moral climate; therefore, rehabilitation is not possible until the world climate changes

22._____

96

C. *correct;* if juvenile delinquents are severely punished, rehabilitation will follow
D. *not correct;* each case of juvenile delinquency is different and, for most effective treatment, must be handled on an individual basis
E. *correct;* if the proper general procedure is set up, it always can be applied

23. A police officer observes a young man, who is obviously very excited, walking unusually fast and repeatedly halting to look behind him. Upon stopping the young man, the police officer finds that he is carrying a gun and has just held up a liquor store a few blocks away.
This incident illustrates that

   A. circumstances that are not suspicious in themselves frequently provide clues for the solution of crimes
   B. an experienced police officer can pick the criminal type out of a crowd by alert observation
   C. action is always to be preferred to thought
   D. a police officer should investigate suspicious circumstances
   E. a police officer who stops to think may sometimes fail to get his man

24. When making arrests, the police officer should treat all suspects in the same manner.
This suggested rule is

   A. *undesirable;* the specific problems presented should govern the police officer's actions
   B. *desirable;* this is the only democratic solution to the problem
   C. *undesirable;* police officers should not be expected to abide by rules as criminals do not
   D. *desirable;* only by setting up fixed and rigid rules can police officers know what is expected of them
   E. *undesirable;* persons who are only suspected are not criminals and should not be treated as such

25. One of the most difficult questions in a crime prevention program is to decide how many men are needed to police a particular area. There have been a number of attempts to invent a simple formula, but none has so far been successful.
Of the following reasons for this, the *MOST* probable is that

   A. men, not formulas, patrol beats
   B. many factors are involved whose relative importance has not been determined
   C. there is no information on which to base such a formula
   D. such a formula even if it were accurate would be of little use as it would be too theoretical
   E. police problems in no two areas in the city are alike in any way

KEY (CORRECT ANSWERS)

1. C
2. D
3. D
4. D
5. C

6. B
7. B
8. D
9. C
10. D

11. C
12. D
13. D
14. B
15. C

16. E
17. D
18. B
19. C
20. E

21. E
22. D
23. D
24. A
25. B

TEST 3

DIRECTIONS: Each question or incomplete statement is followed by several suggested answers or completions. Select the one that BEST answers the question or completes the statement. *PRINT THE LETTER OF THE CORRECT ANSWER IN THE SPACE AT THE RIGHT.*

1. A police officer is testifying at the jury trial of a suspect he arrested.
   Which one of the following actions, taken by the officer while on the witness stand, is *most likely* to FAVORABLY affect the acceptance of his testimony? The officer

   A. refers to his memo book before he answers each question
   B. directs his testimony to the jury, not to the judge or counsel
   C. responds to obviously silly questions with equally silly answers
   D. carefully presents both the facts asked for and also the conclusions he is able to draw from them
   E. adds explanations and support to his answers, rather than merely replying to a question with a direct answer

2. A police officer is interviewing the person who called the police to the scene of a crime. The officer wants to know whether the witness, when he entered the room to call the police, saw someone who might be the person who committed the crime.
   Which one of the following is the *BEST* way for the officer to phrase his question to the witness?

   A. "What did you observe when you entered the room?"
   B. "Didn't you see anyone when you entered the room?"
   C. "Was the person who committed the crime still in the room when you entered?"
   D. "Was someone who could have committed the crime in the room when you entered?"
   E. "Didn't you see someone who could have committed the crime when you entered the room?"

3. Because of the effect that certain physical conditions have on human perception, testimony of well-intentioned witnesses is sometimes unreliable.
   Which one of the following claims by a witness (all of which are affected by physical conditions), is *most likely* to be reliable? A witness

   A. claims that a taxicab, parked at night under a sodium vapor street lamp, was yellow and not white
   B. who is farsighted, claims that he saw clearly a robbery suspect, 25 feet away, even though he was not wearing glasses at the time
   C. who had just entered a dark house from a brightly lighted street, claims that he can identify the prowler he saw escaping through the window of the house at that moment
   D. who was in a very dimly lighted area, claims to have seen a certain man wearing blue pants and a jacket of a color he could not identify
   E. who had been sitting in a movie theatre for about an hour, claims that he did not see a blue flashing light, but did see a red "exit" light; the lights were later found to be of equal brightness

4. Two patrol officers responding to a "dispute" call find the complainant is a woman who says her neighbor is beating his child. They knock on his door and interview the man. He is drunk and alone with his 7-year-old son. The boy is badly beaten and the father is still in a rage and yells at the officers to get out.
Which one of the following, if any, MOST accurately states the person or agency that is both in the best position to promptly remove the child against the father's will in this situation and that also has the authority to do so?

   A. A patrol supervisor
   B. The patrol officers on the scene
   C. A youth aid division officer
   D. The family court, through issuance of a warrant authorizing the police to remove the child
   E. None of the above has authority to remove the child against the father's will.

5. A police officer has responded to a gas station robbery and is interviewing the victim. Among other things, he asks whether the victim can remember the exact words of the suspect and his manner of speech.
Which one of the following BEST states both whether or not this is an important area of investigation and also the best reason therefor?

   A. It *is not* important, because it could not be admissible as evidence in court
   B. It *is* important, because it is necessary to prove the element of intent in robbery
   C. It *is not* important, because most robbers don't say enough to determine any identifying characteristic
   D. It *is not* important, because a robbery victim will be too upset to be very accurate on this matter
   E. It *is* important, because the robber's choice of phrases is often highly characteristic and, therefore, helpful in identification

6. If the primary purpose of traffic law enforcement is the prevention of accidents, then which one of the following is the MOST appropriate attitude for the police to have regarding enforcing traffic laws?

   A. Police officers should attempt to issue as many citations as time permits
   B. Police officers should avoid using warnings because warnings have very little prevention value
   C. Motorists should be encouraged to comply voluntarily with traffic laws and educated regarding such laws, whenever possible
   D. To the extent possible, all traffic laws should be enforced equally, without regard to time, place, or type of violation
   E. Enforcement of traffic laws should be the sole responsibility of specialists who devote full time to accident prevention

7. A foot-patrol officer in a business district observes a man walking in front of him whom he recognizes as a wanted felon. They are at an intersection crowded with people. The suspect is not aware of the patrol officer's presence and continues across the intersection.
Which one of the following is the BEST place at which to make the arrest?

   A. In a restaurant or store if the suspect should enter
   B. Immediately at the intersection where he has observed the suspect
   C. At the first intersection which has little or no pedestrian movement

D. In the middle of the first block which has little or no pedestrian traffic
E. In the middle of the next block, but only if this block is still congested with pedestrians

8. Which one of the following cars is most *likely* to appear to a witness to be traveling FASTER than its *true* speed? A

    A. large car
    B. noisy car
    C. quiet car
    D. car painted a solid color
    E. car painted two or more colors

9. A certain police officer was patrolling a playground area where adolescent gangs had been causing trouble and holding drinking parties. He approached a teenage boy who was alone and drinking from a large paper cup. He asked the boy what he was drinking and the boy replied "Coke." The officer asked the boy for the cup and the boy refused to give it to him. The officer then explained that he wanted to check the contents, and the boy still refused to give it to him. The officer then demanded the cup and the boy reluctantly gave it to him. The officer smelled the contents of the cup and determined that it was, in fact, Coke. He then told the boy to move along, and emptied the Coke on the ground.
Which one of the following is the MOST serious error, if any, made by the officer in handling this situation?

    A. The officer should not have made any effort to determine what was in the cup
    B. The officer should not have explained to the boy why he wanted to have the cup
    C. The officer should have returned the Coke to the boy and allowed the boy to stay where he was
    D. The officer should have first placed the boy under arrest before taking the cup from him
    E. None of the above since the officer made no error in handling the situation

10. A police officer assigned to some clerical duties accidentally destroys an important document which was to be presented in court as evidence in a few days.
The BEST action for him to take FIRST in this situation is to

    A. suggest that the case be postponed until more evidence can be obtained
    B. immediately contact the person from whom the document was obtained and request another copy of it
    C. say nothing at this time, but admit the destruction of the document when asked for it by his superior
    D. notify his superior of the destruction of the document

11. Assume that you are a probationary police officer newly assigned to perform a certain duty. Your superior has given you specific orders concerning a job to be done. An older and more experienced officer who has no authority over you criticizes what you are doing and gives you orders to do things his way.
The BEST action for you to take is to

    A. ask your superior to direct the older patrolman to cease criticizing and giving orders
    B. continue working in accordance with the orders given you by your superior

C. stop doing the job until you have asked your superior about the situation
D. seek the advice of other experienced officers and, if they agree, follow the orders of the older officer

12. Authorities believe that delinquent behavior of children tends strongly to develop into criminal adult behavior.
The CHIEF significance of this statement to a police officer is that he should

   A. pay particular attention to the children of known criminals
   B. arrest all children committing delinquent acts
   C. try to correct early evidences of bad behavior
   D. administer a reasonable degree of physical punishment to the children committing such delinquent acts and warn them of immediate arrest the next time they engage in such activities

13. Of the following, the CHIEF reason for requiring the registration of certain firearms is that

   A. it will reduce law enforcement problems created by home-made guns
   B. uncontrolled availability of guns tends to increase law enforcement problems
   C. most criminals will not use a registered gun in committing a crime
   D. unregistered guns are often found at the scene of a crime

14. In most states no crime can occur unless there is a written law forbidding the act, and, even though an act may not be exactly in harmony with public policy, such act is not a crime unless it is expressly forbidden by legislative enactment.
According to the above statement,

   A. all acts not in harmony with public policy should be expressly forbidden by law
   B. a crime is committed only with reference to a particular law
   C. nothing contrary to public policy can be done without legislative authority
   D. legislative enactments frequently forbid actions which are exactly in harmony with public policy

15. When starting to unload a revolver, it is safest for the police officer to have the muzzle pointing

   A. upward   B. downward   C. to the left   D. to the right

16. When approaching a suspect to make an arrest, it is LEAST important for the police officer to guard against the possibility that the suspect may

   A. be diseased   B. have a gun
   C. use physical force   D. run away

17. The printed departmental rules may *logically* be expected to include instructions on

   A. which posts are the most dangerous
   B. where to purchase uniforms and equipment cheaply
   C. how many days a week overtime work will be required
   D. what information must be included in an accident report

18. It is well known that some people refrain from breaking the law only because they fear   18.____
    subsequent punishment. This statement is *LEAST* likely to apply to the person who

    A. waits to light his cigarette after he reaches the street instead of lighting it in the station
    B. stops his car at a red light where there is a traffic officer
    C. returns the excess change he has received from a bus operator
    D. finds a brief case full of 20-dollar bills and turns it over to the police

---

KEY (CORRECT ANSWERS)

1.	B	11.	B
2.	A	12.	C
3.	B	13.	B
4.	A	14.	B
5.	E	15.	B
6.	C	16.	A
7.	D	17.	D
8.	D	18.	C
9.	C		
10.	D		

EXAMINATION SECTION
TEST 1

DIRECTIONS: Each question or incomplete statement is followed by several suggested answers or completions. Select the one that BEST answers the question or completes the statement. *PRINT THE LETTER OF THE CORRECT ANSWER IN THE SPACE AT THE RIGHT.*

1. _____ refers to a ranger's power or right to give commands, enforce obedience, take action and make decisions.

    A. Jurisdiction
    B. License
    C. Authority
    D. Sanction

2. The primary objective of most of a park ranger's enforcement actions is

    A. correction and punishment
    B. establishing authority and control
    C. education and information
    D. decreasing liability

3. Which of the following ranger services is LEAST likely to be provided through visitor contact?

    A. Interpretive
    B. Resource management
    C. Safety
    D. Search, rescue and recovery

4. A ranger comes upon a location that she believes to be a crime scene, but she has no training in criminal investigation. As the first park official on the scene, she should

    A. disperse everyone in the area
    B. record existing and relevant data in a notebook
    C. straighten or clean up the scene
    D. interview available witnesses

5. In most automobiles, the VIN plate is on the

    A. driver's side doorjamb
    B. driver's side windshield post
    C. driver's side dashboard
    D. passenger's side dashboard

6. A park's "situation map" should be marked on a surface of

    A. wood or plywood
    B. paper
    C. enamel or clear acetate
    D. canvas

7. The Rhomberg test is a field test most useful for indicating _____ intoxication.

   A. alcohol
   B. marijuana
   C. cocaine
   D. methamphetamine

8. A ranger on patrol should imagine his/her key responsibility to be

   A. conservation
   B. prevention
   C. surveillance
   D. observation

9. The form of federal jurisdiction that a park ranger will encounter most rarely is _____ jurisdiction, which means the federal government has been granted the right by a state to exercise certain state authorities.

   A. partial
   B. proprietary
   C. multiple
   D. concurrent

10. One of the actions within a park ranger's continuum of enforcement levels is the verbal warning. The key to issuing a verbal warning is for a park ranger to

    A. maintain a stern and authoritative tone of voice
    B. convince the offender of the seriousness of the offense
    C. convince the offender that the warning is really just a friendly chat
    D. be certain he has the authority to implement the consequences if it becomes necessary

11. For most park agencies, the most appropriate training vehicle for providing training to rangers who will have law enforcement authority includes a
    I. basic agency-wide course of 40 to 80 hours
    II. 20- to 40-hour orientation course at the assigned park
    III. 3- to 6-month on-the-job training program at the assigned park
    IV. participation in special training courses as opportunities arise.

    A. I and II
    B. II and III
    C. II, III and IV
    D. I, II, III and IV

12. Generally, the use of vehicles for park patrol
    I. greatly increases a ranger's ability to respond quickly to emergencies
    II. is the optimal method for increasing personal contact with visitors
    III. affords the ranger a degree of protection
    IV. offers the most efficient method of patrol with limited man power

    A. I, II and III
    B. I, III and IV
    C. II and III
    D. I, II, III and IV

13. Whenever a suitable wall surface isn't available for conducting a search of an offender, a kneeling search may be appropriate. In a standard kneeling search, the

    A. offender's knees should be together
    B. offender's feet should be spread apart
    C. offender's hand should be raised high above his head
    D. ranger should search from behind the offender

14. When initiating communication with visitors in an enforcement situation, the ranger's most immediate responsibility is to

    A. help the visitor understand the seriousness of the offense
    B. create a supportive rather than defensive climate
    C. make sure the visitor is aware of the ranger's authority to enforce
    D. ensure that the visitor is physically incapable of mounting an attack

15. Which of the following types of knots is used to attach a rope to the middle of another rope?

    A. Prusik
    B. Clove hitch
    C. Square lashing
    D. Shear lashing

16. Listening is usually thought of as being accomplished on four levels. The highest level involves

    A. listening with understanding of the speaker's point of view
    B. making sense out of sound
    C. critically evaluating what is said
    D. understanding the literal meaning of what is said

17. Which of the following structures may generally be entered unconditionally by a ranger in an enforcement situation?
    I. Park administrative building
    II. Public restrooms
    III. Visitor abodes
    IV. Concessionaire's leased building

    A. I and II
    B. I, II and III
    C. II and III
    D. I, II, III and IV

18. Which of the following is most likely to be a standard item for a mounted patrol?

    A. Animal noose
    B. Survival kit
    C. Flares
    D. Hydraulic jack

19. "Thumbnail" descriptions of persons include each of the following, EXCEPT

   A. Hair color
   B. Eyes
   C. Clothing
   D. Race

20. A ranger is reading a park map grid reference. On such maps, a four-digit grid reference number refers to the grid square located to the _____ the point of intersection of the lines relating to the grid numbers.

   A. right and above
   B. right and below
   C. left and above
   D. left and below

21. It is usually permissible to search an offender incidental to an arrest. Which of the following statements about such searches is TRUE?

   A. During a legal search, a ranger may seize items that are not only in actual possession, but within reach of the person at the time of the search.
   B. Evidence of a crime other than the one for which the ranger has an arrest warrant is generally not seizable.
   C. Stop-and-frisk searches are permitted under most situations.
   D. A legal search may usually be conducted by any ranger who has arrest powers.

22. A ranger is helping to compose the interpretive text for visitor center exhibits. The best text-on-background color combination in terms of legibility would be

   A. black on white
   B. green on white
   C. green on red
   D. blue on white

23. Before conducting a search, a park ranger should always obtain a search warrant if there is time, or whenever there is doubt as to whether one is necessary. Generally, a search warrant is required if

   A. exceptional circumstances create probable cause that contraband or other evidence will soon be destroyed
   B. the search is of a motor vehicle that is capable of being moved out of the ranger's control and there is probable cause to believe that someone in the vehicle has been involved in the commission of a crime
   C. the search is of a habitable dwelling on park grounds that is owned by the park, but occupied by the suspect as a camping abode
   D. the search is incidental to a lawful arrest and confined to the offender's person

24. A ranger should consider the primary objective of a park agency's interpretive services to be

   A. informing
   B. dispelling commonly held assumptions
   C. furthering an agenda
   D. inciting the visitor to some action or feeling

25. In certain circumstances, search of a person or premises may be appropriate even though legal grounds are weak or absent. Such searches may be conducted with consent. Which of the following statements concerning consent searches is TRUE?   25.____

    A. The person granting consent does not necessarily have to be aware of the right to refuse consent.
    B. A consent to enter premises implies a consent to search.
    C. A statement welcoming a search implies that a warrant is not demanded.
    D. Consent may be revoked at any time, but the revocation does not invalidate any evidence seized prior to the revocation.

KEY (CORRECT ANSWERS)

1.	C	11.	C
2.	C	12.	B
3.	B	13.	D
4.	B	14.	B
5.	C	15.	A
6.	C	16.	A
7.	A	17.	A
8.	D	18.	C
9.	A	19.	B
10.	D	20.	A

21. A
22. D
23. C
24. D
25. D

TEST 2

DIRECTIONS: Each question or incomplete statement is followed by several suggested answers or completions. Select the one that BEST answers the question or completes the statement. *PRINT THE LETTER OF THE CORRECT ANSWER IN THE SPACE AT THE RIGHT.*

1. In most cases it is appropriate for a park ranger to think of visitors as
    I. not dependent on the ranger; it is the ranger who is dependent on them
    II. the most important people the ranger will come into contact with
    III. not an interruption of the ranger's work, but the main reason for it
    IV. outsiders who will alter the park, rather than an integral part of the environment

    A. I and II
    B. I, II and III
    C. II, III and IV
    D. I, II, III and IV

    1._____

2. Which of following legal terms is used to denote the proof that a crime has occurred?

    A. *Corpus delicti*
    B. *Habeus corpus*
    C. *Respondent superior*
    D. Probable cause

    2._____

3. In the continuum of a park ranger's enforcement priorities, "Priority 1" situations deal with

    A. the protection of visitors from each other
    B. situations in which neither the park nor its visitors are in any immediate danger
    C. the protection of the park's resources from the visitor
    D. the protection of visitors from hazardous conditions created by park resources

    3._____

4. The strongest ropes are generally made of

    A. polypropylene
    B. nylon
    C. manila
    D. Dacron

    4._____

5. A ranger is helping to compose the interpretive text for visitor center exhibits. For one exhibit, visitors will be about 15 feet from the text. The letters for this text should be at least _____ high.

    A. a half-inch
    B. an inch
    C. an inch-and-a-half
    D. two inches

    5._____

6. The primary purposes of patrol include
    I. providing resource protection
    II. making assistance available to visitors
    III. providing a deterrent for destructive behavior
    IV. observing the park and visitor behavior

    A. I and II
    B. II and IV
    C. II, III and IV
    D. I, II, III and IV

    6._____

110

7. A ranger is one of the first officials to arrive at the scene of a crime. Preliminary procedures that will ordinarily be undertaken by the investigating ranger include each of the following, EXCEPT

   A. safeguarding the area
   B. conducting a methodic crime scene search
   C. separating witnesses from bystanders and obtaining statements
   D. rendering assistance to the injured

8. In areas of _____ jurisdiction, only state law is considered to be in effect, meaning that federal officers may enforce rules and regulations only such as Title 36, CFR and other federal laws allow regardless of jurisdiction.

   A. partial
   B. proprietary
   C. concurrent
   D. exclusive

9. To be legal, a search warrant should specifically identify the
   I. property to be seized
   II. place to be searched
   III. limits of the search
   IV. probable cause upon which the search is based

   A. I and II
   B. II, III and IV
   C. III and IV
   D. I, II, III and IV

10. Which of the following is a guideline that should be followed in handling a domestic dispute on park property?

    A. If the situation seems to justify the intervention of a professional counselor, recommend counseling in a general way.
    B. Offer legal advice if either of the parties is considering legal action.
    C. Ask questions that will determine who is at fault or who began the altercation.
    D. Try to stay out of such disputes unless it becomes clear that someone is in danger of imminent physical harm.

11. Rangers are often brought into contact with groups who represent "subcultures"-groups of a similar age, race, occupation or other grouping characteristics that may lead to the development of a kind of dialect or language system all their own. In communicating with these groups—especially in enforcement situations—it is important for the ranger to

    A. acknowledge only standard grammatical English
    B. understand the "language" of the subculture, but not to use it
    C. try to communicate with these groups using their own dialect or jargon
    D. try to speak as little as possible

12. Rangers without law enforcement authority are empowered, in some situations, to
    I. issue citations
    II. detain visitors
    III. search visitors
    IV. seize property

    A. I only
    B. I and II
    C. I, II and III
    D. I, II, III and IV

13. Which of the following is a disadvantage associated with foot patrol?

    A. Ranger's presence is suggested, rather than seen or heard
    B. Restricted to extensive-use areas
    C. Direct contact with visitors is inhibited
    D. Limited ability to respond to situations outside the immediate area

14. Guidelines for search-and-rescue operations within a park include
    I. Radio-equipped searchers should be sent to danger or vantage points.
    II. If dogs are used, they should be on a leash.
    III. Searches should generally not be continued after dark unless a life-or-death situation exists.
    IV. Each searcher should periodically call out the name(s) of the lost person(s).

    A. I and II
    B. I, II and III
    C. IV only
    D. I, II, III and IV

15. The ability of park rangers to implement enforcement services is dependent upon a number of factors. Which of the following is LEAST likely to be one of these factors?

    A. The park agency's policies
    B. The ranger's level of certainty about the appropriateness of enforcement
    C. The individual ranger's level of training and expertise
    D. The authority and jurisdiction authorized by law

16. Good listening skills for rangers include
    I. Forming judgements before listening to the speaker, based on appearance and demeanor
    II. Considering listening to be an active process
    III. Always taking notes while listening
    IV. Listening to how something is being said before concentrating on the actual content of the message

    A. I and II
    B. II only
    C. II, III and IV
    D. I, II, III and IV

17. Which of the following is NOT generally considered part of the standard frisk procedure?

   A. Offender's feet spread about two feet apart.
   B. Offender's hands extended above the head, with fingers spread.
   C. Ranger moves fingertips over all searchable areas, crushing clothing to locate concealed weapons.
   D. Offenders considered dangerous should be handcuffed prior to the frisk.

18. One of the signs that a person has overdosed on a stimulant is

   A. cold, clammy skin
   B. fatigue
   C. slurred speech
   D. convulsions

19. Which of the following is NOT a guideline that should usually be followed in conducting patrols?

   A. Patrols should always follow the same method, route, and schedule.
   B. Patrol rangers should periodically stop at "overview" points.
   C. Open patrol is, in most situations, preferred to hidden patrol.
   D. Whenever possible, patrols should be conducted by a team of two.

20. In relaying a description of an individual, the first detail given is usually

   A. sex   B. age   C. race   D. height

21. Normally, searches of vehicles by a park ranger require a search warrant. Exceptions include
   I. whenever probable cause to search exists
   II. the search is incidental to an arrest
   III. items are in open view through the vehicle's window
   IV. the vehicle has stopped at an authorized roadblock

   A. I only
   B. I and II
   C. I, II and III
   D. I, II, III and IV

22. Which of the following is LEAST likely to be a standard item for a cycle patrol?

   A. Portable spotlight
   B. First aid kit
   C. Maps and brochures
   D. Folding shovel

23. A ranger must attempt to stop a moving vehicle to implement an enforcement action. While in motion, the ranger should stay within _____ feet of the vehicle.

   A. 15 and 20   B. 25 and 40   C. 50 and 75   D. 100 and 200

24. Research demonstrates that _____ percent of a ranger's duty time involves some form of communication.

    A. 55-65
    B. 65-75
    C. 75-85
    D. 85-95

25. A ranger is called on to approach an offender who is belligerent. Guidelines to follow during such an encounter include
    I. making sure that a weapon is visible and at the ready
    II. trying to bargain with the offender for better behavior
    III. if you do not have the authority to make an arrest, trying to give the impression that you do
    IV. regardless of the provocation, never exhibiting anger or impatience

    A. I only
    B. I and II
    C. IV only
    D. II, III and IV

KEY (CORRECT ANSWERS)

1.	B	11.	B
2.	A	12.	A
3.	A	13.	D
4.	B	14.	D
5.	B	15.	B
6.	D	16.	B
7.	B	17.	C
8.	B	18.	D
9.	D	19.	A
10.	A	20.	A

21. C
22. D
23. C
24. C
25. C

TEST 3

DIRECTIONS: Each question or incomplete statement is followed by several suggested answers or completions. Select the one that BEST answers the question or completes the statement. *PRINT THE LETTER OF THE CORRECT ANSWER IN THE SPACE AT THE RIGHT.*

1. A ranger is composing a sketch of an accident scene. He will need to discriminate between temporary, short-lived, and long-lived evidence. Which of the following would be considered short-lived evidence?

    A. Gasoline puddles
    B. Vehicle debris
    C. Skid marks
    D. Gouges in the pavement

    1.____

2. In most situations, the best attitude for the park ranger to adopt is one that is _____ oriented.

    A. service
    B. enterprise
    C. task
    D. staff

    2.____

3. In the park setting, courts have ruled that search-and-seizure laws apply to visitor abodes (motor homes, trailers, screen canopies, rented cabins), as well as the area surrounding the abode and normally considered a part thereof (campsite, trash can, storage shed, etc.). The legal term for this surrounding area is

    A. environs
    B. curtilage
    C. quadrangle
    D. milieu

    3.____

4. Which of the following is NOT a guideline that a park ranger should use in handling a complaint?

    A. Remember that some complaints should be taken more seriously than others
    B. Focus initially on the facts surrounding the situation or problem
    C. Always thank the complainant for his or her interest
    D. Notify the complainant when corrective action has been taken

    4.____

5. Guidelines for a park ranger's enforcement actions include
    I. the use of physical force should be limited to the minimum necessary to implement the action
    II. the vigor or severity of enforcement actions should be dependent on the attitude of the offender
    III. whenever a ranger is unable to secure cooperation, he should withdraw from the immediate area and seek appropriate assistance
    IV. whenever doubt exists as to whether a situation actually constitutes a violation, or whether the suspect is in fact the perpetrator, the ranger should rule in favor of the visitor and try to resolve the doubt

    A. I and II
    B. I, III and IV
    C. I and IV
    D. I, II, III and IV

    5.____

6. A park ranger should usually think of her primary duty as

    A. assuring each park visitor a quality experience
    B. enforcing the existing rules within park boundaries
    C. observing visitor behaviors and being prepared for any problems that might arise
    D. protecting the park's most important resources

7. Which of the following is NOT a principle that should guide the composition and delivery of interpretive services in a park?

    A. Interpretation should tell the whole story, rather than just a part of it.
    B. Interpretation should arouse curiosity in addition to giving facts.
    C. The best interpretation sticks to information within the "comfort zone" of visitors.
    D. The best interpretation occurs through person-to-person communication.

8. _____ patrol is the method that provides the greatest amount of visitor access, but usually prohibits extensive observation of visitor behavior and park conditions.

    A. Cycle
    B. Mounted
    C. Foot
    D. Vehicle

9. One of the signs that a person has overdosed on a depressant is

    A. hallucinations
    B. slow pulse
    C. cold, clammy skin
    D. constricted pupils

10. A ranger is conducting a field interview to determine the cause of an incident. The ranger should know that of all the behaviors that suggest an untruthful response, the one most commonly demonstrated by deceitful people is

    A. bringing the hand to the head
    B. interrupting the questioner
    C. hesitation
    D. crossing the arms over the chest

11. A ranger is conducting a field interview to record a visitor's perceptions of an event. In recording the visitor's account, the ranger should remember each of the following general truths about human perception EXCEPT that

    A. people tend to overestimate the length of verticals while underestimating the width of horizontals
    B. danger and stress cause people to underestimate duration and distance
    C. light-colored objects tend to be seen as heavier and nearer than dark objects of the same size and distance away
    D. people usually recall actions and events better than objects

12. If a DWI suspect refuses to submit to a chemical test, many jurisdictions accept this as an admission of intoxication resulting in the revocation of driving privileges for a period of time. This result, however, is predicated on several criteria. Which of the following is NOT one of these criteria?

    A. The ranger has probable cause to believe the suspect is DWI.
    B. The suspect has already completed a standard' field sobriety test.
    C. The ranger placed the suspect under arrest.
    D. The ranger specifically requested the suspect to submit to a chemical test.

13. A ranger is reading a park map grid reference. On this map, the numbers are read from

    A. left to right and top to bottom
    B. left to right and bottom to top
    C. right to left and top to bottom
    D. right to left and bottom to top

14. Defensive measures consist of several levels of defense. The level known as "defensive opposition" involves

    A. warding off blows with limbs or a baton
    B. the use of a firearm
    C. the use of chemical irritants
    D. simply ignoring verbal and visual abuse

15. Which of the following is NOT an element of the "legal scope" of a park ranger's jurisdiction?

    A. The park's physical boundaries
    B. Traffic codes
    C. Fish and game laws
    D. Criminal statutes

16. Which of the following is an example of a "transitional" interpretive experience?

    A. Slide presentation
    B. Visitor center exhibit
    C. Outdoor interpretive stations
    D. Automobile tour

17. A ranger is designing an interpretive activity for a group of elementary school children who are all about eight years old. For children at this age,

    A. ideas, rather than objects, are very important
    B. relations with others are based primarily on self-interest
    C. there is a strong desire for independence from adults
    D. peer relationships are very important

18. Which of the following is most likely to be a standard item for a foot patrol?

    A. Jumper cables
    B. Tranquilizer gun
    C. Folding stretcher
    D. Transceiver

19. In the continuum of a park ranger's enforcement priorities, "Priority 3" situations deal with

   A. the protection of visitors from hazardous conditions created by park resources
   B. the protection of the park's resources from the visitor
   C. the protection of visitors from each other
   D. situations in which neither the park nor its visitors are in any immediate danger

20. Recreational resources may be managed under the guidance of several viewpoints. The _____ viewpoint holds that resources should be used in an essentially "as is" manner, and that visitor use should blend with the resource base.

   A. preservationist
   B. landscape maintenance
   C. conservationist
   D. recreation activity

21. Which of the following is NOT a guideline that should be used for the conduct of station duty?

   A. Whenever rangers are in conversation with visitors, they should stand.
   B. Each question should be answered as if it were the first time the ranger has heard it.
   C. Rangers should remain sitting or standing behind a counter.
   D. Rangers should attempt to serve all visitors who need assistance.

22. Which of the following statements about search warrants is typically FALSE?

   A. Searchers may remain only a sufficient length of time as is "reasonably" necessary to search for and seize the property described in the search warrant.
   B. Generally, searchers may not seize items relating to criminal activity that are not specifically identified in the search warrant
   C. Search warrants for the premises do not permit a search of all persons present in the premises
   D. In most situations, real estate can be seized under a search warrant

23. A ranger's boundary maintenance responsibilities typically include each of the following functions EXCEPT

   A. physically locating the boundary line, either by previous marks or survey
   B. identifying trespass and/or encroachment
   C. marking and signing the boundary
   D. preventing erosion of coastal/shoreline boundaries

24. The park's public relations program must
   I. emphasize specific stages in a process, rather than ultimate goals
   II. solve the problems of others while solving the problems of the park
   III. focus on challenges and shortcomings that are in need of assistance or support
   IV. consist of actions that are coordinated and integrated

   A. I only
   B. I, II and III
   C. II and IV
   D. I, II, III and IV

25. Arrests can normally be made by park rangers
    I. on an arrest warrant
    II. on view of a felony being committed
    III. on reasonable suspicion of a felony
    IV. on reasonable suspicion of a misdemeanor

    A. I only
    B. I and II
    C. I, II and III
    D. I, II, III and IV

KEY (CORRECT ANSWERS)

1.	C	11.	B
2.	A	12.	B
3.	B	13.	B
4.	A	14.	A
5.	B	15.	A
6.	A	16.	D
7.	C	17.	D
8.	C	18.	D
9.	C	19.	B
10.	A	20.	C

21. C
22. D
23. D
24. C
25. C

READING COMPREHENSION
UNDERSTANDING AND INTERPRETING WRITTEN MATERIAL
EXAMINATION SECTION
TEST 1

DIRECTIONS: Each question or incomplete statement is followed by several suggested answers or completions. Select the one that BEST answers the question or completes the statement. *PRINT THE LETTER OF THE CORRECT ANSWER IN THE SPACE AT THE RIGHT.*

Questions 1-3.

DIRECTIONS: Answer Questions 1 through 3 *SOLELY* on the basis of the following statement:
    The final step in an accident investigation is the making out of the police report. In the case of a traffic accident, the officer should go right from the scene to his office to write up the report. However, if a person was injured in the accident and taken to a hospital, the officer should visit him there before going to his office to prepare his report. This personal visit to the injured person does not mean that the office must make a physical examination; but he should make an effort to obtain a statement from the injured person or persons. If this is not possible, information should be obtained from the attending physician as to the extent of the injury. In any event, without fail, the name of the physician should be secured and the report should state the name of the physician and the fact that he told the officer that, at a certain stated time on a certain stated date, the injuries were of such and such a nature. If the injured person dies before the officer arrives at the hospital, it may be necessary to take the responsible person into custody at once.

1. When a person has been injured in a traffic accident, the one of the following actions which it is necessry for a police officer to take in connection with the accident report is to 1.____

    A. prepare the police report immediately after the accident, and then go to the hospital to speak to the victim
    B. do his utmost to verify the victim's story prior to preparing the official police report of the incident
    C. be sure to include the victim's statement in the police report in every case
    D. try to get the victim's version of the accident prior to preparing the police report

2. When one of the persons injured in a motor vehicle accident dies, the above paragraph provides that the police officer 2.____

    A. must immediately take the responsible person into custody, if the injured person is already dead when the officer appears at the scene of the accident
    B. must either arrest the responsible person or get a statement from him, if the injured person dies after arrival at the hospital
    C. may have to immediately arrest the responsible person, if the injured person dies in the hospital prior to the officer's arrival there
    D. may refrain from arresting the responsible person, but only if the responsible person is also seriously injured

3. When someone has been injured in a collision between two automobiles and is given medical treatment shortly thereafter by a physician, the *one* of the following actions which the police officer *MUST* take with regard to the physician is to

   A. obtain his name and his diagnosis of the injuries, regardless of the place where treatment was given
   B. obtain his approval of the portion of the police report relating to the injured person and the treatment given him prior to and after his arrival at the hospital
   C. obtain his name, his opinion of the extent of the person's injuries, and his signed statement of the treatment he gave the injured person
   D. set a certain stated time on a certain stated date for interviewing him, unless he is an attending physician in a hospital

Questions 4-7.

DIRECTIONS: Answer Questions 4 through 7 *SOLELY* on the basis of the following statement:

Because of the importance of preserving physical evidence, the patrolman should not enter a scene of a crime if it can be examined visually from one position and if no other pressing duty requires his presence there. However, there are some responsibilities that take precedence over preservation of evidence. Some examples are: rescue work, disarming dangerous persons, quelling a disturbance. However, the patrolman should learn how to accomplish these more vital tasks, while at the same time preserving as much evidence as possible. If he finds it necessary to enter upon the scene, he should quickly study the place of entry to learn if any evidence will suffer by his contact; then he should determine the routes to be used in walking to the spot where his presence is required. Every place where a foot will fall or where a hand or other part of his body will touch, should be examined with the eye. Objects should not be touched or moved unless there is a definite and compelling reason. For identification of most items of physical evidence at the initial investigation, it is seldom necessary to touch or move them.

4. The *one* of the following titles which is the *MOST* appropriate for the above paragraph is:

   A. Determining the Priority of Tasks at the Scene of a Crime
   B. The Principal Reasons for Preserving Evidence at the Scene of a Crime
   C. Precautions to Take at the Scene of a Crime
   D. Evidence to be Examined at the Scene of a Crime

5. When a patrolman feels that it is essential for him to enter the immediate area where a crime has been committed, he *should*

   A. quickly but carefully glance around to determine whether his entering the area will damage any evidence present
   B. remove all objects of evidence from his predetermined route in order to avoid stepping on them
   C. carefully replace any object immediately if it is moved or touched by his hands or any other part of his body
   D. use only the usual place of entry to the scene in order to avoid disturbing any possible clues left on rear doors and windows by the criminal

6. The one of the following which is the LEAST urgent duty of a police officer who has just reported to the scene of a crime is to

   A. disarm the hysterical victim of the crime who is wildly waving a loaded gun in all directions
   B. give first aid to a possible suspect who has been injured while attempting to leave the scene of the crime
   C. prevent observers from attacking and injuring the persons suspected of having committed the crime
   D. preserve from damage or destruction any evidence necessary for the proper prosecution of the case against the criminals

6.____

7. A police officer has just reported to the scene of a crime in response to a phone call. The BEST of the following actions for him to take with respect to objects of physical evidence present at the scene is to

   A. make no attempt to enter the crime scene if his entry will disturb any vital physical evidence
   B. map out the shortest straight path to follow in walking to the spot where the most physical evidence may be found
   C. move such objects of physical evidence as are necessary to enable him to assist the wounded victim of the crime
   D. quickly examine all objects of physical evidence in order to determine which objects may be touched and which may not

7.____

Questions 8-11.

DIRECTIONS: Answer Questions 8 through 11 SOLELY on the basis of the following statement:

After examining a document and comparing the characters with specimens of other handwritings, the laboratory technician may conclude that a certain individual definitely did write the questioned document. This opinion could be based on a large number of similar, as well as a small number of dissimilar but explainable, characteristics. On the other hand, if the laboratory technician concludes that the person in question did not write the questioned document, such an opinion could be based on the large number of characteristics which are dissimilar, or even on a small number which are dissimilar provided that these are of overriding significance, and despite the presence of explainable similarities. The laboratory expert is not always able to give a positive opinion. He may state that a certain individual probably did or did not write the questioned document. Such an opinion is usually the result of insufficient material, either in the questioned document or in the specimens submitted for comparison. Finally, the expert may be unable to come to any conclusion at all because of insufficient material submitted for comparison or because of improper specimens.

8. The one of the following which is the MOST appropriate title for the above statement is:

   A. Similar and Dissimilar Characteristics in Handwriting
   B. The Limitations of Handwriting Analysis in Identifying the Writer
   C. The Positive Identification of Suspects Through Their Handwriting
   D. The Inability to Identify an Individual Through His Handwriting

8.____

9. When a handwriting expert compares the handwriting on two separate documents and decides that they were written by the same person, his conclusions are *generally* based on the fact that

    A. a large number of characteristics in both documents are dissimilar but the few similar characteristics are more important
    B. all the characteristics are alike in both documents
    C. similar characteristics need to be explained as to the cause for their similarity
    D. most of the characteristics in both documents are alike and their few differences are readily explainable

10. If a fingerprint technician carefully examines a handwritten threatening letter and compares it with specimens of handwriting made by a suspect, he would be *most likely* to decide that the suspect did *NOT* write the threatening letter when the handwriting specimens and the letter have

    A. a small number of dissimilarities
    B. a small number of dissimilar but explainable characteristics
    C. important dissimilarities despite the fact that these may be few
    D. some similar characteristics that are easily imitated or disguised

11. There are instances when even a trained handwriting expert cannot decide definitely whether or not a certain document and a set of handwriting specimens were written by the same person. This inability to make a positive decision *generally* arises in situations where

    A. only one document of considerable length is available for comparison with a sufficient supply of handwriting specimens
    B. the limited nature of the handwriting specimens submitted restricts their comparability with the questioned document
    C. the dissimilarities are not explainable
    D. the document submitted for comparison does not include all the characteristics included in the handwriting specimens

Questions 12-14.

DIRECTIONS: Answer Questions 12 through 14 *SOLELY* on the basis of the following statement:

In cases of drunken driving, or of disorderly conduct while intoxicated, too many times some person who had been completely under the influence of alcoholic liquor at the time of his arrest has walked out of court without any conviction just because an officer failed to make the proper observation. Many of the larger cities and counties make use of various scientific methods to determine the degree of intoxication of a person, such as breath, urine, and blood tests. Many of the smaller cities, however, do not have the facilities to make these various tests, and must, therefore, rely on the observation tests given at the scene. These consist, among other things, of noticing how the subject walked, talked, and acted. One test that is usually given at night is the eye reaction to light, which the officer gives by shining his flashlight into the eyes of the subject. The manner in which the pupils of the eyes react to the light helps to determine the sobriety of a person. If he is intoxicated, the pupils of his eyes are dilated more at night than the eyes of a sober person. Also, when a light is flashed into the eyes of a sober person, his pupils contract instantly, but in the case of a person under the influence of liquor, the pupils contract very slowly.

12. Many persons who have been arrested on a charge of driving while completely intoxicated have been acquitted by a judge because the arresting officer had *neglected* to

   A. bring the driver to court while he was still under the influence of alcohol
   B. make the required scientific tests to fully substantiate his careful personal observations of the driver's intoxicated condition
   C. submit to the court any test results showing the driver's condition or degree of drunkenness
   D. watch the driver closely for some pertinent facts which would support the officer's suspicions of the driver's intoxicated condition

12.____

13. When a person is arrested for acting in a disorderly and apparently intoxicated manner in public, the kind of test which would fit in *BEST* with the thought of the above statement is:

   A. In many smaller cities, a close watch on his behavior and of his reactions to various blood and body tests
   B. In many smaller cities, having him walk a straight line
   C. In most larger counties, a close watch of the speed of his reactions to the flashlight test
   D. In most cities of all sizes, the application of the latest scientific techniques in the analysis of his breath

13.____

14. When a person suspected of driving a motor vehicle while intoxicated is being examined to determine whether or not he actually is intoxicated, one of the methods used is to shine the light of a flashlight into his eyes. When this method is used, the *normal* result is that the pupils of the suspect's eyes will

   A. expand instantly if he is fully intoxicated, and remain unchanged if he is completely sober
   B. expand very slowly if he has had only a small amount of alcohol, and very rapidly if he has had a considerable amount of alcohol
   C. grow smaller at once if he is sober, and grow smaller more slowly if he is intoxicated
   D. grow smaller very slowly if he is fully sober, and grow smaller instantaneously if he is fully intoxicated

14.____

Questions 15-17.

DIRECTIONS: Answer Questions 15 through 17 *SOLELY* on the basis of the following statement:

Where an officer has personal knowledge of facts, sufficient to constitute reasonable grounds to believe that a person has committed or is committing a felony, he may arrest him, and, after having lawfully placed him under arrest, may search and take into his possession any incriminating evidence. The right of an officer to make an arrest and search is not limited to cases where the officer has personal knowledge of the commission of a felony, because he may act upon information conveyed to him by third persons which he believes to be reliable. Where an officer, charged with the duty of enforcing the law, receives information from apparently reliable sources, which would induce in the mind of the prudent person a belief that a felony was being or had been committed, he may make an arrest and search the person of a defendant, but he is not justified in acting on anonymous information alone.

15. When a felony has been committed, an officer would be acting MOST properly if he arrested a man

   A. when he, the officer, has a police report that the man is suspected of having been involved in several minor offenses
   B. when he, the officer, has received information from a usually reliable source that the man was involved in the crime
   C. only when he, the officer, has personal knowledge that the man has committed the felony
   D. when he, the officer, knows for a fact that the man has associated in the past with several persons who had been seen near the scene of the felony

16. An officer would be acting MOST properly if he searched a suspect for incriminating evidence

   A. *when* he has received detailed information concerning the fact that the suspect is going to commit a felony
   B. *only* after having lawfully arrested the suspect and charged him with having committed a felony
   C. *when* he has just received an anonymous tip that the suspect had just committed a felony and is in illegal possession of stolen goods
   D. *in order to* find in his possession legally admissible evidence on the basis of which the officer could then proceed to arrest the suspect for having committed a felony

17. A police officer has received information from an informant that a crime has been committed. The informant has also named two persons who he says committed the crime. The officer's decision to *both* arrest and search the two suspects would be:

   A. *Correct,* if it would not be unreasonable to assume that the crime committed is a felony, and if the informant has been trustworthy in the past
   B. *Incorrect,* if the informant has no proof but his own word to offer that a felony has been committed, although he has always been trustworthy in the past
   C. *Correct,* if it would be logical and prudent to assume that the information is accurate regardless of whether the offense committed is a felony or a less serious crime
   D. *Incorrect,* even if the informant produces objective and seemingly convincing proof that a felony has been committed, but has a reputation of occasional past unreliability

Questions 18-20.

DIRECTIONS: Answer Questions 18 through 20 SOLELY on the basis of the following statement:

If there are many persons at the scene of a hit-and-run accident, it would be a waste of time to question all of them; the witness needed is the one who can best describe the missing auto. Usually the person most qualified to do this is a youth of fifteen or sixteen years of age. He is more likely to be able to tell the make and year of a car than most other persons. A woman may be a good witness as to how the accident occurred, but usually will be unable to tell the make of the car. As soon as any information with regard to the missing car or its description is obtained, the officer should call or radio headquarters and have the information put on the air. This should be done without waiting for further details, for time is an important factor. If a good description of the wanted car is obtained, then the next task is to get a description of the driver. In this hunt, it is found that a woman is often a more accurate witness than a man. Usually she will be able to state the color of clothes worn by the driver. If the wanted driver is a woman, another woman will often be able to tell the color and sometimes even the material of the clothing worn.

18. A hit-and-run accident has occurred and a police officer is attempting to obtain information from persons who had witnessed the incident. It would generally be *BEST* for him to question a

    A. boy in his late teens, when the officer is seeking an accurate description of the age, coloring, and physical build of the driver of the car
    B. man, when the officer is seeking an accurate description of the driver of the car and the color and material of his coat, suit, and hat
    C. woman, when the officer is seeking an accurate description of the driver of the car
    D. young teenage girl, when the officer is seeking an accurate description of the style and color of the clothes worn by the driver of the car

19. Time is an important factor when an attempt is being made to apprehend the guilty driver in a hit-and-run accident. However, the *EARLIEST* moment when the police should broadcast a radio announcement of the crime is *when* a(n)

    A. description of the missing car or any facts concerning it have been obtained
    B. tentative identification of the driver of the missing car has been made
    C. detailed description of the missing car and its occupants has been obtained
    D. eyewitness account has been obtained of the accident, including the identity of the victim, the extent of injuries, and the make and license number of the car

20. The time when it would be *MOST* desirable to get a description of the driver of the hit-and-run car is

    A. *after* getting a description of the car itself
    B. *before* transmitting information concerning the car to headquarters for broadcasting
    C. *as soon as* the officer arrives at the scene of the accident
    D. *as soon as* the victim of the accident has been given needed medical assistance

KEY (CORRECT ANSWERS)

1.	D	11.	B
2.	C	12.	D
3.	A	13.	B
4.	C	14.	C
5.	A	15.	B
6.	D	16.	B
7.	C	17.	A
8.	B	18.	C
9.	D	19.	A
10.	C	20.	A

TEST 2

Questions 1-4.

DIRECTIONS: Answer Questions 1 through 4 SOLELY on the basis of the following statement:

Automobile tire tracks found at the scene of a crime constitute an important link in the chain of physical evidence. In many cases, these are the only clues available. In some areas, unpaved ground adjoins the highway or paved streets. A suspect will often park his car off the paved portion of the street when committing a crime, sometimes leaving excellent tire tracks. Comparison of the tire track impressions with the tires is possible only when the vehicle has been found. However, the intial problem facing the police is the task of determining what kind of car probably made the impressions found at the scene of the crime. If the make, model,and year of the car which made the impressions can be determined, it is obvsious that the task of elimination is greatly lessened.

1. The one of the following which is the MOST appropriate title for the above paragraph is:

    A. The Use of Automobiles in the Commission of Crimes
    B. The Use of Tire Tracks in Police Work
    C. The Capture of Criminals by Scientific Police Work
    D. The Positive Identification of Criminals Through Their Cars

2. When searching for clear signs left by the car used in the commission of a crime, the MOST likely place for the police to look would be on the

    A. highway adjoining unpaved streets
    B. highway adjacent to paved street
    C. paved street adjacent to the highway
    D. unpaved ground adjacent to a highway

3. Automobile tire tracks found at the scene of a crime are of *value* as evidence in that they are

    A. generally sufficient to trap and convict a suspect
    B. the most important link in the chain of physical evidence
    C. often the only evidence at hand
    D. circumstantial rather than direct

4. The PRIMARY reason for the police to try to find out which make, model, and year of car was involved in the commission of a crime, is to

    A. compare the tire tracks left at the scene of the crime with the type of tires used on cars of that make
    B. determine if the mud on the tires of the suspected car matches the mud in the unpaved road near the scene of the crime
    C. reduce to a large extent the amount of work involved in determining the particular car used in the commission of a crime
    D. alert the police patrol forces to question the occupants of all automobiles of this type

Questions 5-8.

DIRECTIONS: Answer Questions 5 through 8 SOLELY on the basis of the following statement:

When stopping vehicles on highways to check for suspects or fugitives, the police use an automobile roadblock whenever possible. This consists of three cars placed in prearranged positions. Car number one is parked across the left lane of the roadway with the front diagonally facing toward the center line. Car number two is parked across the right lane, with the front of the vehicle also toward the center line, in a position perpendicular to car number one and approximately twenty feet to the rear. Continuing another twenty feet to the rear along the highway, car number three is parked in an identical manner to car number one. The width of the highway determines the angle or position in which the autos should be placed. In addition to the regular roadblock signs and the use of flares at night only, there is an officer located at both the entrance and exit to direct and control traffic from both directions. This type of roadblock forces all approaching autos to reduce speed and zigzag around the police cars. Officers standing behind the parked cars can most safely and carefully view all passing motorists. Once a suspect is inside the block it becomes extremely difficult to crash out.

5. Of the following, the MOST appropriate title for this statement is:

    A. The Construction of an Escape-Proof Roadblock
    B. Regulation of Automobile Traffic Through a Police Roadblock
    C. Safety Precautions Necessary in Making an Automobile Roadblock
    D. Structure of a Roadblock to Detain Suspects or Fugitives

6. When setting up a three-car roadblock, the *relative* positions of the cars should be *such that*

    A. the front of car number one is placed diagonally to the center line and faces car number three
    B. car number three is placed parallel to the center line and its front faces the right side of the road
    C. car number two is placed about 20 feet from car number one and its front faces the left side of the road
    D. car number three is parallel to and about 20 feet away from car number one

7. Officers can observe occupants of all cars passing through the roadblock with GREATEST safety when

    A. warning flares are lighted to illuminate the area sufficiently at night
    B. warning signs are put up at each end of the roadblock
    C. they are stationed at both the exit and the entrance of the roadblock
    D. they take up positions behind cars in the roadblock

8. The type of automobile roadblock described in the above paragraph is *of value* in police work because

    A. a suspect is unable to escape its confines by using force
    B. it is frequently used to capture suspects with no danger to the police
    C. it requires only two officers to set up and operate
    D. vehicular traffic within its confines is controled as to speed and direction

Questions 9-11.

DIRECTIONS: Answer Questions 9 through 11 SOLELY on the basis of the following statement:

A problem facing the police department in one area of the city was to try to reduce the number of bicycle thefts which had been increasing at an alarming rate in the past three or four years. A new program was adopted to get at the root of the problem. Tags were printed, reminding youngsters that bicycles left unlocked can be easily stolen. The police concentrated on such places as theaters, a municipal swimming pool, an athletic field, and the local high school, and tied tags on all bicycles which were not locked. The majority of bicycle thefts took place at the swimming pool. In 2006, during the first two weeks the pool was open, an average of 10 bicycles was stolen there daily. During the same two-week period, 30 bicycles a week were stolen at the athletic field, 15 at the high school, and 11 at all theaters combined. In 2007, after tagging the unlocked bicycles, it was found that 20 bicycles a week were stolen at the pool and 5 at the high school. It was felt that the police tags had helped the most, although the school officials had helped to a great extent in this program by distributing "locking" notices to parents and children, and the use of the loudspeaker at the pool urging children to lock their bicycles had also been very helpful.

9. The one of the following which had the GREATEST effect in the campaign to reduce bicycle stealing was the

   A. distribution of "locking" notices by the school officials
   B. locking of all bicycles left in public places
   C. police tagging of bicycles left unlocked by youngsters
   D. use of the loudspeaker at the swimming pool

10. The tagging program was instituted by the police department CHIEFLY to

    A. determine the areas where most bicycle thieves operated
    B. instill in youngsters the importance of punishing bicycle thieves
    C. lessen the rising rate of bicycle thefts
    D. recover as many as possible of the stolen bicycles

11. The figures showing the number of bicycle thefts in the various areas surveyed indicate that in 2006

    A. almost as many thefts occurred at the swimming pool as at all the theaters combined
    B. fewer thefts occurred at the athletic field than at both the high school and all theaters combined
    C. more than half the thefts occurred at the swimming pool
    D. twice as many thefts occurred at the high school as at the athletic field

Questions 12-13.

DIRECTIONS: Answer Questions 12 and 13 SOLELY on the bais of the following statement:
A survey has shown that crime prevention work is most successful if the officers are assigned on rotating shifts to provide for around-the-clock coverage. An officer may work days for a time and then be switched to nights. The prime object of the night work is to enable the officer to spot conditions inviting burglars. Complete lack of, or faulty locations of, night lights and other conditions that may invite burglars, which might go unnoticed during daylight

hours, can be located and corrected more readily through night work. Night work also enables the officer to check local hangouts of juveniles, such as bus and railway depots, certain cafes or pool halls, the local roller rink, and the building where a juvenile dance is held every Friday night. Detectives also join patrolmen cruising in radio patrol cars to check on juveniles loitering late at night and to spot-check local bars for juveniles.

12. The MOST important purpose of assigning officers to night shifts is to make it possible for them to

    A. correct conditions which may not be readily noticed during the day
    B. discover the location of, and replace, missing and faulty night lights
    C. locate criminal hangouts
    D. notice things at night which cannot be noticed during the daytime

13. The type of shifting of officers which BEST prevents crime is to have

    A. day-shift officers rotated to night work
    B. rotating shifts provide sufficient officers for coverage 24 hours daily
    C. an officer work around the clock on a 24-hour basis as police needs arise
    D. rotating shifts to give the officers varied experience

Questions 14-15.

DIRECTIONS: Answer Questions 14 and 15 SOLELY on the basis of the following statement:
Proper firearms training is one phase of law enforcement which cannot be ignored. No part of the training of a police officer is more important or more valuable. The officer's life and often the lives of his fellow officers depend directly upon his skill with the weapon he is carrying. Proficiency with the revolver is not attained exclusively by the volume of ammunition used and the number of hours spent on the firing line. Supervised practice and the use of training aids and techniques help make the shooter. It is essential to have a good firing range where new officers are trained and older personnel practice in scheduled firearms sessions. The fundamental points to be stressed are grip, stance, breathing, sight alignment and trigger squeeze. Coordination of thought, vision, and motion must be achieved before the officer gains confidence in his shooting ability. Attaining this ability will make the student a better officer and enhance his value to the force.

14. A police officer will gain confidence in his shooting ability *only after* he has

    A. spent the required number of hours on the firing line
    B. been given sufficient supervised practice
    C. learned the five fundamental points
    D. learned to coordinate revolver movement with his sight and thought

15. Proper training in the use of firearms is one aspect of law enforcement which must be given serious consideration CHIEFLY because it is the

    A. most useful and essential single factor in the training of a police officer
    B. one phase of police officer training which stresses mental and physical coordination
    C. costliest aspect of police officer training, involving considerable expense for the ammunition used in target practice
    D. most difficult part of police officer training, involving the expenditure of many hours on the firing line

Questions 16-20.

DIRECTIONS: Answer Questions 16 through 20 *SOLELY* on the basis of the following statement:

Lifting consists of transferring a print that has been dusted with powder to a transfer medium in order to preserve the print. Chemically developed prints cannot be lifted. Proper lifting of fingerprints is difficult and should be undertaken only when other means of recording the print are neither available nor suitable. Lifting should not be attempted from a porous surface. There are two types of commercial lifting tape which, are good transfer mediums: rubber adhesive lift, one side of which is gummed and covered with thin, transparent celluloid; and transparent lifting tape, made of cellophane, one side of which is gummed. A package of acetate covers, frosted on one side and used to cover and protect the lifted print, accompanies each roll. If commercial tape is not available, transparent scotch tape may be used. The investigator should remove the celluloid or acetate cover from the lifting tape; smooth the tape, gummy side down, firmly and evenly over the entire print; gently peel the tape off the surface; replace the cover; and attach pertinent identifying data to the tape. All parts of the print should come in contact with the tape; air pockets should be avoided. The print will adhere to the lifting tape. The cover permits the print to be viewed and protects it from damage. Transparent lifting tape does not reverse the print. If a rubber adhesive lift is utilized, the print is reversed. Before a direct comparison can be made, the lifted print must be photographed, the negative reversed, and a positive made.

16. An investigator wishing to preserve a record of fingerprints on a highly porous surface *should*

    A. develop them chemically before attempting to lift them
    B. lift them with scotch tape only when no other means of recording the prints are available
    C. employ some method other than lifting
    D. dust them with powder before attempting to lift them with rubber adhesive lift

17. Disregarding all other considerations, the *SIMPLEST* process to use in lifting a fingerprint from a window pane is *that* involving the use of

    A. rubber adhesive lift, because it gives a positive print in one step
    B. dusting powder and a camera, because the photograph is less likely to break than the window pane
    C. a chemical process, because it both develops and preserves the print at the same time
    D. transparent lifting tape, because it does not reverse the print

18. When a piece of commercial lifting tape is being used by an investigator wishing to lift a clear fingerprint from a smoothly-finished metal safe-door, he *should*

    A. prevent the ends of the tape from getting stuck to the metal surface because of the danger of forming air-pockets and thus damaging the print
    B. make certain that the tape covers all parts of the print and no air-pockets are formed
    C. carefully roll the tape over the most significant parts of the print only to avoid forming air-pockets
    D. be especially cautious not to destroy the air-pockets since this would tend to blur the print

19. When fingerprints lifted from an object found at the scene of a crime are to be compared with the fingerprints of a suspect, the lifted print

   A. can be compared directly only if a rubber adhesive lift was used
   B. cannot be compared directly if transparent scotch tape was used
   C. can be compared directly if transparent scotch tape was used
   D. must be photographed first and a positive made if any commercial lifting tape was used

20. When a rubber adhesive lift is to be used to lift a fingerprint, the one of the following which must be gently peeled off FIRST is the

   A. acetate cover
   B. celluloid strip
   C. dusted surface
   D. tape off the print surface

KEY (CORRECT ANSWERS)

1. B	11. C
2. D	12. A
3. C	13. B
4. C	14. D
5. D	15. A
6. C	16. C
7. D	17. D
8. D	18. B
9. C	19. C
10. C	20. B

PREPARING WRITTEN MATERIAL IN A POLICE SETTING

These questions test for the ability to prepare the types of reports that police personnel write. Some questions test for the ability to present information clearly and accurately. They consist of restatements of information given in note form. You must choose the best version from each set of four choices. Other questions test for the ability to organize paragraphs. They consist of paragraphs with their sentences out of order. For each of the paragraphs you must choose, from four suggestions, the best order of the sentences.

TYPE 1:

TEST TASK: You will be presented with some notes about an incident. You must determine which one of four choices expresses the facts presented in the notes in phrasing and punctuation that results in a clear and accurate presentation of those facts.

SAMPLE QUESTION 1:

The following are taken from notes you have kept while following a suspect and observing his activities. In a "real" situation, part of your assignment would be to prepare a narrative report based on the notes.

NOTES: Brown left work at about 1:00 a.m.

Brown met Johnson in Sam's Bar
Johnson threatened Brown
Brown left the bar quickly
Brown went to Charlie's Place

In the following, select the one choice which is the most CLEAR and ACCURATE presentation of the information from the notes. Considerations of grammar and style are important only when they affect clarity and accuracy.

- A. Brown met Johnson in Sam's Bar, and he left the bar quickly after Johnson threatened him.
- B. Brown met Johnson in Sam's Bar, and he left the bar quickly after he threatened him.
- C. Brown met Johnson in Sam's Bar; he threatened him, and then he left the bar quickly.
- D. Johnson threatened Brown when he met him in Sam's Bar; then he left the bar quickly.

The correct answer to this sample question is A.

SOLUTION: *To answer this question, evaluate all the choices.*
Choice B *makes it unclear who did the threatening, and who left the bar, but it leaves the impression it was Brown who did the threatening.*

Choice C *is also unclear, and it implies even more strongly that Brown threatened Johnson.*

Choice D *is clear about Johnson doing the threatening, but it makes it seem it was also Johnson who left the bar quickly.*

Only choice A *is a clear and accurate presentation of material from the notes. Choice A is therefore the best choice.*
Note that the information from the first and last lines of the "notes" did not appear in any of the four choices. It therefore was not relevant to this particular question.

TYPE 2:

TEST TASK: You will be presented with a set of numbered sentences which form a paragraph. For each of the paragraphs you must choose, from four suggestions, the best order of the sentences.

SAMPLE QUESTION:

DIRECTIONS: The following question is based upon a group of sentences. The sentences are shown out of sequence, but when they are correctly arranged they form a connected, well-organized paragraph. Read the sentences; then answer the question about the best arrangement of the sentences.

1. Eventually, they piece all of this information together, make a choice, and act upon their decision.

2. Before actually deciding upon a job, people usually think about several possibilities.

3. They imagine themselves in different situations, and in so doing, they probably think about their interests, goals, and abilities.

4. Choosing an occupation is an important decision to make.

Which one of the following is the best arrangement of these sentences?

A. 2-3-1-4
B. 2-3-4-1
C. 4-2-1-3
D. 4-2-3-1

The correct answer to this sample question is D.

SOLUTION:

The best arrangement of the sentences is 4-2-3-1. Sentence 4 introduces the main idea of the paragraph: "choosing an occupation." Sentences 2-3-1 then follow up on this idea by describing, in order, the steps involved in making such a choice. Choice D is the BEST ANSWER to the question

TYPE 3:

TEST TASK: You will be presented with some notes about an incident. You must determine which one of four choices expresses the facts presented in the notes in phrasing and punctuation that results in a clear and accurate presentation of those facts.

SAMPLE QUESTION: Following is a portion of notes about an incident.

> NOTES: Responded to a call from 26 Arbor Ave. Residence of Tessa and John Wynter. Pulled in driveway. Saw woman on Wynters' porch. Identified herself as Mrs. Orvis, a neighbor.
>
> QUESTION: Which one of the following choices most clearly and accurately expresses the facts presented in the notes?
>
> 1. I responded to a call from 26 Arbor Avenue, the residence of Tessa and John Wynter. When I pulled into the driveway, I saw a woman on their porch. She identified herself as Mrs. Orvis, a neighbor.
>
> 2. Responding to a call from 26 Arbor Avenue, the residence of Tessa and John Wynter, and pulling into the driveway, I saw a neighbor on their porch, who identified herself as Mrs. Orvis.
>
> 3. When I responded to a call from 26 Arbor Avenue, the residence of Tessa and John Wynter, I saw pulling into their driveway a woman on their porch who identified herself as Mrs. Orris, a neighbor.
>
> 4. Responding to a call from 26 Arbor Avenue, I saw a woman on the porch of Tessa and John Wynter's residence. She identified herself as Mrs. Orvis, a neighbor.

The answer is A.

SOLUTION: *To answer this question, evaluate all the choices.*

Choice A: This choice presents all the information in the notes in the correct sequence. This choice says that the officer responded to a call from the Wynter residence, pulled into the driveway, and saw a woman on their porch who identified herself as Mrs. Orvis, a neighbor.

Choice B: "I saw a neighbor on their porch" suggests that the officer knew that it was a neighbor on the porch before Mrs. Onus told the officer who she was. This choice is incorrect.

Choice C: "I saw pulling into the driveway a woman on their porch" is not phrased and punctuated correctly. For C to be correctly written, there should be a period after "Wynter," and the next sentence should begin: "Pulling into the driveway, I saw..." This choice is incorrect.

Choice D: This choice does not identify 26 Arbor Avenue as the residence of Tessa and John Wynter. Also, another piece of information is missing: the officer does not say that he/she pulled into the driveway. In police writing, every detail is important. This choice is incorrect.

PREPARING WRITTEN MATERIAL

EXAMINATION SECTION
TEST 1

DIRECTIONS: Each question or incomplete statement is followed by several suggested answers or completions. Select the one that BEST answers the question or completes the statement. *PRINT THE LETTER OF THE CORRECT ANSWER IN THE SPACE AT THE RIGHT.*

1. The one of the following sentences which is LEAST acceptable from the viewpoint of correct usage is:

   A. The police thought the fugitive to be him.
   B. The criminals set a trap for whoever would fall into it.
   C. It is ten years ago since the fugitive fled from the city.
   D. The lecturer argued that criminals are usually cowards.
   E. The police removed four bucketfuls of earth from the scene of the crime.

1.____

2. The one of the following sentences which is LEAST acceptable from the viewpoint of correct usage is:

   A. The patrolman scrutinized the report with great care.
   B. Approaching the victim of the assault, two bruises were noticed by the patrolman.
   C. As soon as I had broken down the door, I stepped into the room.
   D. I observed the accused loitering near the building, which was closed at the time.
   E. The storekeeper complained that his neighbor was guilty of violating a local ordinance.

2.____

3. The one of the following sentences which is LEAST acceptable from the viewpoint of correct usage is:

   A. I realized immediately that he intended to assault the woman, so I disarmed him.
   B. It was apparent that Mr. Smith's explanation contained many inconsistencies.
   C. Despite the slippery condition of the street, he managed to stop the vehicle before injuring the child.
   D. Not a single one of them wish, despite the damage to property, to make a formal complaint.
   E. The body was found lying on the floor.

3.____

4. The one of the following sentences which contains NO error in usage is:

   A. After the robbers left, the proprietor stood tied in his chair for about two hours before help arrived.
   B. In the cellar I found the watchmans' hat and coat.
   C. The persons living in adjacent apartments stated that they had heard no unusual noises.
   D. Neither a knife or any firearms were found in the room.
   E. Walking down the street, the shouting of the crowd indicated that something was wrong.

4.____

5. The one of the following sentences which contains NO error in usage is:

   A. The policeman lay a firm hand on the suspect's shoulder.
   B. It is true that neither strength nor agility are the most important requirement for a good patrolman.
   C. Good citizens constantly strive to do more than merely comply the restraints imposed by society.
   D. No decision was made as to whom the prize should be awarded.
   E. Twenty years is considered a severe sentence for a felony.

6. Which of the following is NOT expressed in standard English usage?

   A. The victim reached a pay-phone booth and manages to call police headquarters.
   B. By the time the call was received, the assailant had left the scene.
   C. The victim has been a respected member of the community for the past eleven years.
   D. Although the lighting was bad and the shadows were deep, the storekeeper caught sight of the attacker.
   E. Additional street lights have since been installed, and the patrols have been strengthened.

7. Which of the following is NOT expressed in standard English usage?

   A. The judge upheld the attorney's right to question the witness about the missing glove.
   B. To be absolutely fair to all parties is the jury's chief responsibility.
   C. Having finished the report, a loud noise in the next room startled the sergeant.
   D. The witness obviously enjoyed having played a part in the proceedings.
   E. The sergeant planned to assign the case to whoever arrived first.

8. In which of the following is a word misused?

   A. As a matter of principle, the captain insisted that the suspect's partner be brought for questioning.
   B. The principle suspect had been detained at the station house for most of the day.
   C. The principal in the crime had no previous criminal record, but his closest associate had been convicted of felonies on two occasions.
   D. The interest payments had been made promptly, but the firm had been drawing upon the principal for these payments.
   E. The accused insisted that his high school principal would furnish him a character reference.

9. Which of the following statements is ambiguous?

   A. Mr. Sullivan explained why Mr. Johnson had been dismissed from his job.
   B. The storekeeper told the patrolman he had made a mistake.
   C. After waiting three hours, the patients in the doctor's office were sent home.
   D. The janitor's duties were to maintain the building in good shape and to answer tenants' complaints.
   E. The speed limit should, in my opinion, be raised to sixty miles an hour on that stretch of road.

10. In which of the following is the punctuation or capitalization faulty?   10.____

    A. The accident occurred at an intersection in the Kew Gardens section of Queens, near the bus stop.
    B. The sedan, not the convertible, was struck in the side.
    C. Before any of the patrolmen had left the police car received an important message from headquarters.
    D. The dog that had been stolen was returned to his master, John Dempsey, who lived in East Village.
    E. The letter had been sent to 12 Hillside Terrace, Rutland, Vermont 05701.

Questions 11-25.

DIRECTIONS: Questions 11 through 25 are to be answered in accordance with correct English usage; that is, standard English rather than nonstandard or substandard. Nonstandard and substandard English includes words or expressions usually classified as slang, dialect, illiterate, etc., which are not generally accepted as correct in current written communication. Standard English also requires clarity, proper punctuation and capitalization and appropriate use of words. Write the letter of the sentence NOT expressed in standard English usage in the space at the right.

11. A. There were three witnesses to the accident.   11.____
    B. At least three witnesses were found to testify for the plaintiff.
    C. Three of the witnesses who took the stand was uncertain about the defendant's competence to drive.
    D. Only three witnesses came forward to testify for the plaintiff.
    E. The three witnesses to the accident were pedestrians.

12. A. The driver had obviously drunk too many martinis before leaving for home.   12.____
    B. The boy who drowned had swum in these same waters many times before.
    C. The petty thief had stolen a bicycle from a private driveway before he was apprehended.
    D. The detectives had brung in the heroin shipment they intercepted.
    E. The passengers had never ridden in a converted bus before.

13. A. Between you and me, the new platoon plan sounds like a good idea.   13.____
    B. Money from an aunt's estate was left to his wife and he.
    C. He and I were assigned to the same patrol for the first time in two months.
    D. Either you or he should check the front door of that store.
    E. The captain himself was not sure of the witness's reliability.

14. A. The alarm had scarcely begun to ring when the explosion occurred.   14.____
    B. Before the firemen arrived on the scene, the second story had been destroyed.
    C. Because of the dense smoke and heat, the firemen could hardly approach the now-blazing structure.
    D. According to the patrolman's report, there wasn't nobody in the store when the explosion occurred.
    E. The sergeant's suggestion was not at all unsound, but no one agreed with him.

15. A. The driver and the passenger they were both found to be intoxicated. 15.____
    B. The driver and the passenger talked slowly and not too clearly.
    C. Neither the driver nor his passengers were able to give a coherent account of the accident.
    D. In a corner of the room sat the passenger, quietly dozing.
    E. The driver finally told a strange and unbelievable story, which the passenger contradicted.

16. A. Under the circumstances I decided not to continue my examination of the premises. 16.____
    B. There are many difficulties now not comparable with those existing in 1960.
    C. Friends of the accused were heard to announce that the witness had better been away on the day of the trial.
    D. The two criminals escaped in the confusion that followed the explosion.
    E. The aged man was struck by the considerateness of the patrolman's offer.

17. A. An assemblage of miscellaneous weapons lay on the table. 17.____
    B. Ample opportunities were given to the defendant to obtain counsel.
    C. The speaker often alluded to his past experience with youthful offenders in the armed forces.
    D. The sudden appearance of the truck aroused my suspicions.
    E. Her studying had a good affect on her grades in high school.

18. A. He sat down in the theater and began to watch the movie. 18.____
    B. The girl had ridden horses since she was four years old.
    C. Application was made on behalf of the prosecutor to cite the witness for contempt.
    D. The bank robber, with his two accomplices, were caught in the act.
    E. His story is simply not credible.

19. A. The angry boy said that he did not like those kind of friends. 19.____
    B. The merchant's financial condition was so precarious that he felt he must avail himself of any offer of assistance.
    C. He is apt to promise more than he can perform.
    D. Looking at the messy kitchen, the housewife felt like crying.
    E. A clerk was left in charge of the stolen property.

20. A. His wounds were aggravated by prolonged exposure to sub-freezing temperatures. 20.____
    B. The prosecutor remarked that the witness was not averse to changing his story each time he was interviewed.
    C. The crime pattern indicated that the burglars were adapt in the handling of explosives.
    D. His rigid adherence to a fixed plan brought him into renewed conflict with his subordinates.
    E. He had anticipated that the sentence would be delivered by noon.

21. A. The whole arraignment procedure is badly in need of revision.
     B. After his glasses were broken in the fight, he would of gone to the optometrist if he could.
     C. Neither Tom nor Jack brought his lunch to work.
     D. He stood aside until the quarrel was over.
     E. A statement in the psychiatrist's report disclosed that the probationer vowed to have his revenge.

21.____

22. A. His fiery and intemperate speech to the striking employees fatally affected any chance of a future reconciliation.
     B. The wording of the statute has been variously construed.
     C. The defendant's attorney, speaking in the courtroom, called the official a demagogue who contempuously disregarded the judge's orders.
     D. The baseball game is likely to be the most exciting one this year.
     E. The mother divided the cookies among her two children.

22.____

23. A. There was only a bed and a dresser in the dingy room.
     B. John is one of the few students that have protested the new rule.
     C. It cannot be argued that the child's testimony is negligible; it is, on the contrary, of the greatest importance.
     D. The basic criterion for clearance was so general that officials resolved any doubts in favor of dismissal.
     E. Having just returned from a long vacation, the officer found the city unbearably hot.

23.____

24. A. The librarian ought to give more help to small children.
     B. The small boy was criticized by the teacher because he often wrote careless.
     C. It was generally doubted whether the women would permit the use of her apartment for intelligence operations.
     D. The probationer acts differently every time the officer visits him.
     E. Each of the newly appointed officers has 12 years of service.

24.____

25. A. The North is the most industrialized region in the country.
     B. L. Patrick Gray 3d, the bureau's acting director, stated that, while "rehabilitation is fine" for some convicted criminals, "it is a useless gesture for those who resist every such effort."
     C. Careless driving, faulty mechanism, narrow or badly kept roads all play their part in causing accidents.
     D. The childrens' books were left in the bus.
     E. It was a matter of internal security; consequently, he felt no inclination to rescind his previous order.

25.____

KEY (CORRECT ANSWERS)

1.	C	11.	C
2.	B	12.	D
3.	D	13.	B
4.	C	14.	D
5.	E	15.	A
6.	A	16.	C
7.	C	17.	E
8.	B	18.	D
9.	B	19.	A
10.	C	20.	C

21.	B
22.	E
23.	B
24.	B
25.	D

TEST 2

DIRECTIONS: Each question or incomplete statement is followed by several suggested answers or completions. Select the one that BEST answers the question or completes the statement. *PRINT THE LETTER OF THE CORRECT ANSWER IN THE SPACE AT THE RIGHT.*

Questions 1-6.

DIRECTIONS: Each of Questions 1 through 6 consists of a statement which contains a word (one of those underlined) that is either incorrectly used because it is not in keeping with the meaning the quotation is evidently intended to convey, or is misspelled. There is only one INCORRECT word in each quotation. Of the four underlined words, determine if the first one should be replaced by the word lettered A, the second replaced by the word lettered B, the third replaced by the word lettered C, or the fourth replaced by the word lettered D. *PRINT THE LETTER OF THE REPLACEMENT WORD YOU HAVE SELECTED IN THE SPACE AT THE RIGHT.*

1. Whether one depends on fluorescent or artificial light or both, adequate standards should be maintained by means of systematic tests.

    A. natural
    B. safeguards
    C. established
    D. routine

2. A police officer has to be prepared to assume his knowledge as a social scientist in the community.

    A. forced
    B. role
    C. philosopher
    D. street

3. It is practically impossible to indicate whether a sentence is too long simply by measuring its length.

    A. almost   B. tell   C. very   D. guessing

4. Strong leaders are required to organize a community for delinquency prevention and for dissemination of organized crime and drug addiction.

    A. tactics   B. important   C. control   D. meetings

5. The demonstrators who were taken to the Criminal Courts building in Manhattan (because it was large enough to accommodate them), contended that the arrests were unwarrented.

    A. demonstraters
    B. Manhatten
    C. accomodate
    D. unwarranted

6. They were guaranteed a calm atmosphere, free from harrassment, which would be conducive to quiet consideration of the indictments.

    A. guarenteed
    B. atmospher
    C. harassment
    D. inditements

145

Questions 7-11.

DIRECTIONS: Each of Questions 7 through 11 consists of a statement containing four words in capital letters. One of these words in capital letters is not in keeping with the meaning which the statement is evidently intended to carry. The four words in capital letters in each statement are reprinted after the statement. Print the capital letter preceding the one of the four words which does MOST to spoil the true meaning of the statement in the space at the right.

7. Retirement and pension systems are essential not only to provide employees with a means of support in the future, but also to prevent longevity and CHARITABLE considerations from UPSETTING the PROMOTIONAL opportunities for RETIRED members of the career service.

   A. charitable B. upsetting
   C. promotional D. retired

8. Within each major DIVISION in a properly set up public or private organization, provision is made so that each NECESSARY activity is CARED for and lines of authority and responsibility are clear-cut and INFINITE.

   A. division   B. necessary   C. cared   D. infinite

9. In public service, the scale of salaries paid must be INCIDENTAL to the services rendered, with due CONSIDERATION for the attraction of the desired MANPOWER and for the maintenance of a standard of living COMMENSURATE with the work to be performed.

   A. incidental B. consideration
   C. manpower   D. commensurate

10. An understanding of the AIMS of an organization by the staff will AID greatly in increasing the DEMAND of the correspondence work of the office, and will to a large extent DETERMINE the nature of the correspondence.

    A. aims   B. aid   C. demand   D. determine

11. BECAUSE the Civil Service Commission strongly feels that the MERIT system is a key factor in the MAINTENANCE of democratic government, it has adopted as one of its major DEFENSES the progressive democratization of its own procedures in dealing with candidates for positions in the public service.

    A. Because B. merit
    C. maintenance D. defenses

Questions 12-14.

DIRECTIONS: Questions 12 through 14 consist of one sentence each. Each sentence contains an incorrectly used word. First, decide which is the incorrectly used word. Then, from among the options given, decide which word, when substituted for the incorrectly used word, makes the meaning of the sentence clear.

EXAMPLE:
The U.S. national income exhibits a pattern of long term deflection.
A. reflection B. subjection
C. rejoicing D. growth

The word *deflection* in the sentence does not convey the meaning the sentence evidently intended to convey. The word *growth* (Answer D), when substituted for the word *deflection,* makes the meaning of the sentence clear. Accordingly, the answer to the question is D.

12. The study commissioned by the joint committee fell compassionately short of the mark and would have to be redone.

    A. successfully B. insignificantly
    C. experimentally D. woefully

13. He will not idly exploit any violation of the provisions of the order.

    A. tolerate B. refuse C. construe D. guard

14. The defendant refused to be virile and bitterly protested service.

    A. irked B. feasible C. docile D. credible

Questions 15-25.

DIRECTIONS: Questions 15 through 25 consist of short paragraphs. Each paragraph contains one word which is INCORRECTLY used because it is NOT in keeping with the meaning of the paragraph. Find the word in each paragraph which is INCORRECTLY used and then select as the answer the suggested word which should be substituted for the incorrectly used word.

SAMPLE QUESTION:
In determining who is to do the work in your unit, you will have to decide just who does what from day to day. One of your lowest responsibilities is to assign work so that everybody gets a fair share and that everyone can do his part well.
A. new B. old C. important D. performance

EXPLANATION:
The word which is NOT in keeping with the meaning of the paragraph is *lowest*. This is the INCORRECTLY used word. The suggested word *important* would be in keeping with the meaning of the paragraph and should be substituted for *lowest*. Therefore, the CORRECT answer is choice C.

15. If really good practice in the elimination of preventable injuries is to be achieved and held in any establishment, top management must refuse full and definite responsibility and must apply a good share of its attention to the task.

    A. accept B. avoidable C. duties D. problem

16. Recording the human face for identification is by no means the only service performed by the camera in the field of investigation. When the trial of any issue takes place, a word picture is sought to be distorted to the court of incidents, occurrences, or events which are in dispute.

A. appeals B. description
C. portrayed D. deranged

17. In the collection of physical evidence, it cannot be emphasized too strongly that a haphazard systematic search at the scene of the crime is vital. Nothing must be overlooked. Often the only leads in a case will come from the results of this search.

   A. important B. investigation
   C. proof D. thorough

17.____

18. If an investigator has reason to suspect that the witness is mentally stable, or a habitual drunkard, he should leave no stone unturned in his investigation to determine if the witness was under the influence of liquor or drugs, or was mentally unbalanced either at the time of the occurrence to which he testified or at the time of the trial.

   A. accused B. clue C. deranged D. question

18.____

19. The use of records is a valuable step in crime investigation and is the main reason every department should maintain accurate reports. Crimes are not committed through the use of departmental records alone but from the use of all records, of almost every type, wherever they may be found and whenever they give any incidental information regarding the criminal.

   A. accidental B. necessary
   C. reported D. solved

19.____

20. In the years since passage of the Harrison Narcotic Act of 1914, making the possession of opium amphetamines illegal in most circumstances, drug use has become a subject of considerable scientific interest and investigation. There is at present a voluminous literature on drug use of various kinds.

   A. ingestion B. derivatives
   C. addiction D. opiates

20.____

21. Of course, the fact that criminal laws are extremely patterned in definition does not mean that the majority of persons who violate them are dealt with as criminals. Quite the contrary, for a great many forbidden acts are voluntarily engaged in within situations of privacy and go unobserved and unreported.

   A. symbolic B. casual
   C. scientific D. broad-gauged

21.____

22. The most punitive way to study punishment is to focus attention on the pattern of punitive action: to study how a penalty is applied, to study what is done to or taken from an offender.

   A. characteristic B. degrading
   C. objective D. distinguished

22.____

23. The most common forms of punishment in times past have been death, physical torture, mutilation, branding, public humiliation, fines, forfeits of property, banishment, transportation, and imprisonment. Although this list is by no means differentiated, practically every form of punishment has had several variations and applications.

   A. specific B. simple
   C. exhaustive D. characteristic

23.____

24. There is another important line of inference between ordinary and professional criminals, and that is the source from which they are recruited. The professional criminal seems to be drawn from legitimate employment and, in many instances, from parallel vocations or pursuits.   24._____

    A. demarcation
    B. justification
    C. superiority
    D. reference

25. He took the position that the success of the program was insidious on getting additional revenue.   25._____

    A. reputed
    B. contingent
    C. failure
    D. indeterminate

KEY (CORRECT ANSWERS)

1.	A	11.	D
2.	B	12.	D
3.	B	13.	A
4.	C	14.	C
5.	D	15.	A
6.	C	16.	C
7.	D	17.	D
8.	D	18.	C
9.	A	19.	D
10.	C	20.	B

21. D
22. C
23. C
24. A
25. B

TEST 3

DIRECTIONS: Each question or incomplete statement is followed by several suggested answers or completions. Select the one that BEST answers the question or completes the statement. *PRINT THE LETTER OF THE CORRECT ANSWER IN THE SPACE AT THE RIGHT.*

Questions 1-5.

DIRECTIONS: Question 1 through 5 are to be answered on the basis of the following:

You are a supervising officer in an investigative unit. Earlier in the day, you directed Detectives Tom Dixon and Sal Mayo to investigate a reported assault and robbery in a liquor store within your area of jurisdiction.

Detective Dixon has submitted to you a preliminary investigative report containing the following information:

- At 1630 hours on 2/20, arrived at Joe's Liquor Store at 350 SW Avenue with Detective Mayo to investigate A & R.
- At store interviewed Rob Ladd, store manager, who stated that he and Joe Brown (store owner) had been stuck up about ten minutes prior to our arrival.
- Ladd described the robbers as male whites in their late teens or early twenties. Further stated that one of the robbers displayed what appeared to be an automatic pistol as he entered the store, and said, *Give us the money or we'll kill you.* Ladd stated that Brown then reached under the counter where he kept a loaded .38 caliber pistol. Several shots followed, and Ladd threw himself to the floor.
- The robbers fled, and Ladd didn't know if any money had been taken.
- At this point, Ladd realized that Brown was unconscious on the floor and bleeding from a head wound.
- Ambulance called by Ladd, and Brown was removed by same to General Hospital.
- Personally interviewed John White, 382 Dartmouth Place, who stated he was inside store at the time of occurrence. White states that he hid behind a wine display upon hearing someone say, *Give us the money.* He then heard shots and saw two young men run from the store to a yellow car parked at the curb. White was unable to further describe auto. States the taller of the two men drove the car away while the other sat on passenger side in front.
- Recovered three spent .38 caliber bullets from premises and delivered them to Crime Lab.
- To General Hospital at 1800 hours but unable to interview Brown, who was under sedation and suffering from shock and a laceration of the head.
- Alarm #12487 transmitted for car and occupants.
- Case Active.

Based solely on the contents of the preliminary investigation submitted by Detective Dixon, select one sentence from the following groups of sentences which is MOST accurate and is grammatically correct.

1. A. Both robbers were armed.
    B. Each of the robbers were described as a male white.
    C. Neither robber was armed.
    D. Mr. Ladd stated that one of the robbers was armed.

2. A. Mr. Brown fired three shots from his revolver.
    B. Mr. Brown was shot in the head by one of the robbers.
    C. Mr. Brown suffered a gunshot wound of the head during the course of the robbery.
    D. Mr. Brown was taken to General Hospital by ambulance.

3. A. Shots were fired after one of the robbers said, *Give us* the money or we'll kill you.
    B. After one of the robbers demanded the money from Mr. Brown, he fired a shot.
    C. The preliminary investigation indicated that although Mr. Brown did not have a license for the gun, he was justified in using deadly physical force.
    D. Mr. Brown was interviewed at General Hospital.

4. A. Each of the witnesses were customers in the store at the time of occurrence.
    B. Neither of the witnesses interviewed was the owner of the liquor store.
    C. Neither of the witnesses interviewed were the owner of the store.
    D. Neither of the witnesses was employed by Mr. Brown.

5. A. Mr. Brown arrived at General Hospital at about 5:00 P.M.
    B. Neither of the robbers was injured during the robbery.
    C. The robbery occurred at 3:30 P.M. on February 10.
    D. One of the witnesses called the ambulance.

Questions 6-10.

DIRECTIONS: Each of Questions 6 through 10 consists of information given in outline form and four sentences labelled A, B, C, and D. For each question, choose the one sentence which CORRECTLY expresses the information given in outline form and which also displays PROPER English usage.

6. Client's Name - Joanna Jones
    Number of Children - 3
    Client's Income - None
    Client's Marital Status - Single

    A. Joanna Jones is an unmarried client with three children who have no income.
    B. Joanna Jones, who is single and has no income, a client she has three children.
    C. Joanna Jones, whose three children are clients, is single and has no income.
    D. Joanna Jones, who has three children, is an unmarried client with no income.

7. Client's Name - Bertha Smith
    Number of Children - 2
    Client's Rent - $105 per month
    Number of Rooms - 4

A. Bertha Smith, a client, pays $105 per month for her four rooms with two children.
B. Client Bertha Smith has two children and pays $105 per month for four rooms.
C. Client Bertha Smith is paying $105 per month for two children with four rooms.
D. For four rooms and two children client Bertha Smith pays $105 per month.

8. Name of Employee - Cynthia Dawes
   Number of Cases Assigned - 9
   Date Cases were Assigned - 12/16
   Number of Assigned Cases Completed - 8

   A. On December 16, employee Cynthia Dawes was assigned nine cases; she has completed eight of these cases.
   B. Cynthia Dawes, employee on December 16, assigned nine cases, completed eight.
   C. Being employed on December 16, Cynthia Dawes completed eight of nine assigned cases.
   D. Employee Cynthia Dawes, she was assigned nine cases and completed eight, on December 16.

8.____

9. Place of Audit - Broadway Center
   Names of Auditors - Paul Cahn, Raymond Perez
   Date of Audit - 11/20
   Number of Cases Audited - 41

   A. On November 20, at the Broadway Center 41 cases was audited by auditors Paul Cahn and Raymond Perez.
   B. Auditors Raymond Perez and Paul Cahn has audited 41 cases at the Broadway Center on November 20.
   C. At the Broadway Center, on November 20, auditors Paul Cahn and Raymond Perez audited 41 cases.
   D. Auditors Paul Cahn and Raymond Perez at the Broadway Center, on November 20, is auditing 41 cases.

9.____

10. Name of Client - Barbra Levine
    Client's Monthly Income - $210
    Client's Monthly Expenses - $452

    A. Barbra Levine is a client, her monthly income is $210 and her monthly expenses is $452.
    B. Barbra Levine's monthly income is $210 and she is a client, with whose monthly expenses are $452.
    C. Barbra Levine is a client whose monthly income is $210 and whose monthly expenses are $452.
    D. Barbra Levine, a client, is with a monthly income which is $210 and monthly expenses which are $452.

10.____

Questions 11-13.

DIRECTIONS: Questions 11 through 13 involve several statements of fact presented in a very simple way. These statements of fact are followed by 4 choices which attempt to incorporate all of the facts into one logical sentence which is properly constructed and grammatically correct.

4 (#3)

11. I.   Mr. Brown was sweeping the sidewalk in front of his house.
    II. He was sweeping it because it was dirty.
    III. He swept the refuse into the street
    IV. Police Officer Green gave him a ticket.
    Which one of the following BEST presents the information given above?

    A. Because his sidewalk was dirty, Mr. Brown received a ticket from Officer Green when he swept the refuse into the street.
    B. Police Officer Green gave Mr. Brown a ticket because his sidewalk was dirty and he swept the refuse into the street.
    C. Police Officer Green gave Mr. Brown a ticket for sweeping refuse into the street because his sidewalk was dirty.
    D. Mr. Brown, who was sweeping refuse from his dirty sidewalk into the street, was given a ticket by Police Officer Green.

12. I.   Sergeant Smith radioed for help.
    II. The sergeant did so because the crowd was getting larger.
    III. It was 10:00 A.M. when he made his call.
    IV. Sergeant Smith was not in uniform at the time of occurrence.
    Which one of the following BEST presents the information given above?

    A. Sergeant Smith, although not on duty at the time, radioed for help at 10 o'clock because the crowd was getting uglier.
    B. Although not in uniform, Sergeant Smith called for help at 10:00 A.M. because the crowd was getting uglier.
    C. Sergeant Smith radioed for help at 10:00 A.M. because the crowd was getting larger.
    D. Although he was not in uniform, Sergeant Smith radioed for help at 10:00 A.M. because the crowd was getting larger.

13. I.   The payroll office is open on Fridays.
    II. Paychecks are distributed from 9:00 A.M. to 12 Noon.
    III. The office is open on Fridays because that's the only day the payroll staff is available.
    IV. It is open for the specified hours in order to permit employees to cash checks at the bank during lunch hour.
    The choice below which MOST clearly and accurately presents the above idea is:

    A. Because the payroll office is open on Fridays from 9:00 A.M. to 12 Noon, employees can cash their checks when the payroll staff is available.
    B. Because the payroll staff is only available on Fridays until noon, employees can cash their checks during their lunch hour.
    C. Because the payroll staff is available only on Fridays, the office is open from 9:00 A.M. to 12 Noon to allow employees to cash their checks.
    D. Because of payroll staff availability, the payroll office is open on Fridays. It is open from 9:00 A.M. to 12 Noon so that distributed paychecks can be cashed at the bank while employees are on their lunch hour.

Questions 14-16.

DIRECTIONS: In each of Questions 14 through 16, the four sentences are from a paragraph in a report. They are not in the right order. Which of the following arrangements is the BEST one?

14. I. An executive may answer a letter by writing his reply on the face of the letter itself instead of having a return letter typed.
II. This procedure is efficient because it saves the executive's time, the typist's time, and saves office file space.
III. Copying machines are used in small offices as well as large offices to save time and money in making brief replies to business letters.
IV. A copy is made on a copying machine to go into the company files, while the original is mailed back to the sender.
The CORRECT answer is:

A. I, II, IV, III
B. I, IV, II, III
C. III, I, IV, II
D. III, IV, II, I

15. I. Most organizations favor one of the types but always include the others to a lesser degree.
II. However, we can detect a definite trend toward greater use of symbolic control.
III. We suggest that our local police agencies are today primarily utilizing material control.
IV. Control can be classified into three types: physical, material, and symbolic.
The CORRECT answer is:

A. IV, II, III, I
B. II, I, IV, III
C. III, IV, II, I
D. IV, I, III, II

16. I. They can and do take advantage of ancient political and geographical boundaries, which often give them sanctuary from effective police activity.
II. This country is essentially a country of small police forces, each operating independently within the limits of its jurisdiction.
III. The boundaries that define and limit police operations do not hinder the movement of criminals, of course.
IV. The machinery of law enforcement in America is fragmented, complicated, and frequently overlapping.
The CORRECT answer is:

A. III, I, II, IV
B. II, IV, I, III
C. IV, II, III, I
D. IV, III, II, I

17. Examine the following sentence, and then choose from below the words which should be inserted in the blank spaces to produce the best sentence.
The unit has exceeded _____ goals and the employees are satisfied with _____ accomplishments.

A. their, it's
B. it's, it's
C. its, there
D. its, their

18. Examine the following sentence, and then choose from below the words which should be inserted in the blank spaces to produce the best sentence.
Research indicates that employees who _____ no opportunity for close social relationships often find their work unsatisfying, and this _____ of satisfaction often reflects itself in low production.

   A. have, lack
   B. have, excess
   C. has, lack
   D. has, excess

19. Words in a sentence must be arranged properly to make sure that the intended meaning of the sentence is clear. The sentence below that does NOT make sense because a clause has been separated from the word on which its meaning depends is:

   A. To be a good writer, clarity is necessary.
   B. To be a good writer, you must write clearly.
   C. You must write clearly to be a good writer.
   D. Clarity is necessary to good writing.

Questions 20-21.

DIRECTIONS: Each of Questions 20 and 21 consists of a statement which contains a word (one of those underlined) that is either incorrectly used because it is not in keeping with the meaning the quotation is evidently intended to convey, or is misspelled. There is only one INCORRECT word in each quotation. Of the four underlined words, determine if the first one should be replaced by the word lettered A, the second one replaced by the word lettered B, the third one replaced by the word lettered C, or the fourth one replaced by the word lettered D. *PRINT THE LETTER OF THE REPLACEMENT WORD YOU HAVE SELECTED IN THE SPACE AT THE RIGHT.*

20. The alleged killer was occasionally permitted to excercise in the corridor.

   A. alledged
   B. ocasionally
   C. permited
   D. exercise

21. Defense counsel stated, in affect, that their conduct was permissible under the First Amendment.

   A. council
   B. effect
   C. there
   D. permissable

Question 22.

DIRECTIONS: Question 22 consists of one sentence. This sentence contains an incorrectly used word. First, decide which is the incorrectly used word. Then, from among the options given, decide which word, when substituted for the incorrectly used word, makes the meaning of the sentence clear.

22. As today's violence has no single cause, so its causes have no single scheme.

   A. deference   B. cure   C. flaw   D. relevance

7 (#3)

23. In the sentence, *A man in a light-grey suit waited thirty-five minutes in the ante-room for the all-important document,* the word IMPROPERLY hyphenated is   23._____

    A. light-grey
    B. thirty-five
    C. ante-room
    D. all-important

24. In the sentence, *The candidate wants to file his application for preference before it is too late,* the word *before* is used as a(n)   24._____

    A. preposition
    B. subordinating conjunction
    C. pronoun
    D. adverb

25. In the sentence, *The perpetrators ran from the scene,* the word *from* is a   25._____

    A. preposition
    B. pronoun
    C. verb
    D. conjunction

KEY (CORRECT ANSWERS)

1.	D	11.	D
2.	D	12.	D
3.	A	13.	D
4.	B	14.	C
5.	D	15.	D
6.	D	16.	C
7.	B	17.	D
8.	A	18.	A
9.	C	19.	A
10.	C	20.	D

21. B
22. B
23. C
24. B
25. A

PREPARING WRITTEN MATERIAL

PARAGRAPH REARRANGEMENT
COMMENTARY

The sentences which follow are in scrambled order. You are to rearrange them in proper order and indicate the letter choice containing the correct answer at the space at the right.

Each group of sentences in this section is actually a paragraph presented in scrambled order. Each sentence in the group has a place in that paragraph; no sentence is to be left out. You are to read each group of sentences and decide upon the best order in which to put the sentences so as to form as well-organized paragraph.

The questions in this section measure the ability to solve a problem when all the facts relevant to its solution are not given.

More specifically, certain positions of responsibility and authority require the employee to discover connections between events sometimes, apparently, unrelated. In order to do this, the employee will find it necessary to correctly infer that unspecified events have probably occurred or are likely to occur. This ability becomes especially important when action must be taken on incomplete information.

Accordingly, these questions require competitors to choose among several suggested alternatives, each of which presents a different sequential arrangement of the events. Competitors must choose the MOST logical of the suggested sequences.

In order to do so, they may be required to draw on general knowledge to infer missing concepts or events that are essential to sequencing the given events. Competitors should be careful to infer only what is essential to the sequence. The plausibility of the wrong alternatives will always require the inclusion of unlikely events or of additional chains of events which are NOT essential to sequencing the given events.

It's very important to remember that you are looking for the best of the four possible choices, and that the best choice of all may not even be one of the answers you're given to choose from.

There is no one right way to solve these problems. Many people have found it helpful to first write out the order of the sentences, as they would have arranged them, on their scrap paper before looking at the possible answers. If their optimum answer is there, this can save them some time. If it isn't, this method can still give insight into solving the problem. Others find it most helpful to just go through each of the possible choices, contrasting each as they go along. You should use whatever method feels comfortable, and works, for you.

While most of these types of questions are not that difficult, we've added a higher percentage of the difficult type, just to give you more practice. Usually there are only one or two questions on this section that contain such subtle distinctions that you're unable to answer confidently, and you then may find yourself stuck deciding between two possible choices, neither of which you're sure about.

PREPARING WRITTEN MATERIAL
EXAMINATION SECTION
TEST 1

DIRECTIONS: The sentences that follow are in scrambled order. You are to rearrange them in proper order and indicate the letter choice containing the CORRECT answer. *PRINT THE LETTER OF THE CORRECT ANSWER IN THE SPACE AT THE RIGHT.*

1. Police Officer Jenner responds to the scene of a burglary at 2106 La Vista Boulevard. He is approached by an elderly man named Richard Jenkins, whose account of the incident includes the following five sentences:
    I. I saw that the lock on my apartment door had been smashed and the door was open.
    II. My apartment was a shambles; my belongings were everywhere and my television set was missing.
    III. As I walked down the hallway toward the bedroom, I heard someone opening a window.
    IV. I left work at 5:30 P.M. and took the bus home.
    V. At that time, I called the police.
   The MOST logical order for the above sentences to appear in the report is

   A. I, V, IV, II, III
   B. IV, I, II, III, V
   C. I, V, II, III, IV
   D. IV, III, II, V, I

   1.____

2. Police Officer LaJolla is writing an Incident Report in which back-up assistance was required. The report will contain the following five sentences:
    I. The radio dispatcher asked what my location was and he then dispatched patrol cars for back-up assistance.
    II. At approximately 9:30 P.M., while I was walking my assigned footpost, a gunman fired three shots at me.
    III. I quickly turned around and saw a white male, approximately 5'10", with black hair, wearing blue jeans, a yellow T-shirt, and white sneakers, running across the avenue carrying a handgun.
    IV. When the back-up officers arrived, we searched the area but could not find the suspect.
    V. I advised the radio dispatcher that a gunman had just fired a gun at me, and then I gave the dispatcher a description of the man.
   The MOST logical order for the above sentences to appear in the report is

   A. III, V, II, IV, I
   B. II, III, V, I, IV
   C. III, II, IV, I, V
   D. II, V, I, III, IV

   2.____

3. Police Officer Durant is completing a report of a robbery and assault. The report will contain the following five sentences:
    I. I went to Mount Snow Hospital to interview a man who was attacked and robbed of his wallet earlier that night.
    II. An ambulance arrived at 82nd Street and 3rd Avenue and took an intoxicated, wounded man to Mount Snow Hospital.
    III. Two youths attacked the man and stole his wallet.
    IV. A well-dressed man left Hanratty's Bar very drunk, with his wallet hanging out of his back pocket.
    V. A passerby dialed 911 and requested police and ambulance assistance.

   3.____

159

The MOST logical order for the above sentences to appear in the report is

   A. I, II, IV, III, V   B. IV, III, V, II, I
   C. IV, V, II, III, I   D. V, IV, III, II, I

4. Police Officer Boswell is preparing a report of an armed robbery and assault which will contain the following five sentences:
   I. Both men approached the bartender and one of them drew a gun.
   II. The bartender immediately went to grab the phone at the bar.
   III. One of the men leaped over the counter and smashed a bottle over the bartender's head.
   IV. Two men in a blue Buick drove up to the bar and went inside.
   V. I found the cash register empty and the bartender unconscious on the floor, with the phone still dangling off the hook.

   The MOST logical order for the above sentences to appear in the report is

      A. IV, I, II, III, V   B. V, IV, III, I, II
      C. IV, III, II, V, I   D. II, I, III, IV, V

5. Police Officer Mitzler is preparing a report of a bank robbery, which will contain the following five sentences:
   I. The teller complied with the instructions on the note, but also hit the silent alarm.
   II. The perpetrator then fled south on Broadway.
   III. A suspicious male entered the bank at approximately 10:45 A.M.
   IV. At this time, an undetermined amount of money has been taken.
   V. He approached the teller on the far right side and handed her a note.

   The MOST logical order for the above sentences to appear in the report is

      A. III, V, I, II, IV   B. I, III, V, II, IV
      C. III, V, IV, I, II   D. III, V, II, IV, I

6. A Police Officer is preparing an Accident Report for an accident which occurred at the intersection of East 119th Street and Lexington Avenue. The report will include the following five sentences:
   I. On September 18, 1990, while driving ten children to school, a school bus driver passed out.
   II. Upon arriving at the scene, I notified the dispatcher to send an ambulance.
   III. I notified the parents of each child once I got to the station house.
   IV. He said the school bus, while traveling west on East 119th Street, struck a parked Ford which was on the southwest corner of East 119th Street.
   V. A witness by the name of John Ramos came up to me to describe what happened.

   The MOST logical order for the above sentences to appear in the Accident Report is

      A. I, II, V, III, IV   B. I, II, V, IV, III
      C. II, V, I, III, IV   D. II, V, I, IV, III

7. A Police Officer is preparing a report concerning a dispute. The report will contain the following five sentences:
   I. The passenger got out of the back of the taxi and leaned through the front window to complain to the driver about the fare.
   II. The driver of the taxi caught up with the passenger and knocked him to the ground; the passenger then kicked the driver and a scuffle ensued.
   III. The taxi drew up in front of the high-rise building and stopped.
   IV. The driver got out of the taxi and followed the passenger into the lobby of the apartment building.
   V. The doorman tried but was unable to break up the fight, at which point he called the precinct.

   The MOST logical order for the above sentences to appear in the report is

   A. III, I, IV, II, V
   B. III, IV, I, II, V
   C. III, IV, II, V, I
   D. V, I, III, IV, II

8. Police Officer Morrow is writing an Incident Report. The report will include the following four sentences:
   I. The man reached into his pocket and pulled out a gun.
   II. While on foot patrol, I identified a suspect, who was wanted for six robberies in the area, from a wanted picture I was carrying.
   III. I drew my weapon and fired six rounds at the suspect, killing him instantly.
   IV. I called for back-up assistance and told the man to put his hands up.

   The MOST logical order for the above sentences to appear in the report is

   A. II, III, IV, I
   B. IV, I, III, II
   C. IV, I, II, III
   D. II, IV, I, III

9. Sergeant Allen responds to a call at 16 Grove Street regarding a missing child. At the scene, the Sergeant is met by Police Officer Samuels, who gives a brief account of the incident consisting of the following five sentences:
   I. I transmitted the description and waited for you to arrive before I began searching the area.
   II. Mrs. Banks, the mother, reports that she last saw her daughter Julie about 7:30 A.M. when she took her to school.
   III. About 6 P.M., my partner and I arrived at this location to investigate a report of a missing 8 year-old girl.
   IV. When Mrs. Banks left her, Julie was wearing a red and white striped T-shirt, blue jeans, and white sneakers.
   V. Mrs. Banks dropped her off in front of the playground of P.S. 11.

   The MOST logical order for the above sentences to appear in the report is

   A. III, V, IV, II, I
   B. III, II, V, IV, I
   C. III, IV, I, II, V
   D. III, II, IV, I, V

10. Police Officer Franco is completing a report of an assault. The report will contain the following five sentences:
    I. In the park I observed an elderly man lying on the ground, bleeding from a back wound.
    II. I applied first aid to control the bleeding and radioed for an ambulance to respond.

III. The elderly man stated that he was sitting on the park bench when he was attacked from behind by two males.
IV. I received a report of a man's screams coming from inside the park, and I went to investigate.
V. The old man could not give a description of his attackers.

The MOST logical order for the above sentences to appear in the report is

A. IV, I, II, III, V
B. V, III, I, IV, II
C. IV, III, V, II, I
D. II, I, V, IV, III

11. Police Officer Williams is completing a Crime Report. The report contains the following five sentences:
    I. As Police Officer Hanson and I approached the store, we noticed that the front door was broken.
    II. After determining that the burglars had fled, we notified the precinct of the burglary.
    III. I walked through the front door as Police Officer Hanson walked around to the back.
    IV. At approximately midnight, an alarm was heard at the Apex Jewelry Store.
    V. We searched the store and found no one.

    The MOST logical order for the above sentences to appear in the report is

    A. I, IV, II, III, V
    B. I, IV, III, V, II
    C. IV, I, III, II, V
    D. IV, I, III, V, II

12. Police Officer Clay is giving a report to the news media regarding someone who has jumped from the Empire State Building. His report will include the following five sentences:
    I. I responded to the 86th floor, where I found the person at the edge of the roof.
    II. A security guard at the building had reported that a man was on the roof at the 86th floor.
    III. At 5:30 P.M., the person jumped from the building.
    IV. I received a call from the radio dispatcher at 4:50 P.M. to respond to the Empire State Building.
    V. I tried to talk to the person and convince him not to jump.

    The MOST logical order for the above sentences to appear in the report is

    A. I, II, IV, III, V
    B. III, IV, I, II, V
    C. II, IV, I, III, V
    D. IV, II, I, V, III

13. The following five sentences are part of a report of a burglary written by Police Officer Reed:
    I. When I arrived at 2400 1st Avenue, I noticed that the door was slightly open.
    II. I yelled out, *Police, don't move!*
    III. As I entered the apartment, I saw a man with a TV set passing it through a window to another man standing on a fire escape.
    IV. While on foot patrol, I was informed by the radio dispatcher that a burglary was in progress at 2400 1st Avenue.
    V. However, the burglars quickly ran down the fire escape.

    The MOST logical order for the above sentences to appear in the report is

    A. I, III, IV, V, II
    B. IV, I, III, V, II
    C. IV, I, III, II, V
    D. I, IV, III, II, V

14. Police Officer Jenkins is preparing a report for Lost or Stolen Property. The report will include the following five sentences:
    I. On the stairs, Mr. Harris slipped on a wet leaf and fell on the landing.
    II. It wasn't until he got to the token booth that Mr. Harris realized his wallet was no longer in his back pants pocket.
    III. A boy wearing a football jersey helped him up and brushed off the back of Mr. Harris' pants.
    IV. Mr. Harris states he was walking up the stairs to the elevated subway at Queensborough Plaza.
    V. Before Mr. Harris could thank him, the boy was running down the stairs to the street.

    The MOST logical order for the above sentences to appear in the report is

    A. IV, III, V, I, II
    B. IV, I, III, V, II
    C. I, IV, II, III, V
    D. I, II, IV, III, V

15. Police Officer Hubbard is completing a report of a missing person. The report will contain the following five sentences:
    I. I visited the store at 7:55 P.M. and asked the employees if they had seen a girl fitting the description I had been given.
    II. She gave me a description and said she had gone into the local grocery store at about 6:15 P.M.
    III. I asked the woman for a description of her daughter.
    IV. The distraught woman called the precinct to report that her daughter, aged 12, had not returned from an errand.
    V. The storekeeper said a girl matching the description had been in the store earlier, but he could not give an exact time.

    The MOST logical order for the above sentences to appear in the report is

    A. I, III, II, V, IV
    B. IV, III, II, I, V
    C. V, I, II, III, IV
    D. III, I, II, IV, V

16. A police officer is completing an entry in his Daily Activity Log regarding traffic summonses which he issued. The following five sentences will be included in the entry:
    I. I was on routine patrol parked 16 yards west of 170th Street and Clay Avenue.
    II. The summonses were issued for unlicensed operator and disobeying a steady red light.
    III. At 8 A.M. hours, I observed an auto traveling westbound on 170th Street not stop for a steady red light at the intersection of Clay Avenue and 170th Street.
    IV. I stopped the driver of the auto and determined that he did not have a valid driver's license.
    V. After a brief conversation, I informed the motorist that he was receiving two summonses.

    The MOST logical order for the above sentences to appear in the report is

    A. I, III, IV, V, II
    B. III, IV, II, V, I
    C. V, II, I, III, IV
    D. IV, V, II, I, III

17. The following sentences appeared on an Incident Report:
    I. Three teenagers who had been ejected from the theater were yelling at patrons who were now entering.
    II. Police Officer Dixon told the teenagers to leave the area.
    III. The teenagers said that they were told by the manager to leave the theater because they were talking during the movie.
    IV. The theater manager called the precinct at 10:20 P.M. to report a disturbance outside the theater.
    V. A patrol car responded to the theater at 10:42 P.M. and two police officers went over to the teenagers.

    The MOST logical order for the above sentences to appear in the Incident Report

    A. I, V, IV, III, II
    B. IV, I, V, III, II
    C. IV, I, III, V, II
    D. IV, III, I, V, II

18. Activity Log entries are completed by police officers. Police Officer Samuels has written an entry concerning vandalism and part of it contains the following five sentences:
    I. The man, in his early twenties, ran down the block and around the corner.
    II. A man passing the store threw a brick through a window of the store.
    III. I arrived on the scene and began to question the witnesses about the incident.
    IV. Malcolm Holmes, the owner of the Fast Service Shoe Repair Store, was working in the back of the store at approximately 3 P.M.
    V. After the man fled, Mr. Holmes called the police.

    The MOST logical order for the above sentences to appear in the Activity Log is

    A. IV, II, I, V, III
    B. II, IV, I, III, V
    C. II, I, IV, III, V
    D. IV, II, V, III, I

19. Police Officer Buckley is preparing a report concerning a dispute in a restaurant. The report will contain the following five sentences:
    I. The manager, Charles Chin, and a customer, Edward Green, were standing near the register arguing over the bill.
    II. The manager refused to press any charges providing Green pay the check and leave.
    III. While on foot patrol, I was informed by a passerby of a disturbance in the Dragon Flame Restaurant.
    IV. Green paid the $7.50 check and left the restaurant.
    V. According to witnesses, the customer punched the owner in the face when Chin asked him for the amount due.

    The MOST logical order for the above sentences to appear in the report is

    A. III, I, V, II, IV
    B. I, II, III, IV, V
    C. V, I, III, II, IV
    D. III, V, II, IV, I

20. Police Officer Wilkins is preparing a report for leaving the scene of an accident. The report will include the following five sentences:
    I. The Dodge struck the right rear fender of Mrs. Smith's 1980 Ford and continued on its way.
    II. Mrs. Smith stated she was making a left turn from 40th Street onto Third Avenue.
    III. As the car passed, Mrs. Smith noticed the dangling rear license plate #412AEJ.
    IV. Mrs. Smith complained to police of back pains and was removed by ambulance to Bellevue Hospital.
    V. An old green Dodge traveling up Third Avenue went through the red light at 40th Street and Third Avenue.

    The MOST logical order for the above sentences to appear in the report is

    A. V, III, I, II, IV
    B. I, III, II, V, IV
    C. IV, V, I, II, III
    D. II, V, I, III, IV

21. Detective Simon is completing a Crime Report. The report contains the following five sentences:
    I. Police Officer Chin, while on foot patrol, heard the yelling and ran in the direction of the man.
    II. The man, carrying a large hunting knife, left the High Sierra Sporting Goods Store at approximately 10:30 A.M.
    III. When the man heard Police Officer Chin, he stopped, dropped the knife, and began to cry.
    IV. As Police Officer Chin approached the man, he drew his gun and yelled, *Police, freeze.*
    V. After the man left the store, he began yelling, over and over, *I am going to 'kill myself!*

    The MOST logical order for the above sentences to appear in the report is

    A. V, II, I, IV, III
    B. II, V, I, IV, III
    C. II, V, IV, I, III
    D. II, I, V, IV, III

22. Police Officer Miller is preparing a Complaint Report which will include the following five sentences:
    I. From across the lot, he yelled to the boys to get away from his car.
    II. When he came out of the store, he noticed two teenage boys trying to break into his car.
    III. The boys fled as Mr. Johnson ran to his car.
    IV. Mr. Johnson stated that he parked his car in the municipal lot behind Tams Department Store.
    V. Mr. Johnson saw that the door lock had been broken, but nothing was missing from inside the auto.

    The MOST logical order for the above sentences to appear in the report is

    A. IV, I, II, V, III
    B. II, III, I, V, IV
    C. IV, II, I, III, V
    D. I, II, III, V, IV

23. Police Officer O'Hara completes a Universal Summons for a motorist who has just passed a red traffic light. The Universal Summons includes the following five sentences:
    I. As the car passed the light, I followed in the patrol car.
    II. After the driver stopped the car, he stated that the light was yellow, not red.
    III. A blue Cadillac sedan passed the red light on the corner of 79th Street and 3rd Avenue at 11:25 P.M.
    IV. As a result, the driver was informed that he did pass a red light and that his brake lights were not working.
    V. The driver in the Cadillac stopped his car as soon as he saw the patrol car, and I noticed that the brake lights were not working.

    The MOST logical order for the above sentences to appear in the Universal Summons is

    A. I, III, V, II, IV
    B. III, I, V, II, IV
    C. III, I, V, IV, II
    D. I, III, IV, II, V

24. Detective Egan is preparing a follow-up report regarding a homicide on 170th Street and College Avenue. An unknown male was found at the scene. The report will contain the following five sentences:
    I. Police Officer Gregory wrote down the names, addresses, and phone numbers of the witnesses.
    II. A 911 operator received a call of a man shot and dispatched Police Officers Worth and Gregory to the scene.
    III. They discovered an unidentified male dead on the street.
    IV. Police Officer Worth notified the Precinct Detective Unit immediately.
    V. At approximately 9:00 A.M., an unidentified male shot another male in the chest during an argument.

    The MOST logical order for the above sentences to appear in the report is

    A. V, II, III, IV, I
    B. II, III, V, IV, I
    C. IV, I, V, II, III
    D. V, III, II, IV, I

25. Police Officer Tracey is preparing a Robbery Report which will include the following five sentences:
    I. I ran around the corner and observed a man pointing a gun at a taxidriver.
    II. I informed the man I was a police officer and that he should not move.
    III. I was on the corner of 125th Street and Park Avenue when I heard a scream coming from around the corner.
    IV. The man turned around and fired one shot at me.
    V. I fired once, shooting him in the arm and causing him to fall to the ground.

    The MOST logical order for the above sentences to appear in the report is

    A. I, III, IV, II, V
    B. IV, V, II, I, III
    C. III, I, II, IV, V
    D. III, I, V, II, IV

KEY (CORRECT ANSWERS)

1.	B	11.	D
2.	B	12.	D
3.	B	13.	C
4.	A	14.	B
5.	A	15.	B
6.	B	16.	A
7.	A	17.	B
8.	D	18.	A
9.	B	19.	A
10.	A	20.	D

21. B
22. C
23. B
24. A
25. C

TEST 2

DIRECTIONS: The sentences that follow are in scrambled order. You are to rearrange them in proper order and indicate the letter choice containing the CORRECT answer. *PRINT THE LETTER OF THE CORRECT ANSWER IN THE SPACE AT THE RIGHT.*

1. Police Officer Weiker is completing a Complaint Report which will contain the following five sentences:
    I. Mr. Texlor was informed that the owner of the van would receive a parking ticket and that the van would be towed away.
    II. The police tow truck arrived approximately one half hour after Mr. Texlor complained.
    III. While on foot patrol on West End Avenue, I saw the owner of Rand's Restaurant arrive to open his business.
    IV. Mr. Texlor, the owner, called to me and complained that he could not receive deliveries because a van was blocking his driveway.
    V. The van's owner later reported to the precinct that his van had been stolen, and he was then informed that it had been towed.

   The MOST logical order for the above sentences to appear in the report is

   A. III, V, I, II, IV B. III, IV, I, II, V
   C. IV, III, I, II, V D. IV, III, II, I, V

2. Police Officer Ames is completing an entry in his Activity Log. The entry contains the following five sentences:
    I. Mr. Sands gave me a complete description of the robber.
    II. Alvin Sands, owner of the Star Delicatessen, called the precinct to report he had just been robbed.
    III. I then notified all police patrol vehicles to look for a white male in his early twenties wearing brown pants and shirt, a black leather jacket, and black and white sneakers.
    IV. I arrived on the scene after being notified by the precinct that a robbery had just occurred at the Star Delicatessen.
    V. Twenty minutes later, a man fitting the description was arrested by a police officer on patrol six blocks from the delicatessen.

   The MOST logical order for the above sentences to appear in the Activity Log is

   A. II, I, IV, III, V B. II, IV, III, I, V
   C. II, IV, I, III, V D. II, IV, I, V, III

3. Police Officer Benson is completing a Complaint Report concerning a stolen taxicab, which will include the following five sentences:
    I. Police Officer Benson noticed that a cab was parked next to a fire hydrant.
    II. Dawson *borrowed* the cab for transportation purposes since he was in a hurry.
    III. Ed Dawson got into his car and tried to start it, but the battery was dead.
    IV. When he reached his destination, he parked the cab by a fire hydrant and placed the keys under the seat.
    V. He looked around and saw an empty cab with the engine running.

   The MOST logical order for the above sentences to appear in the report is

A.	I, III, II, IV, V	B.	III, I, II, V, IV
C.	III, V, II, IV, I	D.	V, II, IV, III, I

4. Police Officer Hatfield is reviewing his Activity Log entry prior to completing a report. The entry contains the following five sentences:
    I. When I arrived at Zand's Jewelry Store, I noticed that the door was slightly open.
    II. I told the burglar I was a police officer and that he should stand still or he would be shot.
    III. As I entered the store, I saw a man wearing a ski mask attempting to open the safe in the back of the store.
    IV. On December 16, 1990, at 1:38 A.M., I was informed that a burglary was in progress at Zand's Jewelry Store on East 59th Street.
    V. The burglar quickly pulled a knife from his pocket when he saw me.

The MOST logical order for the above sentences to appear in the report is

A.	IV, I, III, V, II	B.	I, IV, III, V, II
C.	IV, III, II, V, I	D.	I, III, IV, V, II

5. Police Officer Lorenz is completing a report of a murder. The report will contain the following five statements made by a witness:
    I. I was awakened by the sound of a gunshot coming from the apartment next door, and I decided to check.
    II. I entered the apartment and looked into the kitchen and the bathroom.
    III. I found Mr. Hubbard's body slumped in the bathtub.
    IV. The door to the apartment was open, but I didn't see anyone.
    V. He had been shot in the head.

The MOST logical order for the above sentences to appear in the report is

A.	I, III, II, IV, V	B.	I, IV, II, III, V
C.	IV, II, I, III, V	D.	III, I, II, IV, V

6. Police Officer Baldwin is preparing an accident report which will include the following five sentences:
    I. The old man lay on the ground for a few minutes, but was not physically hurt.
    II. Charlie Watson, a construction worker, was repairing some brick work at the top of a building at 54th Street and Madison Avenue.
    III. Steven Green, his partner, warned him that this could be dangerous, but Watson ignored him.
    IV. A few minutes later, one of the bricks thrown by Watson smashed to the ground in front of an old man, who fainted out of fright.
    V. Mr. Watson began throwing some of the bricks over the side of the building.

The MOST logical order for the above sentences to appear in the report is

A.	II, V, III, IV, I	B.	I, IV, II, V, III
C.	III, II, IV, V, I	D.	II, III, I, IV, V

7. Police Officer Porter is completing an incident report concerning her rescue of a woman being held hostage by a former boyfriend. Her report will contain the following five sentences:
   I. I saw a man holding .25 caliber gun to a woman's head, but he did not see me.
   II. I then broke a window and gained access to the house.
   III. As I approached the house on foot, a gunshot rang out and I heard a woman scream.
   IV. A decoy van brought me as close as possible to the house where the woman was being held hostage.
   V. I ordered the man to drop his gun, and he released the woman and was taken into custody.

   The MOST logical order for the above sentences to appear in the report is

   A. I, III, II, IV, V　　B. IV, III, II, I, V
   C. III, II, I, IV, V　　D. V, I, II, III, IV

8. Police Officer Byrnes is preparing a crime report concerning a robbery. The report will consist of the following five sentences:
   I. Mr. White, following the man's instructions, opened the car's hood, at which time the man got out of the auto, drew a revolver, and ordered White to give him all the money in his pockets.
   II. Investigation has determined there were no witnesses to this incident.
   III. The man asked White to check the oil and fill the tank.
   IV. Mr. White, a gas attendant, states that he was working alone at the gas station when a black male pulled up to the gas pump in a white Mercury.
   V. White was then bound and gagged by the male and locked in the gas station's rest room.

   The MOST logical order for the above sentences to appear in the report is

   A. IV, I, III, II, V　　B. III, I, II, V, IV
   C. IV, III, I, V, II　　D. I, III, IV, II, V

9. Police Officer Gale is preparing a report of a crime committed against Mr. Weston. The report will consist of the following five sentences:
   I. The man, who had a gun, told Mr. Weston not to scream for help and ordered him back into the apartment.
   II. With Mr. Weston disposed of in this fashion, the man proceeded to ransack the apartment.
   III. Opening the door to see who was there, Mr. Weston was confronted by a tall white male wearing a dark blue jacket and white pants.
   IV. Mr. Weston was at home alone in his living room when the doorbell rang.
   V. Once inside, the man bound and gagged Mr. Weston and locked him in the bathroom.

   The MOST logical order for the above sentences to appear in the report is

   A. III, V, II, I, IV　　B. IV, III, I, V, II
   C. III, V, IV, II, I　　D. IV, III, V, I, II

10. A police officer is completing a report of a robbery, which will contain the following five sentences:
    I. Two police officers were about to enter the Red Rose Coffee Shop on 47th Street and 8th Avenue.
    II. They then noticed a male running up the street carrying a brown paper bag.
    III. They heard a woman standing outside the Broadway Boutique yelling that her store had just been robbed by a young man, and she was pointing up the street.
    IV. They caught up with him and made an arrest.
    V. The police officers pursued the male, who ran past them on 8th Avenue.

    The MOST logical order for the above sentences to appear in the report is

    A. I, III, II, V, IV
    B. III, I, II, V, IV
    C. IV, V, I, II, III
    D. I, V, IV, III, II

11. Police Officer Capalbo is preparing a report of a bank robbery. The report will contain the following five statements made by a witness:
    I. Initially, all I could see were two men, dressed in maintenance uniforms, sitting in the area reserved for bank officers.
    II. I was passing the bank at 8 P.M. and noticed that all the lights were out, except in the rear section.
    III. Then I noticed two other men in the bank, coming from the direction of the vault, carrying a large metal box.
    IV. At this point, I decided to call the police.
    V. I knocked on the window to get the attention of the men in the maintenance uniforms, and they chased the two men carrying the box down a flight of steps.

    The MOST logical order for the above sentences to appear in the report is

    A. IV, I, II, V, III
    B. I, III, II, V, IV
    C. II, I, III, V, IV
    D. II, III, I, V, IV

12. Police Officer Roberts is preparing a crime report concerning an assault and a stolen car. The report will contain the following five sentences:
    I. Upon leaving the store to return to his car, Winters noticed that a male unknown to him was sitting in his car.
    II. The man then re-entered Winters' car and drove away, fleeing north on 2nd Avenue.
    III. Mr. Winters stated that he parked his car in front of 235 East 25th Street and left the engine running while he went into the butcher shop at that location.
    IV. Mr. Robert Gering, a witness, stated that the male is known in the neighborhood as Bobby Rae and is believed to reside at 323 East 114th Street.
    V. When Winters approached the car and ordered the man to get out, the man got out of the auto and struck Winters with his fists, knocking him to the ground.

    The MOST logical order for the above sentences to appear in the report is

    A. III, II, V, I, IV
    B. III, I, V, II, IV
    C. I, IV, V, II, III
    D. III, II, I, V, IV

13. Police Officer Robinson is preparing a crime report concerning the robbery of Mr. Edwards' store. The report will consist of the following five sentences:
    I. When the last customer left the store, the two men drew revolvers and ordered Mr. Edwards to give them all the money in the cash register.
    II. The men proceeded to the back of the store as if they were going to do some shopping.
    III. Janet Morley, a neighborhood resident, later reported that she saw the men enter a green Ford station wagon and flee northbound on Albany Avenue.
    IV. Edwards complied after which the gunmen ran from the store.
    V. Mr. Edwards states that he was stocking merchandise behind the store counter when two white males entered the store.

    The MOST logical order for the above sentences to appear in the report is

    A. V, II, III, I, IV
    B. V, II, I, IV, III
    C. II, I, V, IV, III
    D. III, V, II, I, IV

14. Police Officer Wendell is preparing an accident report for a 6-car accident that occurred at the intersection of Bath Avenue and Bay Parkway. The report will consist of the following five sentences:
    I. A 2006 Volkswagen Beetle, traveling east on Bath Avenue, swerved to the left to avoid the Impala, and struck a 2004 Ford station wagon which was traveling west on Bath Avenue.
    II. The Seville then mounted the curb on the northeast corner of Bath Avenue and Bay Parkway and struck a light pole.
    III. A 2003 Buick Lesabre, traveling northbound on Bay Parkway directly behind the Impala, struck the Impala, pushing it into the intersection of Bath Avenue and Bay Parkway.
    IV. A 2005 Chevy Impala, traveling northbound on Bay Parkway, had stopped for a red light at Bath Avenue.
    V. A 2007 Toyota, traveling westbound on Bath Avenue, swerved to the right to avoid hitting the Ford station wagon, and struck a 2007 Cadillac Seville double-parked near the corner.

    The MOST logical order for the above sentences to appear in the report is

    A. IV, III, V, II, I
    B. III, IV, V, II, I
    C. IV, III, I, V, II
    D. III, IV, V, I, II

15. The following five sentences are part of an Activity Log entry Police Officer Rogers made regarding an explosion,
    I. I quickly treated the pedestrian for the injury.
    II. The explosion caused a glass window in an office building to shatter.
    III. After the pedestrian was treated, a call was placed to the precinct requesting additional police officers to evacuate the area.
    IV. After all the glass settled to the ground, I saw a pedestrian who was bleeding from the arm
    V. While on foot patrol near 5th Avenue and 53rd Street, I heard a loud explosion.

    The MOST logical order for the above sentences to appear in the report is

    A. II, V, IV, I, III
    B. V, II, IV, III, I
    C. V, II, I, IV, III
    D. V, II, IV, I, III

16. Police Officer David is completing a report regarding illegal activity near the entrance to Madison Square Garden during a recent rock concert. The report will contain the following five sentences:
    I. As I came closer to the man, he placed what appeared to be tickets in his pocket and began to walk away.
    II. After the man stopped, I questioned him about *scalping* tickets.
    III. While on assignment near the Madison Square Garden entrance, I observed a man apparently selling tickets.
    IV. I stopped the man by stating that I was a police officer.
    V. The man was then given a summons, and he left the area.
    The MOST logical order for the above sentences to appear in the report is
    A. I, III, IV, II, V
    B. III, I, IV, V, II
    C. III, IV, I, II, V
    D. III, I, IV, II, V

17. Police Officer Sampson is preparing a report concerning a dispute in a bar. The report will contain the following five sentences:
    I. John Evans, the bartender, ordered the two men out of the bar.
    II. Two men dressed in dungarees entered the C and D Bar at 5:30 P.M.
    III. The two men refused to leave and began to beat up Evans.
    IV. A customer in the bar saw me on patrol and yelled to me to come separate the three men.
    V. The two men became very drunk and loud within a short time.
    The MOST logical order for the above sentences to appear in the report is
    A. II, I, V, III, IV
    B. II, III, IV, V, I
    C. III, I, II, V, IV
    D. II, V, I, III, IV

18. A police officer is completing a report concerning the response to a crime in progress. The report will include the following five sentences:
    I. The officers saw two armed men run out of the liquor store and into a waiting car.
    II. Police Officers Lunty and Duren received the call and responded to the liquor store.
    III. The robbers gave up without a struggle.
    IV. Lunty and Duren blocked the getaway car with their patrol car.
    V. A call came into the precinct concerning a robbery in progress at Jane's Liquor Store.
    The MOST logical order for the above sentences to appear in the report is
    A. V, II, I, IV, III
    B. II, V, I, III, IV
    C. V, I, IV, II, III
    D. I, V, II, III, IV

19. Police Officer Jenkins is preparing a Crime Report which will consist of the following five sentences:
    I. After making inquiries in the vicinity, Smith found out that his next door neighbor, Viola Jones, had seen two local teenagers, Michael Heinz and Vincent Gaynor, smash his car's windshields with a crowbar.
    II. Jones told Smith that the teenagers live at 8700 19th Avenue.
    III. Mr. Smith heard a loud crash at approximately 11:00 P.M., looked out his apartment window, and saw two white males running away from his car.
    IV. Smith then reported the incident to the precinct, and Heinz and Gaynor were arrested at the address given.

V. Leaving his apartment to investigate further, Smith discovered that his car's front and rear windshields had been smashed.

The MOST logical order for the above sentences to appear in the report is

- A. III, IV, V, I, II
- B. III, V, I, II, IV
- C. III, I, V, II, IV
- D. V, III, I, II, IV

20. Sergeant Nancy Winston is reviewing a Gun Control Report which will contain the following five sentences:
    I. The man fell to the floor when hit in the chest with three bullets from 22 caliber gun.
    II. Merriam'22 caliber gun was seized, and he wasgiven a summons for not having a pistol permit.
    III. Christopher Merriam, the owner of A-Z Grocery, shot a man who attempted to rob him.
    IV. Police Officer Franks responded and asked Merriam for his pistol permit, which he could not produce.
    V. Merriam phoned the police to report he had just shot a man who had attempted to rob him.

    The MOST logical order for the above sentences to appear in the report is

    - A. III, I, V, IV, II
    - B. I, III, V, IV, II
    - C. III, I, V, II, IV
    - D. I, III, II, V, IV

21. Detective John Manville is completing a report for his superior regarding the murder of an unknown male who was shot in Central Park. The report will contain the following five sentences:
    I. Police Officers Langston and Cavers responded to the scene.
    II. I received the assignment to investigate the murder in Central Park from Detective Sergeant Rogers.
    III. Langston notified the Detective Bureau after questioning Jason.
    IV. An unknown male, apparently murdered, was discovered in Central Park by Howard Jason, a park employee, who immediately called the police.
    V. Langston and Cavers questioned Jason.

    The MOST logical order for the above sentences to appear in the report is

    - A. I, IV, V, III, II
    - B. IV, I, V, II, III
    - C. IV, I, V, III, II
    - D. IV, V, I, III, II

22. A police officer is completing a report concerning the arrest of a juvenile. The report will contain the following five sentences:
    I. Sanders then telephoned Jay's parents from the precinct to inform them of their son's arrest.
    II. The store owner resisted, and Jay then shot him and ran from the store.
    III. Jay was transported directly to the precinct by Officer Sanders.
    IV. James Jay, a juvenile, walked into a candy store and announced a hold-up.
    V. Police Officer Sanders, while on patrol, arrested Jay a block from the candy store.

    The MOST logical order for the above sentences to appear in the report is

    - A. IV, V, II, I, III
    - B. IV, II, V, III, I
    - C. II, IV, V, III, I
    - D. V, IV, II, I, III

23. Police Officer Olsen prepared a crime report for a robbery which contained the following five sentences:
    I. Mr. Gordon was approached by this individual who then produced a gun and demanded the money from the cash register.
    II. The man then fled from the scene on foot, southbound on 5th Avenue.
    III. Mr. Gordon was working at the deli counter when a white male, 5'6", 150-160 lbs., wearing a green jacket and blue pants, entered the store.
    IV. Mr. Gordon complied with the man's demands and handed him the daily receipts.
    V. Further investigation has determined there are no other witnesses to this robbery.

    The MOST logical order for the above sentences to appear in the report is

    A. I, III, IV, V, II   B. I, IV, II, III, V
    C. III, IV, I, V, II   D. III, I, IV, , II, V

24. Police Officer Bryant responded to 285 E. 31st Street to take a crime report of a burglary of Mr. Bond's home. The report will contain a brief description of the incident, consisting of the following five sentences:
    I. When Mr. Bond attempted to stop the burglar by grabbing him, he was pushed to the floor.
    II. The burglar had apparently gained access to the home by forcing open the 2nd floor bedroom window facing the fire escape.
    III. Mr. Bond sustained a head injury in the scuffle, and the burglar exited the home through the front door.
    IV. Finding nothing in the dresser, the burglar proceeded downstairs to the first floor, where he was confronted by Mr. Bond who was reading in the dining room.
    V. Once inside, he searched the drawers of the bedroom dresser.

    The MOST logical order for the above sentences to appear in the report is

    A. V, IV, I, II, III   B. II, V, IV, I, III
    C. II, IV, V, III, I   D. III, II, I, V, IV

25. Police Officer Derringer responded to a call of a rape-homicide case in his patrol area and was ordered to prepare an incident report, which will contain the following five sentences:
    I. He pushed Miss Scott to the ground and forcibly raped her.
    II. Mary Scott was approached from behind by a white male, 5'7", 150-160 lbs. wearing dark pants and a white jacket.
    III. As Robinson approached the male, he ordered him to stop.
    IV. Screaming for help, Miss Scott alerted one John Robinson, a local grocer, who chased her assailant as he fled the scene.
    V. The male turned and fired two shots at Robinson, who fell to the ground mortally wounded.

    The MOST logical order for the above' sentences to appear in the report is

    A. IV, III, I, II, V   B. II, IV, III, V, I
    C. II, IV, I, V, III   D. II, I, IV, III, V

KEY (CORRECT ANSWERS)

1. B
2. C
3. C
4. A
5. B

6. A
7. B
8. C
9. B
10. A

11. C
12. B
13. B
14. C
15. D

16. D
17. D
18. A
19. B
20. A

21. C
22. B
23. D
24. B
25. D

REPORT WRITING

EXAMINATION SECTION
TEST 1

DIRECTIONS: Each question or incomplete statement is followed by several suggested answers or completions. Select the one that BEST answers the question or completes the statement. *PRINT THE LETTER OF THE CORRECT ANSWER IN THE SPACE AT THE RIGHT.*

1. Police Officer Johnson responds to the scene of an assault and obtains the following information:
   Time of Occurrence: 8:30 P.M.
   Place of Occurrence: 120-18 119th Avenue, Apt. 2A
   Suspects: John Andrews, victim's ex-husband and unknown white male
   Victim: Susan Andrews
   Injury: Broken right arm
   Officer Johnson is preparing a complaint report on the incident.
   Which one of the following expresses the above information MOST clearly and accurately?

   A. Susan Andrews was assaulted at 120-18 119th Avenue, Apt. 2A. At 8:30 P.M., her ex-husband, John Andrews, and an unknown white male broke her arm.
   B. At 8:30 P.M., Susan Andrews was assaulted at 120-18 119th Avenue, Apt. 2A, by her ex-husband, John Andrews, and an unknown white male. Her right arm was broken.
   C. John Andrews, an unknown white male, and Susan Andrews' ex-husband, assaulted and broke her right arm at 8:30 P.M., at 120-18 119th Avenue, Apt. 2A.
   D. John Andrews, ex-husband of Susan Andrews, broke her right arm with an unknown white male at 120-18 119th Avenue, at 8:30 P.M. in Apt. 2A.

2. While on patrol, Officers Banks and Thompson see a man lying on the ground bleeding. Officer Banks records the following details about the incident:
   Time of Incident: 3:15 P.M.
   Place of Incident: Sidewalk in front of 517 Rock Avenue
   Incident: Tripped and fell
   Name of Injured: John Blake
   Injury: Head wound
   Action Taken: Transported to Merry Hospital
   Officer Banks is completing a report on the incident.
   Which one of the following expresses the above information MOST clearly and accurately?

   A. At 3:15 P.M., Mr. John Blake was transported to Merry Hospital. He tripped and fell, injuring his head on sidewalk in front of 517 Rock Avenue.
   B. Mr. John Blake tripped and fell on the sidewalk at 3:15 P.M. in front of 517 Rock Avenue. He was transported to Merry Hospital while he sustained a head wound.
   C. Mr. John Blake injured his head when he tripped and fell on the sidewalk in front of 517 Rock Avenue at 3:15 P.M. He was transported to Merry Hospital.
   D. A head was wounded on the sidewalk in front of 517 Rock Avenue at 3:15 P.M. Mr. John Blake tripped and fell and was transported to Merry Hospital.

3. When assigned to investigate a complaint, a police officer should
   I. Interview witnesses and obtain facts
   II. Conduct a thorough investigation of circumstances concerning the complaint
   III. Prepare a complaint report
   IV. Determine if the complaint report should be closed or referred for further investigation
   V. Enter complaint report on the Complaint Report Index and obtain a complaint report number at the station house

   While on patrol, Police Officer John is instructed by his supervisor to investigate a complaint by Mr. Stanley Burns, who was assaulted by his brother-in-law, Henry Traub. After interviewing Mr. Burns, Officer John learns that Mr. Traub has been living with Mr. Burns for the past two years. Officer John accompanies Mr. Burns to his apartment but Mr. Traub is not there. Officer John fills out the complaint report and takes the report back to the station house where it is entered on the Complaint Report Index and assigned a complaint report number. Officer John's actions were

   A. *improper,* primarily because he should have stayed at Mr. Burns' apartment and waited for Mr. Traub to return in order to arrest him
   B. *proper,* primarily because after obtaining all the facts, he took the report back to the station house and was assigned a complaint report number
   C. *improper,* primarily because he should have decided whether to close the report or refer it for further investigation
   D. *proper,* primarily because he was instructed by his supervisor to take the report from Mr. Burns even though it involved his brother-in-law

4. Police Officer Waters was the first person at the scene of a fire which may have been the result of arson. He obtained the following information:
   Place of Occurrence: 35 John Street, Apt. 27
   Time of Occurrence: 4:00 P.M.
   Witness: Daisy Logan
   Incident: Fire (possible arson)
   Suspect: Male, white, approximately 18 years old, wearing blue jeans and a plaid shirt, running away from the incident Officer Waters is completing a report on the incident.

   Which one of the following expresses the above information MOST clearly and accurately?

   A. At 4:00 P.M., Daisy Logan saw a white male, approximately 18 years old who was wearing blue jeans and a plaid shirt, running from the scene of a fire at 35 John Street, Apt. 27.
   B. Seeing a fire at 35 John Street, a white male approximately 18 years old, wearing blue jeans and a plaid shirt, was seen running from Apt. 27 at 4:00 P.M. reported Daisy Logan.
   C. Approximately 18 years old and wearing blue jeans and a plaid shirt, Daisy Logan saw a fire and a white male running from 35 John Street, Apt. 27 at 4:00 P.M.
   D. Running from 35 John Street, Apt. 27, the scene of the fire, reported Daisy Logan at 4:00 P.M., was a white male approximately 18 years old and wearing blue jeans and a plaid shirt.

5. Police Officer Sullivan obtained the following information at the scene of a two-car accident:

Place of Occurrence: 2971 William Street
Drivers and Vehicles Involved: Mrs. Wilson, driver of blue 2004 Toyota Camry; Mr. Bailey, driver of white 2001 Dodge
Injuries Sustained: Mr. Bailey had a swollen right eye; Mrs. Wilson had a broken left hand

Which one of the following expresses the above information MOST clearly and accurately?

A. Mr. Bailey, owner of a white 2001 Dodge, at 2971 William Street, had a swollen right eye. Mrs. Wilson, with a broken left hand, is the owner of the blue 2004 Toyota Camry. They were in a car accident.
B. Mrs. Wilson got a broken left hand and Mr. Bailey a swollen right eye at 2971 William Street. The vehicles involved in the car accident were a 2001 Dodge, white, owned by Mr. Bailey, and Mrs. Wilson's blue 2004 Toyota Camry.
C. Mrs. Wilson, the driver of the blue 2004 Toyota Camry, and Mr. Bailey, the driver of the white 2001 Dodge, were involved in a car accident at 2971 William Street. Mr. Bailey sustained a swollen right eye, and Mrs. Wilson broke her left hand.
D. Mr. Bailey sustained a swollen right eye and Mrs. Wilson broke her left hand in a car accident at 2971 William Street. They owned a 2001 white Dodge and a 2004 blue Toyota Camry.

6. Officer Johnson has issued a summons to a driver and has obtained the following information:

Place of Occurrence: Corner of Foster Road and Woodrow Avenue
Time of Occurrence: 7:10 P.M.
Driver: William Grant
Offense: Driving through a red light
Age of Driver: 42
Address of Driver: 23 Richmond Avenue

Officer Johnson is making an entry in his Memo Book regarding the incident.
Which one of the following expresses the above information MOST clearly and accurately?

A. William Grant, lives at 23 Richmond Avenue at 7:10 P.M., went through a red light. He was issued a summons at the corner of Foster Road and Woodrow Avenue. The driver is 42 years old.
B. William Grant, age 42, who lives at 23 Richmond Avenue, was issued a summons for going through a red light at 7:10 P.M. at the corner of Foster Road and Woodrow Avenue.
C. William Grant, age 42, was issued a summons on the corner of Foster Road and Woodrow Avenue for going through a red light. He lives at 23 Richmond Avenue at 7:10 P.M.
D. A 42-year-old man who lives at 23 Richmond Avenue was issued a summons at 7:10 P.M. William Grant went through a red light at the corner of Foster Road and Woodrow Avenue.

7. Police Officer Frome has completed investigating a report of a stolen auto and obtained the following information:
   Date of Occurrence: October 26, 2004
   Place of Occurrence: 51st Street and 8th Avenue
   Time of Occurrence: 3:30 P.M.
   Crime: Auto theft
   Suspect: Michael Wadsworth
   Action Taken: Suspect arrested
   Which one of the following expresses the above information MOST clearly and accurately?

   A. Arrested on October 26, 2004 was a stolen auto at 51st Street and 8th Avenue at 3:30 P.M. driven by Michael Wadsworth.
   B. For driving a stolen auto at 3:30 P.M., Michael Wadsworth was arrested at 51st Street and 8th Avenue on October 26, 2004.
   C. On October 26, 2004 at 3:30 P.M., Michael Wadsworth was arrested at 51st Street and 8th Avenue for driving a stolen auto.
   D. Michael Wadsworth was arrested on October 26, 2004 at 3:30 P.M. for driving at 51st Street and 8th Avenue. The auto was stolen.

8. Police Officer Wright has finished investigating a report of Grand Larceny and has obtained the following information:
   Time of Occurrence: Between 1:00 P.M. and 2:00 P.M.
   Place of Occurrence: In front of victim's home, 85 Montgomery Avenue
   Victim: Mr. Williams, owner of the vehicle
   Crime: Automobile broken into
   Property Taken: Stereo valued at $1,200
   Officer Wright is preparing a report on the incident. Which one of the following expresses the above information MOST clearly and accurately?

   A. While parked in front of his home Mr. Williams states that between 1:00 P.M. and 2:00 P.M. an unknown person broke into his vehicle. Mr. Williams, who lives at 85 Montgomery Avenue, lost his $1,200 stereo.
   B. Mr. Williams, who lives at 85 Montgomery Avenue, states that between 1:00 P.M. and 2:00 P.M. his vehicle was parked in front of his home when an unknown person broke into his car and took his stereo worth $1,200.
   C. Mr. Williams was parked in front of 85 Montgomery Avenue, which is his home, when it was robbed of a $1,200 stereo. When he came out, he observed between 1:00 P.M. and 2:00 P.M. that his car had been broken into by an unknown person.
   D. Mr. Williams states between 1:00 P.M. and 2:00 P.M. that an unknown person broke into his car in front of his home. Mr. Williams further states that he was robbed of a $1,200 stereo at 85 Montgomery Avenue.

9. Police Officer Fontaine obtained the following details relating to a suspicious package:
Place of Occurrence: Case Bank, 2 Wall Street
Time of Occurrence: 10:30 A.M.
Date of Occurrence: October 10, 2004
Complaint: Suspicious package in doorway
Found By: Emergency Service Unit

Officer Fontaine is preparing a report for department records.
Which one of the following expresses the above information MOST clearly and accurately?

 A. At 10:30 A.M., the Emergency Service Unit reported they found a package on October 10, 2004 which appeared suspicious. This occurred in a doorway at 2 Wall Street, Case Bank.
 B. A package which appeared suspicious was in the doorway of Case Bank. The Emergency Service Unit reported this at 2 Wall Street at 10:30 A.M. on October 10, 2004 when found.
 C. On October 10, 2004 at 10:30 A.M., a suspicious package was found by the Emergency Service Unit in the doorway of Case Bank at 2 Wall Street.
 D. The Emergency Service Unit found a package at the Case Bank. It appeared suspicious at 10:30 A.M. in the doorway of 2 Wall Street on October 10, 2004.

10. Police Officer Reardon receives the following information regarding a case of child abuse:
Victim: Joseph Mays
Victim's Age: 10 years old
Victim's Address: Resides with his family at 42 Columbia Street, Apt. 1B
Complainant: Victim's uncle, Kevin Mays
Suspects: Victim's parents

Police Officer Reardon is preparing a report to send to the Department of Social Services.
Which one of the following expresses the above information MOST clearly and accurately?

 A. Kevin Mays reported a case of child abuse to his ten-year-old nephew, Joseph Mays, by his parents. He resides with his family at 42 Columbia Street, Apt. 1B.
 B. Kevin Mays reported that his ten-year-old nephew, Joseph Mays, has been abused by the child's parents. Joseph Mays resides with his family at 42 Columbia Street, Apt. 1B.
 C. Joseph Mays has been abused by his parents. Kevin Mays reported that his nephew resides with his family at 42 Columbia Street, Apt. 1B. He is ten years old.
 D. Kevin Mays reported that his nephew is ten years old. Joseph Mays has been abused by his parents. He resides with his family at 42 Columbia Street, Apt. 1B.

11. While on patrol, Police Officer Hawkins was approached by Harry Roland, a store owner, who found a leather bag valued at $200.00 outside his store. Officer Hawkins took the property into custody and removed the following items:

2 Solex watches, each valued at	$500.00
4 14-kt. gold necklaces, each valued at	$315.00
Cash	$519.00
1 diamond ring, valued at	$400.00

    Officer Hawkins is preparing a report on the found property.
    Which one of the following is the TOTAL value of the property and cash found?

    A. $1,734   B. $3,171   C. $3,179   D. $3,379

12. While on patrol, Police Officer Blake observes a man running from a burning abandoned building. Officer Blake radios the following information:
    Place of Occurrence: 310 Hall Avenue
    Time of Occurrence: 8:30 P.M.
    Type of Building: Abandoned
    Suspect: Male, white, about 35 years old
    Crime: Arson
    Officer Blake is completing a report on the incident.
    Which one of the following expresses the above information
    MOST clearly and accurately?

    A. An abandoned building located at 310 Hall Avenue was on fire at 8:30 P.M. A white male, approximately 35 years old, was observed fleeing the scene.
    B. A white male, approximately 35 years old, at 8:30 P.M. was observed fleeing 310 Hall Avenue. The fire was set at an abandoned building.
    C. An abandoned building was set on fire. A white male, approximately 35 years old, was observed fleeing the scene at 8:30 P.M. at 310 Hall Avenue.
    D. Observed fleeing a building at 8:30 P.M. was a white male, approximately 35 years old. An abandoned building, located at 310 Hall Avenue, was set on fire.

13. Police Officer Winters responds to a call regarding a report of a missing person. The following information was obtained by the Officer:
    Time of Occurrence: 3:30 P.M.
    Place of Occurrence: Harrison Park
    Reported By: Louise Dee - daughter
    Description of Missing
    Person: Sharon Dee, 70 years old, 5'5", brown eyes, black hair - mother
    Officer Winters is completing a report on the incident. Which one of the following expresses the above information MOST clearly and accurately?

    A. Mrs. Sharon Dee, reported missing by her daughter, Louise, was seen in Harrison Park. The last time she saw her was at 3:30 P.M. She is 70 years old with black hair, brown eyes, and 5'5".
    B. Louise Dee reported that her mother, Sharon Dee, is missing. Sharon Dee is 70 years old, has black hair, brown eyes, and is 5'5". She was last seen at 3:30 P.M. in Harrison Park.
    C. Louise Dee reported Sharon, her 70-year-old mother at 3:30 P.M., to be missing after being seen last at Harrison Park. Described as being 5'5", she has black hair and brown eyes.

D. At 3:30 P.M. Louise Dee's mother was last seen by her daughter in Harrison Park. She has black hair and brown eyes. Louise reported Sharon is 5'5" and 70 years old.

14. While on patrol, Police Officers Mertz and Gallo receive a call from the dispatcher regarding a crime in progress.
When the Officers arrive, they obtain the following information:
Time of Occurrence: 2:00 P.M.
Place of Occurrence: In front of 2124 Bristol Avenue
Crime: Purse snatch
Victim: Maria Nieves
Suspect: Carlos Ortiz
Witness: Jose Perez, who apprehended the subject
The Officers are completing a report on the incident.
Which one of the following expresses the above information MOST clearly and accurately?

14.____

A. At 2:00 P.M., Jose Perez witnessed Maria Nieves. Her purse was snatched. The suspect, Carlos Ortiz, was apprehended in front of 2124 Bristol Avenue.
B. In front of 2124 Bristol Avenue, Carlos Ortiz snatched the purse belonging to Maria Nieves. Carlos Ortiz was apprehended by a witness to the crime after Jose Perez saw the purse snatch at 2:00 P.M.
C. At 2:00 P.M., Carlos Ortiz snatched a purse from Maria Nieves in front of 2124 Bristol Avenue. Carlos Ortiz was apprehended by Jose Perez, a witness to the crime.
D. At 2:00 P.M., Carlos Ortiz was seen snatching the purse of Maria Nieves as seen and apprehended by Jose Perez in front of 2124 Bristol Avenue.

15. Police Officers Willis and James respond to a crime in progress and obtain the following information:
Time of Occurrence: 8:30 A.M.
Place of Occurrence: Corner of Hopkin Avenue and Amboy Place
Crime: Chain snatch
Victim: Mrs. Paula Evans
Witness: Mr. Robert Peters
Suspect: White male
Officers Willis and James are completing a report on the incident.
Which one of the following expresses the above information MOST clearly and accurately?

15.____

A. Mrs. Paula Evans was standing on the corner of Hopkin Avenue and Amboy Place at 8:30 A.M. when a white male snatched her chain. Mr. Robert Peters witnessed the crime.
B. At 8:30 A.M., Mr. Robert Peters witnessed Mrs. Paula Evans and a white male standing on the corner of Hopkin Avenue and Amboy Place. Her chain was snatched.
C. At 8:30 A.M., a white male was standing on the corner of Hopkin Avenue and Amboy Place. Mrs. Paula Evans' chain was snatched, and Mr. Robert Peters witnessed the crime.

D. At 8:30 A.M., Mr. Robert Peters reported he witnessed a white male snatching Mrs. Paula Evans' chain while standing on the corner of Hopkin Avenue and Amboy Place.

16. Police Officers Cleveland and Logan responded to an assault that had recently occurred. The following information was obtained at the scene:

Place of Occurrence: Broadway and Roosevelt Avenue
Time of Occurrence: 1:00 A.M.
Crime: Attempted robbery, assault
Victim: Chuck Brown, suffered a broken tooth
Suspect: Lewis Brown, victim's brother

Officer Logan is completing a report on the incident.
Which one of the following expresses the above information MOST clearly and accurately?

A. Lewis Brown assaulted his brother Chuck on the corner of Broadway and Roosevelt Avenue. Chuck Brown reported his broken tooth during the attempted robbery at 1:00 A.M.
B. Chuck Brown had his tooth broken when he was assaulted at 1:00 A.M. on the corner of Broadway and Roosevelt Avenue by his brother, Lewis Brown, while Lewis was attempting to rob him.
C. An attempt at 1:00 A.M. to rob Chuck Brown turned into an assault at the corner of Broadway and Roosevelt Avenue when his brother Lewis broke his tooth.
D. At 1:00 A.M., Chuck Brown reported that he was assaulted during his brother's attempt to rob him. Lewis Brown broke his tooth. The incident occurred on the corner of Broadway and Roosevelt Avenue.

17. Police Officer Mannix has just completed an investigation regarding a hit-and-run accident which resulted in a pedestrian being injured. Officer Mannix has obtained the following information:

Make and Model of Car: Pontiac, Trans Am
Year and Color of Car: 2006, white
Driver of Car: Male, black
Place of Occurrence: Corner of E. 15th Street and 8th Avenue
Time of Occurrence: 1:00 P.M.

Officer Mannix is completing a report on the accident.
Which one of the following expresses the above information MOST clearly and accurately?

A. At 1:00 P.M., at the corner of E. 15th Street and 8th Avenue, a black male driving a white 2006 Pontiac Trans Am was observed leaving the scene of an accident after injuring a pedestrian with the vehicle.
B. On the corner of E. 15th Street and 8th Avenue, a white Pontiac, driven by a black male, a 2006 Trans Am injured a pedestrian and left the scene of the accident at 1:00 P.M.
C. A black male driving a white 2006 Pontiac Trans Am injured a pedestrian and left with the car while driving on the corner of E. 15th Street and 8th Avenue at 1:00 P.M.
D. At the corner of E. 15th Street and 8th Avenue, a pedestrian was injured by a black male. He fled in his white 2006 Pontiac Trans Am at 1:00 P.M.

18. The following details were obtained by Police Officer Dwight at the scene of a family dispute:

Place of Occurrence: 77 Baruch Drive
Victim: Andrea Valdez, wife of Walker
Violator: Edward Walker
Witness: George Valdez, victim's brother
Crime: Violation of Order of Protection
Action Taken: Violator arrested

Police Officer Dwight is preparing a report on the incident.
Which one of the following expresses the above information MOST clearly and accurately?

- A. George Valdez saw Edward Walker violate his sister's Order of Protection at 77 Baruch Drive. Andrea Valdez's husband was arrested for this violation.
- B. Andrea Valdez's Order of Protection was violated at 77 Baruch Drive. George Valdez saw his brother-in-law violate his sister's Order. Edward Walker was arrested.
- C. Edward Walker was arrested for violating an Order of Protection held by his wife, Andrea Valdez. Andrea's brother, George Valdez, witnessed the violation at 77 Baruch Drive.
- D. An arrest was made at 77 Baruch Drive when an Order of Protection held by Andrea Valdez was violated by her husband. George Valdez, her brother, witnessed Edward Walker.

19. The following details were obtained by Police Officer Jackson at the scene of a robbery:

Place of Occurrence: Chambers Street, northbound A platform
Victim: Mr. John Wells
Suspect: Joseph Miller
Crime: Robbery, armed with knife, wallet taken
Action Taken: Suspect arrested

Officer Jackson is completing a report on the incident.
Which one of the following expresses the above information MOST clearly and accurately?

- A. At Chambers Street northbound A platform, Joseph Miller used a knife to remove the wallet of John Wells while waiting for the train. Police arrested him.
- B. Mr. John Wells, while waiting for the northbound A train at Chambers Street, had his wallet forcibly removed at knifepoint by Joseph Miller. Joseph Miller was later arrested.
- C. Joseph Miller was arrested for robbery. At Chambers Street, John Wells stated that his wallet was taken. The incident occurred at knifepoint while waiting on a northbound A platform.
- D. At the northbound Chambers Street platform, John Wells was waiting for the A train. Joseph Miller produced a knife and removed his wallet. He was arrested.

20. Police Officer Bellows responds to a report of drugs being sold in the lobby of an apartment building. He obtains the following information at the scene:

Time of Occurrence: 11:30 P.M.
Place of Occurrence: 1010 Bath Avenue
Witnesses: Mary Markham, John Silver
Suspect: Harry Stoner
Crime: Drug sales
Action Taken: Suspect was gone when police arrived

Officer Bellows is completing a report of the incident. Which one of the following expresses the above information MOST clearly and accurately?

A. Mary Markham and John Silver witnessed drugs being sold and the suspect flee at 1010 Bath Avenue. Harry Stoner was conducting his business at 11:30 P.M. before police arrival in the lobby.
B. In the lobby, Mary Markham reported at 11:30 P.M. she saw Harry Stoner, along with John Silver, selling drugs. He ran from the lobby at 1010 Bath Avenue before police arrived.
C. John Silver and Mary Markham reported that they observed Harry Stoner selling drugs in the lobby of 1010 Bath Avenue at 11:30 P.M. The witnesses stated that Stoner fled before police arrived.
D. Before police arrived, witnesses stated that Harry Stoner was selling drugs. At 1010 Bath Avenue, in the lobby, John Silver and Mary Markham said they observed his actions at 11:30 P.M.

21. While on patrol, Police Officer Fox receives a call to respond to a robbery. Upon arriving at the scene, he obtains the following information:

Time of Occurrence: 6:00 P.M.
Place of Occurrence: Sal's Liquor Store at 30 Fordham Road
Victim: Sal Jones
Suspect: White male wearing a beige parka
Description of Crime: Victim was robbed in his store at gunpoint

Officer Fox is completing a report on the incident. Which one of the following expresses the above information MOST clearly and accurately?

A. I was informed at 6:00 P.M. by Sal Jones that an unidentified white male robbed him at gunpoint at 30 Fordham Road while wearing a beige parka at Sal's Liquor Store.
B. At 6:00 P.M., Sal Jones was robbed at gunpoint in his store. An unidentified white male wearing a beige parka came into Sal's Liquor Store at 30 Fordham Road, he told me.
C. I was informed at 6:00 P.M. while wearing a beige parka an unidentified white male robbed Sal Jones at gunpoint at Sal's Liquor Store at 30 Fordham Road.
D. Sal Jones informed me that at 6:00 P.M. he was robbed at gunpoint in his store, Sal's Liquor Store, located at 30 Fordham Road, by an unidentified white male wearing a beige parka.

22. The following details were obtained by Police Officer Connors at the scene of a bank robbery:

Time of Occurrence: 10:21 A.M.
Place of Occurrence: Westbury Savings and Loan
Crime: Bank Robbery
Suspect: Male, dressed in black, wearing a black woolen face mask
Witness: Mary Henderson of 217 Westbury Ave.
Amount Stolen: $6141 U.S. currency

Officer Connors is completing a report on the incident. Which one of the following expresses the above information MOST clearly and accurately?

    A. At 10:21 A.M., the Westbury Savings and Loan was witnessed being robbed by Mary Henderson of 217 Westbury Avenue. The suspect fled dressed in black with a black woolen face mask. He left the bank with $6141 in U.S. currency.
    B. Dressed in black wearing a black woolen face mask, Mary Henderson of 217 Westbury Avenue saw a suspect flee with $6141 in U.S. currency after robbing the Westbury Savings and Loan. The robber was seen at 10:21 A.M.
    C. At 10:21 A.M., Mary Henderson of 217 Westbury Avenue, witness to the robbery of the Westbury Savings and Loan, reports that a male, dressed in black, wearing a black face mask, did rob said bank and fled with $6141 in U.S. currency.
    D. Mary Henderson, of 217 Westbury Avenue, witnessed the robbery of the Westbury Savings and Loan at 10:21 A.M. The suspect, a male, was dressed in black and was wearing a black woolen face mask. He fled with $6141 in U.S. currency.

23. At the scene of a dispute, Police Officer Johnson made an arrest after obtaining the following information:

Place of Occurrence: 940 Baxter Avenue
Time of Occurrence: 3:40 P.M.
Victim: John Mitchell
Suspect: Robert Holden, arrested at scene
Crime: Menacing
Weapon: Knife
Time of Arrest: 4:00 P.M.

Officer Johnson is completing a report of the incident.
Which one of the following expresses the above information
MOST clearly and accurately?

    A. John Mitchell was menaced by a knife at 940 Baxter Avenue. Robert Holden, owner of the weapon, was arrested at 4:00 P.M., twenty minutes later, at the scene.
    B. John Mitchell reports at 3:40 P.M. he was menaced at 940 Baxter Avenue by Robert Holden. He threatened him with his knife and was arrested at 4:00 P.M. at the scene.
    C. John Mitchell stated that at 3:40 P.M. at 940 Baxter Avenue he was menaced by Robert Holden, who was carrying a knife. Mr. Holden was arrested at the scene at 4:00 P.M.
    D. With a knife, Robert Holden menaced John Mitchell at 3:40 P.M. The knife belonged to him, and he was arrested at the scene of 940 Baxter Avenue at 4:00 P.M.

24. Officer Nieves obtained the following information after he was called to the scene of a large gathering:

Time of Occurrence:	2:45 A.M.
Place of Occurrence:	Mulberry Park
Complaint:	Loud music
Complainant:	Mrs. Simpkins, 42 Mulberry Street, Apt. 25
Action Taken:	Police officer dispersed the crowd

Officer Nieves is completing a report on the incident. Which one of the following expresses the above information MOST clearly and accurately?

- A. Mrs. Simpkins, who lives at 42 Mulberry Street, Apt. 25, called the police to make a complaint. A large crowd of people were playing loud music in Mulberry Park at 2:45 A.M. Officer Nieves responded and dispersed the crowd.
- B. Officer Nieves responded to Mulberry Park because Mrs. Simpkins, the complainant, lives at 42 Mulberry Street, Apt. 25. Due to a large crowd of people who were playing loud music at 2:45 A.M., he immediately dispersed the crowd.
- C. Due to a large crowd of people who were playing loud music in Mulberry Park at 2:45 A.M., Officer Nieves responded and dispersed the crowd. Mrs. Simpkins called the police and complained. She lives at 42 Mulberry Street, Apt. 25.
- D. Responding to a complaint by Mrs. Simpkins, who resides at 42 Mulberry Street, Apt. 25, Officer Nieves dispersed a large crowd in Mulberry Park. They were playing loud music. It was 2:45 A.M.

25. While patroling the subway, Police Officer Clark responds to the scene of a past robbery where he obtains the following information:

Place of Occurrence:	Northbound E train
Time of Occurrence:	6:30 P.M.
Victim:	Robert Brey
Crime:	Wallet and jewelry taken
Suspects:	2 male whites armed with knives

Officer Clark is completing a report on the incident.
Which one of the following expresses the above information MOST clearly and accurately?

- A. At 6:30 P.M., Robert Brey reported he was robbed of his wallet and jewelry. On the northbound E train, two white males approached Mr. Brey. They threatened him before taking his property with knives.
- B. While riding the E train northbound, two white men approached Robert Brey at 6:30 P.M. They threatened him with knives and took his wallet and jewelry.
- C. Robert Brey was riding the E train at 6:30 P.M. when he was threatened by two whites. The men took his wallet and jewelry as he was traveling northbound.
- D. Robert Brey reports at 6:30 P.M. he lost his wallet to two white men as well as his jewelry. They were carrying knives and threatened him aboard the northbound E train.

KEY (CORRECT ANSWERS)

1. B
2. C
3. C
4. A
5. C

6. B
7. C
8. B
9. C
10. B

11. D
12. A
13. B
14. C
15. A

16. B
17. A
18. C
19. B
20. C

21. D
22. D
23. C
24. A
25. B

TEST 2

DIRECTIONS: Each question or incomplete statement is followed by several suggested answers or completions. Select the one that BEST answers the question or completes the statement. *PRINT THE LETTER OF THE CORRECT ANSWER IN THE SPACE AT THE RIGHT.*

1. Police Officer Johnson has just finished investigating a report of a burglary and has obtained the following information:
   Place of Occurrence: Victim's residence
   Time of Occurrence: Between 8:13 P.M. and 4:15 A.M.
   Victim: Paul Mason of 1264 Twentieth Street, Apt. 3D
   Crime: Burglary
   Damage: Filed front door lock
   Officer Johnson is preparing a report of the incident. Which one of the following expresses the above information MOST clearly and accurately?

   A. Paul Mason's residence was burglarized at 1264 Twentieth Street, Apt. 3D, between 8:13 P.M. and 4:15 A.M. by filing the front door lock.
   B. Paul Mason was burglarized by filing the front door lock and he lives at 1264 Twentieth Street, Apt. 3D, between 8:13 P.M. and 4:15 A.M.
   C. Between 8:13 P.M. and 4:15 A.M., the residence of Paul Mason, located at 1264 Twentieth Street, Apt. 3D, was burglarized after the front door lock was filed.
   D. Between 8:13 P.M. and 4:15 A.M., at 1264 Twentieth Street, Apt. 3D, after the front door lock was filed, the residence of Paul Mason was burglarized.

   1._____

2. Police Officer Lowell has just finished investigating a burglary and has received the following information:
   Place of Occurrence: 117-12 Sutphin Boulevard
   Time of Occurrence: Between 9:00 A.M. and 5:00 P.M.
   Victim: Mandee Cotton
   Suspects: Unknown
   Officer Lowell is completing a report on this incident.
   Which one of the following expresses the above information MOST clearly and accurately?

   A. Mandee Cotton reported that her home was burglarized between 9:00 A.M. and 5:00 P.M. Ms. Cotton resides at 117-12 Sutphin Boulevard. Suspects are unknown.
   B. A burglary was committed at 117-12 Sutphin Boulevard reported Mandee Cotton between 9:00 A.M. and 5:00 P.M. Ms. Cotton said unknown suspects burglarized her home.
   C. Unknown suspects burglarized a home at 117-12 Sutphin Boulevard between 9:00 A.M. and 5:00 P.M. Mandee Cotton, homeowner, reported.
   D. Between the hours of 9:00 A.M. and 5:00 P.M., it was reported that 117-12 Sutphin Boulevard was burglarized. Mandee Cotton reported that unknown suspects are responsible.

   2._____

3. Police Officer Dale has just finished investigating a report of attempted theft and has obtained the following information:

Place of Occurrence: In front of 103 W. 105th Street
Time of Occurrence: 11:30 A.M.
Victim: Mary Davis
Crime: Attempted theft
Suspect: Male, black, scar on right side of
face Action Taken: Drove victim around area to locate suspect

Officer Dale is preparing a report on the incident. Which one of the following expresses the above information MOST clearly and accurately?

A. Mary Davis was standing in front of 103 W. 105th Street when Officer Dale arrived after an attempt to steal her pocketbook failed at 11:30 A.M. Officer Dale canvassed the area looking for a black male with a scar on the right side of his face with Ms. Davis in the patrol car.
B. Mary Davis stated that, at 11:30 A.M., she was standing in front of 103 W. 105th Street when a black male with a scar on the right side of his face attempted to steal her pocketbook. Officer Dale canvassed the area with Ms. Davis in the patrol car.
C. Officer Dale canvassed the area by putting Mary Davis in a patrol car looking for a black male with a scar on the right side of his face. At 11:30 A.M. in front of 103 W. 105th Street, she said he attempted to steal her pocketbook.
D. At 11:30 A.M., in front of 103 W. 105th Street, Officer Dale canvassed the area with Mary Davis in a patrol car who said that a black male with a scar on the right side of his face attempted to steal her pocketbook.

4. While on patrol, Police Officer Santoro received a call to respond to the scene of a shooting. The following details were obtained at the scene:

Time of Occurrence: 4:00 A.M.
Place of Occurrence: 232 Senator Street
Victim: Mike Nisman
Suspect: Howard Conran
Crime: Shooting
Witness: Sheila Norris

Officer Santoro is completing a report on the incident.
Which one of the following expresses the above information MOST clearly and accurately?

A. Sheila Norris stated at 4:00 A.M. she witnessed a shooting of her neighbor in front of her building. Howard Conran shot Mike Nisman and ran from 232 Senator Street.
B. Mike Nisman was the victim of a shooting incident seen by his neighbor. At 4:00 A.M., Sheila Norris saw Howard Conran shoot him and run in front of their building. Norris and Nisman reside at 232 Senator Street.
C. Sheila Norris states that at 4:00 A.M. she witnessed Howard Conran shoot Mike Nisman, her neighbor, in front of their building at 232 Senator Street. She further states she saw the suspect running from the scene.
D. Mike Nisman was shot by Howard Conran at 4:00 A.M. His neighbor, Sheila Norris, witnessed him run from the scene in front of their building at 232 Senator Street.

5. Police Officer Taylor responds to the scene of a serious traffic accident in which a car struck a telephone pole, and obtains the following information:
   Place of Occurrence: Intersection of Rock Street and Amboy Place
   Time of Occurrence: 3:27 A.M.
   Name of Injured: Carlos Black
   Driver of Car: Carlos Black
   Action Taken: Injured taken to Beth-El Hospital
   Officer Taylor is preparing a report on the accident. Which one of the following expresses the above information MOST clearly and accurately?

   A. At approximately 3:27 A.M., Carlos Black drove his car into a telephone pole located at the intersection of Rock Street and Amboy Place. Mr. Black, who was the only person injured, was taken to Beth-El Hospital.
   B. Carlos Black, injured at the intersection of Rock Street and Amboy Place, hit a telephone pole. He was taken to Beth-El Hospital after the car accident which occurred at 3:27 A.M.
   C. At the intersection of Rock Street and Amboy Place, Carlos Black injured himself and was taken to Beth-El Hospital. His car hit a telephone pole at 3:27 A.M.
   D. At the intersection of Rock Street and Amboy Place at 3:27 A.M., Carlos Black was taken to Beth-El Hospital after injuring himself by driving into a telephone pole.

6. While on patrol in the Jefferson Housing Projects, Police Officer Johnson responds to the scene of a Grand Larceny.
   The following information was obtained by Officer Johnson:
   Time of Occurrence: 6:00 P.M.
   Place of Occurrence: Rear of Building 12A
   Victim: Maria Lopez
   Crime: Purse snatched
   Suspect: Unknown
   Officer Johnson is preparing a report on the incident.
   Which one of the following expresses the above information MOST clearly and accurately?

   A. At the rear of Building 12A, at 6:00 P.M., by an unknown suspect, Maria Lopez reported her purse snatched in the Jefferson Housing Projects.
   B. Maria Lopez reported that at 6:00 P.M. her purse was snatched by an unknown suspect at the rear of Building 12A in the Jefferson Housing Projects.
   C. At the rear of Building 12A, Maria Lopez reported at 6:00 P.M. that her purse had been snatched by an unknown suspect in the Jefferson Housing Projects.
   D. In the Jefferson Housing Projects, Maria Lopez reported at the rear of Building 12A that her purse had been snatched by an unknown suspect at 6:00 P.M.

4 (#2)

7. Criminal Possession of Stolen Property 2nd Degree occurs when a person knowingly possesses stolen property with intent to benefit himself or a person other than the owner, or to prevent its recovery by the owner, and when the
    I. value of the property exceeds two hundred fifty dollars; or
    II. property consists of a credit card; or
    III. person is a pawnbroker or is in the business of buying, selling, or otherwise dealing in property; or
    IV. property consists of one or more firearms, rifles, or shotguns.
   Which one of the following is the BEST example of Criminal Possession of Stolen Property in the Second Degree?

   A. Mary knowingly buys a stolen camera valued at $225 for her mother's birthday.
   B. John finds a wallet containing $100 and various credit cards. John keeps the money and turns the credit cards in at his local precinct.
   C. Mr. Varrone, a pawnbroker, refuses to buy Mr. Cutter's stolen VCR valued at $230.
   D. Mr. Aquista, the owner of a toy store, knowingly buys a crate of stolen water pistols valued at $260.

   7.____

8. Police Officer Dale has just finished investigating a report of menacing and obtained the following information:
   Time of Occurrence: 10:30 P.M.
   Place of Occurrence: (Hallway) 77 Hill Street
   Victim: Grace Jackson
   Suspect: Susan, white female, 30 years of age
   Crime: Menacing with a knife
   Officer Dale is preparing a report on the incident.
   Which one of the following expresses the above information MOST clearly and accurately?

   A. At 10:30 P.M., Grace Jackson was stopped in the hallway of 77 Hill Street by a 30-year-old white female known to Grace as Susan. Susan put a knife to Grace's throat and demanded that Grace stay out of the building or Susan would hurt her.
   B. Grace Jackson was stopped in the hallway at knifepoint and threatened to stay away from the building located at 77 Hill Street. The female who is 30 years of age known as Susan by Jackson stopped her at 10:30 P.M.
   C. At 10:30 P.M. in the hallway of 77 Hill Street, Grace Jackson reported a white female 30 years of age put a knife to her throat. She knew her as Susan and demanded she stay away from the building or she would get hurt.
   D. A white female 30 years of age known to Grace Jackson as Susan stopped her in the hallway of 77 Hill Street. She put a knife to her throat and at 10:30 P.M. demanded she stay away from the building or she would get hurt.

   8.____

9. Police Officer Bennett responds to the scene of a car accident and obtains the following information from the witness:
   Time of Occurrence: 3:00 A.M.
   Victim: Joe Morris, removed to Methodist Hospital
   Crime: Struck pedestrian and left the scene of accident
   Description of Auto: Blue 2008 Pontiac, license plate BOT-3745
   Officer Bennett is preparing an accident report. Which one of the following expresses the above information MOST clearly and accurately?

   9.____

A. Joe Morris, a pedestrian, was hit at 3:00 A.M. and removed to Methodist Hospital. Also a blue Pontiac, 2008 model left the scene, license plate BOT-3745.
B. A pedestrian was taken to Methodist Hospital after being struck at 3:00 A.M. A blue automobile was seen leaving the scene with license plate BOT-3745. Joe Morris was knocked down by a 2008 Pontiac.
C. At 3:00 A.M., Joe Morris, a pedestrian, was struck by a blue 2008 Pontiac. The automobile, license plate BOT-3745, left the scene. Mr. Morris was taken to Methodist Hospital.
D. Joe Morris, a pedestrian at 3:00 A.M. was struck by a Pontiac. A 2008 model, license plate BOT-3745, blue in color, left the scene and the victim was taken to Methodist Hospital.

10. At 11:30 A.M., Police Officers Newman and Johnson receive a radio call to respond to a reported robbery. The Officers obtained the following information:
Time of Occurrence: 11:20 A.M.
Place of Occurrence: Twenty-four hour newsstand at 2024 86th Street
Victim: Sam Norris, owner
Amount Stolen: $450.00
Suspects: Two male whites
Officer Newman is completing a complaint report on the incident.
Which one of the following expresses the above information MOST clearly and accurately?

A. At 11:20 A.M., it was reported by the newsstand owner that two male whites robbed $450.00 from Sam Norris. The Twenty-four hour newsstand is located at 2024 86th Street.
B. At 11:20 A.M., Sam Norris, the newsstand owner, reported that the Twenty-four hour newsstand located at 2024 86th Street was robbed by two male whites who took $450.00.
C. Sam Norris, the owner of the Twenty-four hour newsstand located at 2024 86th Street, reported that at 11:20 A.M. two white males robbed his newsstand of $450.00.
D. Sam Norris reported at 11:20 A.M. that $450.00 had been taken from the owner of the Twenty-four hour newsstand located at 2024 86th Street by two male whites.

11. While on patrol, Police Officers Carter and Popps receive a call to respond to an assault in progress. Upon arrival, they receive the following information:
Place of Occurrence: 27 Park Avenue
Victim: John Dee
Suspect: Michael Jones
Crime: Stabbing during a fight
Action Taken: Suspect arrested
The Officers are completing a report on the incident.
Which one of the following expresses the above information MOST clearly and accurately?

A. In front of 27 Park Avenue, Michael Jones was arrested for stabbing John Dee during a fight.
B. Michael Jones was arrested for stabbing John Dee during a fight in front of 27 Park Avenue.

C. During a fight, Michael Jones was arrested for stabbing John Dee in front of 27 Park Avenue.
D. John Dee was stabbed by Michael Jones, who was arrested for fighting in front of 27 Park Avenue.

12. Police Officer Gattuso responded to a report of a robbery and obtained the following information regarding the incident:

Place of Occurrence: Princess Grocery, 6 Button Place
Time of Occurrence: 6:00 P.M.
Crime: Robbery of $200
Victim: Sara Davidson, owner of Princess Grocery
Description of Suspect: White, female, red hair, blue jeans, and white T-shirt
Weapon: Knife

Officer Gattuso is preparing a report on the incident.
Which one of the following expresses the above information MOST clearly and accurately?

A. Sara Davidson reported at 6:00 P.M. her store Princess Grocery was robbed at knifepoint at 6 Button Place. A white woman with red hair took $200 from her wearing blue jeans and a white T-shirt.
B. At 6:00 P.M., a red-haired woman took $200 from 6 Button Place at Princess Grocery owned by Sara Davidson, who was robbed by the white woman. She was wearing blue jeans and a white T-shirt and used a knife.
C. In a robbery that occurred at knifepoint, a red-haired white woman robbed the owner of Princess Grocery. Sara Davidson, the owner of the 6 Button Place store which was robbed of $200, said she was wearing blue jeans and a white T-shirt at 6:00 P.M.
D. At 6:00 P.M., Sara Davidson, owner of Princess Grocery, located at 6 Button Place, was robbed of $200 at knifepoint. The suspect is a white female with red hair wearing blue jeans and a white T-shirt.

13. Police Officer Martinez responds to a report of an assault and obtains the following information regarding the incident :

Place of Occurrence: Corner of Frank and Lincoln Avenues
Time of Occurrence: 9:40 A.M.
Crime: Assault
Victim: Mr. John Adams of 31 20th Street
Suspect: Male, white, 5'11", 170 lbs., dressed in gray
Injury: Victim suffered a split lip
Action Taken: Victim transported to St. Mary's Hospital

Officer Martinez is completing a report on the incident. Which one of the following expresses the above information MOST clearly and accurately?

A. At 9:40 A.M., John Adams was assaulted on the corner of Frank and Lincoln Avenues by a white male, 5'11", 170 lbs., dressed in gray, suffering a split lip. Mr. Adams lives at 31 20th Street and was transported to St. Mary's Hospital.
B. At 9:40 A.M., John Adams was assaulted on the corner of Frank and Lincoln Avenues by a white male, 5'11", 170 lbs., dressed in gray, and lives at 31 20th Street. Mr. Adams suffered a split lip and was transported to St. Mary's Hospital.

C. John Adams, who lives at 31 20th Street, was assaulted at 9:40 A.M. on the corner of Frank and Lincoln Avenues by a white male, 5'11", 170 lbs., dressed in gray. Mr. Adams suffered a split lip and was transported to St. Mary's Hospital.
D. Living at 31 20th Street, Mr. Adams suffered a split lip and was transported to St. Mary's Hospital. At 9:40 A.M., Mr. Adams was assaulted by a white male, 5'11", 170 lbs., dressed in gray.

14. The following information was obtained by Police Officer Adams at the scene of an auto accident:

Date of Occurrence:	August 7, 2004
Place of Occurrence:	541 W. Broadway
Time of Occurrence:	12:45 P.M.
Drivers:	Mrs. Liz Smith and Mr. John Sharp
Action Taken:	Summons served to Mrs. Liz Smith

Officer Adams is completing a report on the accident. Which one of the following expresses the above information MOST clearly and accurately?

A. At 541 W. Broadway, Mr. John Sharp and Mrs. Liz Smith had an auto accident at 12:45 P.M. Mrs. Smith received a summons on August 7, 2004.
B. Mrs. Liz Smith received a summons at 12:45 P.M. on August 7, 2004 for an auto accident with Mr. John Sharp at 541 W. Broadway.
C. Mr. John Sharp and Mrs. Liz Smith were in an auto accident. At 541 W. Broadway on August 7, 2004 at 12:45 P.M., Mrs. Smith received a summons.
D. On August 7, 2004 at 12:45 P.M. at 541 W. Broadway, Mrs. Liz Smith and Mr. John Sharp were involved in an auto accident. Mrs. Smith received a summons.

15. Police Officer Gold and his partner were directed by the radio dispatcher to investigate a report of a past burglary. They obtained the following information at the scene:

Date of Occurrence:	April 2, 2004
Time of Occurrence:	Between 7:30 A.M. and 6:15 P.M.
Place of Occurrence:	124 Haring Street, residence of victim
Victim:	Mr. Gerald Palmer
Suspect:	Unknown
Crime:	Burglary
Items Stolen:	Assorted jewelry, $150 cash, TV, VCR

Officer Gold must complete a report on the incident. Which one of the following expresses the above information MOST clearly and accurately?

A. Mr. Gerald Palmer stated that on April 2, 2004, between 7:30 A.M. and 6:15 P.M., while he was at work, someone broke into his house at 124 Haring Street and removed assorted jewelry, a VCR, $150 cash, and a TV.
B. Mr. Gerald Palmer stated while he was at work that somebody broke into his house on April 2, 2004 and between 7:30 A.M. and 6:15 P.M. took his VCR, TV, assorted jewelry, and $150 cash. His address is 124 Haring Street.
C. Between 7:30 A.M. and 6:15 P.M. on April 2, 2004, Mr. Gerald Palmer reported an unknown person at 124 Haring Street took his TV, VCR, $150 cash, and assorted jewelry from his house. Mr. Palmer said he was at work at the time.
D. An unknown person broke into the house at 124 Haring Street and stole a TV, VCR, assorted jewelry, and $150 cash from Mr. Gerald Palmer. The suspect broke in on April 2, 2004 while he was at work, reported Mr. Palmer between 7:30 A.M. and 6:15 P.M.

16. While on patrol, Police Officers Morris and Devine receive a call to respond to a reported burglary. The following information relating to the crime was obtained by the Officers:

Time of Occurrence: 2:00 A.M.
Place of Occurrence: 2100 First Avenue
Witness: David Santiago
Victim: John Rivera
Suspect: Joe Ryan
Crime: Burglary, DVD player stolen

The Officers are completing a report on the incident.
Which one of the following expresses the above information MOST clearly and accurately?

- A. David Santiago, the witness reported at 2:00 A.M. he saw Joe Ryan leave 2100 First Avenue, home of John Rivera, with a DVD player.
- B. At 2:00 A.M. David Santiago reported that he had seen Joe Ryan go into 2100 First Avenue and steal a DVD player. John Rivera lives at 2100 First Avenue.
- C. David Santiago stated that Joe Ryan burglarized John Rivera's house at 2100 First Avenue. He saw Joe Ryan leaving his house at 2:00 A.M. with a DVD player.
- D. David Santiago reported that at 2:00 A.M. he saw Joe Ryan leave John Rivera's house, located at 2100 First Avenue, with Mr. Rivera's DVD player.

16.____

17. When a police officer responds to an incident involving the victim of an animal bite, the officer should do the following in the order given:
    I. Determine the owner of the animal
    II. Obtain a description of the animal and attempt to locate it for an examination if the owner is unknown
    III. If the animal is located and the owner is unknown, comply with the Care and Disposition of Animal procedure
    IV. Prepare a Department of Health Form 480BAA and deliver it to the Desk Officer with a written report
    V. Notify the Department of Health by telephone if the person has been bitten by an animal other than a dog or cat.

Police Officer Rosario responds to 1225 South Boulevard where someone has been bitten by a dog. He is met by John Miller who informs Officer Rosario that he was bitten by a large German Shepard. Mr. Miller also states that he believes the dog belongs to someone in the neighborhood but does not know who owns it. Officer Rosario searches the area for the dog but is unable to find it.
What should Officer Rosario do NEXT?

- A. Locate the owner of the animal.
- B. Notify the Department of Health by telephone.
- C. Prepare a Department of Health Form 480BAA.
- D. Comply with the Care and Disposition of Animal procedure.

17.____

9 (#2)

18. The following details were obtained by Police Officer Howard at the scene of a hit-and-run accident:
    Place of Occurrence: Intersection of Brown Street and Front Street
    Time of Occurrence: 11:15 A.M.
    Victim: John Lawrence
    Vehicle: Red Chevrolet, license plate 727PQA
    Crime: Leaving the scene of an accident
    Officer Howard is completing a report on the incident. Which one of the following expresses the above information MOST clearly and accurately?

    A. A red Chevrolet, license plate 727PQA, hit John Lawrence. It left the scene of the accident at 11:15 A.M. at the intersection of Brown and Front Streets.
    B. At 11:15 A.M., John Lawrence was walking at the intersection of Brown Street and Front Street when he was struck by a red Chevrolet, license plate 727PQA, which left the scene.
    C. It was reported at 11:15 A.M. that John Lawrence was struck at the intersection of Brown Street and Front Street. The red Chevrolet, license plate 727PQA, left the scene.
    D. At the intersection of Brown Street and Front Street, John Lawrence was the victim of a car at 11:15 A.M. which struck him and left the scene. It was a red Chevrolet, license plate 727PQA.

19. Police Officer Donnelly has transported an elderly male to Mt. Hope Hospital after finding him lying on the street. At the hospital, Nurse Baker provided Officer Donnelly with the following information:
    Name: Robert Jones
    Address: 1485 E. 97th St.
    Date of Birth: May 13, 1935
    Age: 73 years old
    Type of Ailment: Heart condition
    Officer Donnelly is completing an Aided Report.
    Which one of the following expresses the above information MOST clearly and accurately?

    A. Mr. Robert Jones, who is 73 years old, born on May 13, 1935, collapsed on the street. Mr. Jones, who resides at 1485 E. 97th Street, suffers from a heart condition.
    B. Mr. Robert Jones had a heart condition and collapsed today on the street, and resides at 1485 E. 97th Street. He was 73 years old and born on May 13, 1935.
    C. Mr. Robert Jones, who resides at 1485 E. 97th Street, was born on May 13, 1935, and is 73 years old, was found lying on the street from a heart condition.
    D. Mr. Robert Jones, born on May 13, 1935, suffers from a heart condition at age 73 and was found lying on the street residing at 1485 E. 97th Street.

20. Police officers on patrol are often called to a scene where a response from the Fire Department might be necessary.
    In which one of the following situations would a request to the Fire Department to respond be MOST critical?

A. A film crew has started a small fire in order to shoot a scene on an October evening.
B. Two manhole covers blow off on a September afternoon.
C. Homeless persons are gathered around a trash can fire on a February morning.
D. A fire hydrant has been opened by people in the neighborhood on a July afternoon.

21. Police Officer Johnson arrives at the National Savings Bank five minutes after it has been robbed at gunpoint.
    The following are details provided by eyewitnesses: Suspect
    Sex: Male
    Ethnicity: White
    Height: 5'10" to 6'2"
    Weight: 180 lbs. to 190 lbs.
    Hair Color: Blonde
    Clothing: Black jacket, blue dungarees
    Weapon: .45 caliber revolver
    Officer Johnson is completing a report on the incident.
    Which one of the following expresses the above information MOST clearly and accurately?
    A white male

    A. weighing 180-190 lbs. robbed the National Savings Bank. He was white with a black jacket with blonde hair, is 5'10" to 6'2", and blue dungarees. The robber was armed with a .45 caliber revolver.
    B. weighing around 180 or 190 lbs. was wearing a black jacket and blue dungarees. He had blonde hair and had a .45 caliber revolver, and was 5'10" to 6'2". He robbed the National Savings Bank.
    C. who was 5'10" to 6'2" and was weighing 180 to 190 lbs., and has blonde hair and wearing blue dungarees and a black jacket with a revolver, robbed the National Savings Bank.
    D. armed with a .45 caliber revolver robbed the National Savings Bank. The robber was described as being between 180-190 lbs., 5'10" to 6'2", with blonde hair. He was wearing a black jacket and blue dungarees.

22. While on patrol, Police Officer Rogers is approached by Terry Conyers, a young woman whose pocketbook has been stolen. Ms. Conyers tells Officer Rogers that the following items were in her pocketbook at the time it was taken:
    4 Traveler's checks, each valued at $20.00
    3 Traveler's checks, each valued at $25.00
    Cash of $212.00
    1 wedding band valued at $450.00
    Officer Rogers is preparing a Complaint Report on the robbery.
    Which one of the following is the TOTAL value of the property and cash taken from Ms. Conyers?
    A. $707   B. $807   C. $817   D. $837

23. While on patrol, Police Officer Scott is dispatched to respond to a reported burglary. Two burglars entered the home of Mr. and Mrs. Walker and stole the following items:
    3 watches valued at $65.00 each
    1 amplifier valued at $340.00
    1 television set valued at $420.00
    Officer Scott is preparing a Complaint Report on the burglary.
    Which one of the following is the TOTAL value of the property stolen?

    A. $707   B. $825   C. $920   D. $955

24. While on patrol, Police Officer Smith is dispatched to investigate a grand larceny. Deborah Paisley, a businesswoman, reports that her 2000 Porsche was broken into. The following items were taken:
    1 car stereo system valued at $2,950.00
    1 car phone valued at $1,060.00
    Ms. Paisley's attache case valued at $200.00 was also taken from the car in the incident. The attache case contained two new solid gold pens valued at $970.00 each.
    Officer Smith is completing a Complaint Report.
    Which one of the following is the TOTAL dollar value of the property stolen from Ms. Paisley's car?

    A. $5,180   B. $5,980   C. $6,040   D. $6,150

25. Police Officer Grundig is writing a Complaint Report regarding a burglary and assault case. Officer Grundig has obtained the following facts:
    Place of Occurrence: 2244 Clark Street
    Victim: Mrs. Willis
    Suspect: Mr. Willis, victim's ex-husband
    Complaint: Unlawful entry; head injury inflicted with a bat
    Officer Grundig is completing a report on the incident. Which one of the following expresses the above information MOST clearly and accurately?

    A. He had no permission or authority to do so and it caused her head injuries, when Mr. Willis entered his ex-wife's premises. Mrs. Willis lives at 2244 Clark Street. He hit her with a bat.
    B. Mr. Willis entered 2244 Clark Street, the premises of his ex-wife. He hit her with a bat, without permission and authority to do so. It caused Mrs. Willis to have head injuries.
    C. After Mr. Willis hit his ex-wife, Mrs. Willis, at 2244 Clark Street, the bat caused her to have head injuries. He had no permission nor authority do so so.
    D. Mr. Willis entered his ex-wife's premises at 2244 Clark Street without her permission or authority. He then struck Mrs. Willis with a bat, causing injuries to her head.

KEY (CORRECT ANSWERS)

1. C
2. A
3. B
4. C
5. A

6. B
7. D
8. A
9. C
10. C

11. B
12. D
13. C
14. D
15. A

16. D
17. C
18. B
19. A
20. B

21. D
22. C
23. D
24. D
25. D